SHAKESPEARE AND SOCIAL CLASS

SHAKESPEARE AND SOCIAL CLASS

Ralph Berry

HUMANITIES PRESS INTERNATIONAL, INC.
Atlantic Highlands, NJ

First published in 1988 in the United States of America by
HUMANITIES PRESS INTERNATIONAL, INC., Atlantic Highlands,
NJ 07716

© 1988 Humanities Press International, Inc.

Library of Congress Cataloging-in-Publication Data
Berry, Ralph, 1931—
  Shakespeare and social class.
  Bibliography: p.
  Includes index.
  1. Shakespeare, William, 1564–1616—Political
and social views. 2. Social classes in literature.
3. England—Social life and customs—16th century.
I. Title.
PR3024.B47 1988   822.3'3   86–27652
ISBN 0–391–03530–4
ISBN 0–391–03531–2 (pbk.)

Printed in the United States of America

For Dick

Contents

Introduction

Shakespeare's characters come from the full range of social classes. His plays contain kings and beggars, laborers and nobles, gentlemen and yeomen. This mingling of high and low is based on exact discriminations between individuals, for Shakespeare has an acute sense of social differentiation. His characters speak and behave in ways that are, on the whole, consistent with their social positions. Their relationships express the social order in which they live. This does not mean, however, that their actions are determined by their social positions. A gentleman may behave in an ungentlemanly manner, and a servant in *King Lear* kills his master, the Duke of Cornwall. It does mean that Shakespeare has a sense of characteristic behavior, the tendency people have to behave in a way appropriate to their social ranks and occupations and to reflect what others expect of them. From this emerges a general sense of social class as formed by rank and occupation. Sometimes, too, matters of social status arise. For instance, Abhorson, the public hangman in *Measure for Measure*, is professionally outraged that Pompey, the bawd, is assigned as his assistant and protests: "Fie upon him! He will discredit our mystery" (4.2.24–25). Income, naturally, comes and goes as an issue that drama reflects as socially significant. "Seven hundred pounds and possibilities is goot gifts" is Sir Hugh Evans's testimony to Anne Page (*The Merry Wives of Windsor* 1.1.56–57). Status and income receive intermittent treatment in Shakespeare's plays. Rank and occupation are there all the time.

These seem, self-evidently, interesting and important aspects of Shakespeare's work. But they have not been much written about. It is now over half a century since *A Companion to Shakespeare Studies* was published. In it, Muriel St. Clare Byrne contributed what is still, I think, the necessary introduction to the subject, in "The Social Background." It was not, however, expanded in *A New Companion to Shakespeare Studies* (1971). On the contrary, in that edition, the corresponding chapter, by Joel Hurstfield, was called "The Historical and Social Background," and its coverage of social class had shrunk to a page or two. This must have reflected the editors' judgment of changing public taste. Yet even so, it seems odd that social class in Shakespeare has attracted so little connected assessment. It is left to writers on Shakespeare's language to point out, here and there, usages that relate to the speaker's social class. I do not know of any general or comprehensive treatment of social class in the plays.

This book aims at an introduction to the subject. Some exclusions are in order. The problems of kingship as they affect high politics are outside my scope. So is the psychology of individuals, beyond what seems directly related to the speaker's rank. I treat Hamlet as a prince, and in no other category. Questions of dowry fall within my province, but not love. Again, the intensity of dramatic interest in social class varies very greatly, though of course the subject is formally present all the time, since all dramatis personae are placed as belonging to some social group. For example, I can find little of social interest in *Antony and Cleopatra*, while *Coriolanus* is founded upon class issues. Therefore, I have not felt obliged to analyze in detail the class structure of *Antony and Cleopatra*: it is obvious that the play's interest lies elsewhere, in the title relationship. At all times, I have concentrated on what seem the salient features of each play, and I have been content to ignore matters that do not bear directly on my inquiry. The extraordinary variety and richness of Shakespeare's playing with class demand a certain flexibility in one who aims to describe it.

The problem is to relate the social classes of Elizabethan England to the dramatis personae of Shakespeare's plays. There are two extreme positions, neither of which works. The first is that Shakespeare holds up a mirror to contemporary life, with a direct transference of social reality to the stage. But drama is not a documentary record, and must serve its own needs. A case much discussed by the social historians is the marriage of Juliet, at the age of thirteen, to Paris. Child-marriages certainly took place in Elizabethan England: Peter Laslett cites the marriage of Elizabeth Manners to the second Earl of Exeter in 1589, when she was thirteen.[1] She bore her first child at around fourteen years and five months. Such marriages were not, however, representative. Laslett believes that in one local sampling, child-marriages cannot have made up one-half of one percent of all marriages. Shakespeare, who has lowered Juliet's age from that found in his sources, is aiming at dramatic intensification, to stress the extreme youth of Paris's child bride. And how far can Renaissance Italy be seen as equivalent to Renaissance England? The second position is that Shakespeare's plays are pure fictions, appeals to fantasy that respect only their internal laws. But this is clearly unrealistic. Shakespeare's plays must, for their effect, keep in touch with the real world. They are not autonomous fantasies.

The truth will have to cover both positions. Shakespeare's plays register the society of his day, and its classes. They are also dramatic artifacts that bend the world into forms suited for the "two hours' traffic" of the stage.

And Shakespeare develops early his characteristic way of reconciling the two positions.

It all comes down to the difference between plays set in England and abroad. The early history plays—which are likely enough the first plays Shakespeare wrote—work to a pattern which the author must have found irksome. The point about the histories is that they are set in England. There is of necessity a direct correspondence between the people onstage and their social equivalents offstage. Shakespeare is working with fixed counters: an Earl is an Earl, a gentleman is a gentleman, a groom is a groom. They are determined by their context, the history and society of England itself. But the majority of Shakespeare's plays are set abroad. From these continental bases, he makes imaginative raids into English territory before retreating. It is like a bridge player who decides to play the hand from deck. As Byrne remarks, "the background of life in the plays is, and at the same time is not, the background of Elizabethan life."[2] So, though social classes are depicted in these non-English settings, they cannot be pinned down. The author is in the clear. What is a "County" (as Paris is)? Are the Montagues and Capulets "noble," as the play declares, or bourgeois? Are the Venetian traders close to merchants operating out of the City of London? What are English knights, Sir Toby and Sir Andrew, doing in Illyria? This loose, flexible system, exact enough to fix impressions but not to document them, is Shakespeare's preferred mode. It is his answer to the problems of depicting the English classes on stage.

The society out of which Shakespeare worked, which essentially is present in all his plays, has been well studied, notably by A. L. Rowse, Lawrence Stone, Peter Laslett, and other historians of the Elizabethan age. To them the reader must turn for proper accounts of English society in that era. But I need here to fix the sense of social class which the Elizabethans were conscious of, and to which Shakespeare responded in his plays. Sir Thomas Smith (1583) saw a fourfold division of English society: first, the nobility; second, the gentry or "minor nobility," which Smith subdivides into knights, esquires, and gentlemen; third, citizens, burgesses, and yeomen; and fourth, "The fourth sort of men which do not rule."[3] These were laborers, husbandmen, and artificers. Below them were the very poor, not even mentioned in Smith's classification. As a ruling principle, says Stone, "the hierarchy of ranks corresponded very roughly to categories of income."[4] There would always be anomalies and variations. And social class has never been based exclusively on wealth.

But there was a general understanding that degrees of rank were related to degrees of wealth. This understanding was illustrated, scandalously so, in the sliding scale for the purchase of titles set up under James I.

The great divide, and it is this that drama is especially interested in, was between gentlemen and the rest. Stone quotes a contemporary of Smith's who saw things with an even bleaker classification: "All sorts of people created from the beginning are divided into 2: noble and ignoble."[5] This is not the richest of classifications, and yet it corresponds to the linguistic convention on which Shakespearean drama is founded, that of blank verse and prose. *Gentleman* is the key term in the stratification of classes.

To be a gentleman placed one within the 4 to 5 percent of the population that exercised power. Characteristically, the gentleman did not work with his hands. He could live off his income. As Smith says:

In these days he is a gentleman who is commonly taken and reputed. And whosoever studieth in the universities, who professeth the liberal sciences and to be short who can live idly and without manual labor and will bear the port, charge and countenance of a gentleman, he shall be called master.[6]

"Master" means here a term of respectful address, the forebear of our "Mr." According to Smith, the main criterion was economic. There's a nice balance in his account. A. L. Rowse speaks of its "easy-going empiricism," into which is assimilated Smith's sardonic view, "As for gentlemen, they be made good cheap in England."[7] The implications of Smith's irony are plain when such shocked observers as Philip Stubbes speak of "every man crying with open mouth I am a gentleman, I am Honorable, I am noble, and I cannot tell what: my father was this, my father was that; I am come of this house, I am come of that."[8] Stubbes abhors the trend toward self-styled gentry and the general social assertiveness of the era. There was obviously a deal of social jostling, coupled with what a later age would know as social mobility. But as Stone says, "Despite the blurring of the line by the devaluation of the word 'gent.' despite the relative ease with which it could be crossed, the division between the gentleman and the rest was basic to Elizabethan society."[9]

Gentleman defies exact definition. Of all the social terms, it casts the widest net. The word contains the ideas of birth, education, wealth, behavior, and values. Yet it allows no single aspect to dominate, nor can any element insist on its presence. It is a moving part that takes the strain of fixed relationships in society. Moreover, *gentleman* is more than a rank.

It is an ideal of conduct, a fact regularly noted in Shakespeare's plays. Hamlet, a prince, is reported to have received Rosencrantz and Guildenstern "most like a gentleman." Don Armado assures Holofernes that "the King is a noble gentleman"—a marvellous line, which combines royalty, nobility, and gentry in a single statement of admiration. *Gentleman* will have to cover personages as diverse as Malvolio and the King of Navarre, Proteus and Coriolanus. It is a chameleon word, lacking solidity of definition.

To be a gentleman is to file a claim. And this is not true of the other major social strata in the same way. Scriveners, servants, grooms, and so on have no claims to make. Their cards of identity are issued, and there is no possibility of revoking them. The nobility may quarrel with one another over precedence—the cast of *Henry VI* does little else—but the matter will be decided, if not by brute force, then by the law, by genealogy. There is a rule book of sorts. Only gentlemen exist in a state of tension and perennial re-definition, since there may be no title deeds. The real gentleman has to assert himself against the usurper, against the inferior classes, against all manner of challenges. "Good Kate, I *am* a gentleman" says Petruchio, putting a distance between himself and the obscenity he has just uttered (*The Taming of the Shrew*, 2.1. 216). Hence the slightly queasy tone often associated with stage gentlemen derives from the claim they make, their push for self-definition. This is the subtext of Henry's encounter with his soldiers before Agincourt. There's a terrier-like reaction of Michael Williams to Henry, a bristling toward the unknown gentleman whose authority is imparted but not explained.

Gentleman brings into focus a wider problem of social class in Shakespeare. It is this: what begins as a simple indicator of rank turns easily into a repository of values. Rank as a metaphor for value is embedded in our language: in the phrase "to reward royally," for instance. The fact that representatives of rank act against its idea does not affect the idea. No doubt there were occasions when courtiers watching the public performance of, say, William IV of England or Charles VII of France murmured to one another, "He's not very royal, is he?" But he was: and *royal* still connotes becoming and generous behavior. Nietzsche seized on this perception long after Shakespeare, and in his *Genealogy of Morals* makes its classic statement:

What is the true etymological significance of the various symbols for the idea "good" which have been coined in the various languages? I then found that they all led back to *the same evolution of the same idea*—that everywhere "aristocrat," "noble" (in the social sense), is the root idea, out of which have necessarily developed "good," in the sense of "with aristocratic soul," "noble," in the sense of "with a soul of high calibre," "with a privileged soul"—a development which invariably runs parallel with that other evolution by which "vulgar," "plebeian," "low" are made to change finally into "bad" (I, 4).[10]

Noble is especially interesting to Shakespeare. It happens to be both adjective and noun (while *gentlemanly, gentleman-like* is cumbersome), and can be used ambivalently for social class and moral values. Usually there is no irony in sight: a noble behaves nobly. The overwhelming majority of cases implies assent to the claimed value: "'Tis nobly spoken," as Henry VIII says of Wolsey. But there are occasions—the eulogies, say, of "noble Timon" and "the noblest Roman of them all"—when the audience is free to ponder if it believes the claim. Irony is available, not coercive. Always there is a latent tension between noun and adjective (or adverb), that is, between rank and conduct.

This tension is available in all terms of rank. "This is not generous, *not gentle*, not humble," says Holofernes, rebuking the young followers of Navarre who are behaving in an ungentlemanly manner (*Love's Labor's Lost*, 5.2.621). *Noble* stands not only for rank, but also for soul and manner: demeanor, loftiness of bearing, a style of behavior. The stage has been skeptical of the word for several decades, as though *noble* were either meaningless or false. But it is not. Shakespeare impresses the word on us with intent to sound its implications; and the theater reviewers who, from time to time, deplore a Hamlet or an Othello who "lacks nobility" are not, I think, making an empty or unreasonable complaint. Hamlet is more than a postgraduate student in need of counseling, and Othello more than "a cultivated Arab businessman," to quote a recent reviewer. Terms of rank flood the text, insistently calling for realization in all their aspects.

Just as the idea of nobility is treated with a tactful but persistent accounting, so is the idea of baseness. Shakespeare shows from the earliest plays on that people in choler turn to class terms as their first refuge. "Churl," "base groom," "peasant" are the basic vocabulary of class invective. It goes without saying that Shakespeare is coolly neutral toward the general rhetoric of class terms. He merely shows us people whose thought, and expression, are impregnated with the equivalence of class and moral values. A nice instance occurs in *1 Henry VI*, when the Temple Garden scene leads to an open quarrel among the nobles. The Duke of Somerset, furious with Plantagenet, says "We grace the yeoman by conversing with him" (2.4. 81). In general usage, "yeoman" is positive enough. A yeoman, says Fuller, "is a gentleman in ore, whom the next age may see refined; and is the wax capable of a gentle impression, when the prince shall stamp it."[11] It is the stratum just beneath gentleman, in line for promotion. But to Somerset, it is a convenient insult, since by it he may degrade Plantagenet. Through the rhetoric of abuse, as with eulogy, one sees class absorbed into a moral system.

Naturally, Shakespearean drama tests these equations. It does so with a patient, cumulative skepticism that is neither subversive nor sycophantic. People are shown making claims for themselves and others via class. What one makes of those claims is part of the essential plot, the real play in performance.

How are the social classes identified in Shakespeare's plays? Usually, although not invariably, the rank or occupation of each member of the cast is easily discoverable. It could hardly be otherwise in an era when class affiliations were apparent through costume and mien, with personal wealth well known. Occupations gave a secure indicator of rank. Characters often refer to other characters by rank or occupation, and announce their own. Some caution is necessary, though, concerning information given in the dramatis personae as listed. That is because only seven of Shakespeare's plays are provided, in the Folio, with a list of dramatis personae. The lists for all other plays have had to be reconstructed by later editors, from Rowe on. And there are some errors in the usual attributions. Editors often, for example, refer to Benedick in *Much Ado About Nothing* as "a young lord." He is not. It is also incorrect to identify Baptista, Katherine's father, as a merchant. He is a well-to-do citizen of Padua. One should read the dramatis personae with some reserve, as a matter of course. But the text will usually offer a straightforward answer to a straightforward question.

Class identification is confirmed through language. From his earliest plays, certainly from *Richard III* on, Shakespeare works to give each speaker an individual mode of expression. And this mode has a class base. A knowledge of tropes, for example, is related to education. Swearing is a great indicator of rank, and Shakespeare is much interested in the freedom and variety with which people vent their feelings. He also, through Hotspur, records the reluctance of the middling classes to join in the vigorous profanity of high and low. The imagery a speaker employs often reveals something of his background. These are matters to be noted on an ad hoc basis, as they present themselves. But there are major conventions to which all classes must subscribe.

Shakespearean drama is grounded in prose and blank verse (with a small quantity of rhyme). This convention offers multiple effects, one of which is to distinguish between the classes. As a general rule, blank verse is the natural medium of gentry, as with nobility and royalty. It is the language of passion, dignity, and moral elevation, hence is equated with social elevation. Prose, says Vickers, "is the vehicle of an inferior class, such as servants and clowns."[12] It is the medium of those who, for reasons which include the social, fall beneath the dignity of verse.

Now this is an indispensable generalization; and yet it is broken all the time. Members of the aristocracy may relax, or condescend, into prose if they wish. It is for them the language of informality. Hamlet speaks prose to Rosencrantz and Guildenstern, as to the Players and the Gravedigger. Falstaff speaks prose virtually all the time, whatever the company. So does Sir Toby Belch. Orsino, who speaks verse most of the time, speaks prose with Feste (5.1), evidently realizing that it would never do to stand on his dignity with the Clown. The patrician Brutus reasons in prose with the Roman crowd. Those who are mad (Ophelia, Lear, Othello) necessarily fall below the level of verse, which implies intellectual control, and express themselves in prose. Conversely—though of this there are far fewer examples—a member of the subordinate classes may, on occasion, be elevated into verse. The Murderers in *Richard III* speak to Clarence in verse, because at that point they take on the dignity of judges. Sometimes the general tone of a scene will demand that everyone in it conform to the prevailing mode, whether verse or prose. At the end of *Richard II*, the Groom speaks to Richard in verse, because he shares in the dignity and passion of Richard's last moments. Shifts of tone and situation must always be taken into account. And yet the basis of the convention is social. Prose is an extra dimension of being, an extra register for those above the line. For those below, it is virtually the only mode. The mass of reservation is formidable. And yet the ruling generalization holds: kings speak verse and commoners speak prose.

A second indicator of rank is the distinction between *you* and *thou*. It is not so far from the German *du/Sie* and the French *tu/vous* conventions. Historically, *you* came to be used as a mark of respect when used in the singular while addressing a social superior. *You/thou* is often taken as a contrast between polite and insulting; but this, says Randolph Quirk, is a gross oversimplification: "The modern linguistic concept of contrast operating through *marked* and *unmarked* members gives us a truer picture. *You* is usually the stylistically unmarked form: it is not so much 'polite' as 'not impolite'; it is not so much 'formal' as 'not informal.' "[13] The distinction bears regularly upon the social standing of the speaker and the person addressed. *Thou* conveys intimacy, whether of warmth or hostility. It closes the distance between people. It is for the social superior in a relationship to choose *thou* (unless, of course, the address can be taken for granted between friends of equal standing). These nuances are regularly observed by Shakespeare. Hamlet addresses Horatio as *thou*, and is addressed by him as *you*. Commonly, a master addresses his servants as *thou*, but it is not for the servant to reciprocate. That is why Kent is so offensively rebellious in his defiance of Lear: "What would'st thou, old man?" G. L. Brook regards *you* as "the usual pronoun used by upper-class speakers to one another," while *thou* is used "by lower-class characters in speaking to other members of the same social class."[14]

Usage can vary between the same sets of speakers. Proteus and Valentine use *thou* at the beginning of *The Two Gentlemen of Verona*, but after a separation use the cooler *you*. Falstaff and Hal use both forms freely, often reverting to the marked *thou* of anger or intimacy: "Dost thou hear me, Hal?" "Ay, and mark thee too, Jack" (*Henry IV Part One*, 2.4. 201–02). Falstaff is asserting his human equality to the Prince. So is Poins, at a tense moment: "I would think thee a most princely hypocrite" (*Henry IV Part Two*, 2.2 50–51). Benedick, after his declaration of love for Beatrice, wavers between the forms: he clearly wants the sustained and reciprocated warmth of *thou*, but Beatrice, who invariably addresses him as *you*, keeps him at a distance as it were (*Much Ado About Nothing*, 4.1). *Thou/you* is an infinitely subtle marker of distance between human beings, constantly moving on the scale. Social nuances fade into the emotional, where we must leave them. But as with the use of verse and prose, one comes back to the social dimension of the matter. The person addressing the other as *thou* has the initiative; he claims a social right for himself. Hamlet, who must spend the play addressing Claudius as *you* (and is so addressed by Claudius: they are not close, those two) ends it with "Here, thou incestuous, murd'rous, damned Dane,/ Drink off this potion." With *thou*, Hamlet releases a social insult, the linguistic analogue to killing the King. And *thou*, as Sir Toby Belch well understands, is a useful provocation if that is one's game. "If thou thou'st him some thrice, it shall not be amiss" (*Twelfth Night*, 3.2. 41–42). If there is any doubt as to the relative social standing of the speakers, the matter can as well be referred to their use of *you/thou* as any other form of arbitration. They always seem to know.

For the actor, as for the playwright, social class is a means of transmitting identity. Every human being is an individual and a member of many groups—indeed, an infinite number of groups. Part of the interest of people lies in the extent to which they are, or seem to be, representative of their groups. Certainly the actor needs something to work on, needs to be able to say: This part reminds me of some people I've known. The individual's experience will be part of a group experience. Glen Byam Shaw, who played the Cripple in Max Reinhardt's production of *The Miracle* (1932) relates that, before he made his first entrance, Reinhardt, instead of wishing him luck, spat at him to put him in the right frame of mind. The actor was to frame himself to the condition, and experience, of cripples.

All parts in Shakespeare may be approached via their general aspects, whether of rank, occupation, or type. Dr. Johnson saw Shakespeare as supremely gifted in his handling of a species. For the Romantics, the individual was all. Today, there would I suppose be general agreement that individual and social aspects of character are balanced. The most important and provocative case for study is Coriolanus. He is shown to be very strongly influenced by his mother, Volumnia, who is a compendium of patrician attitudes. Coriolanus is formed (though not defined) by his class background. We need the class, to account for the individual; without the individual, there is really little point in discussing class. Coriolanus is so fascinating a study because one receives a picture of his upbringing (which is not, of course, true of Shakespeare's characters in general) and is encouraged to assess the factors that went into his making. Through social class, one gains insight into how people think and feel. Class is an ellipsis of motivation.

Chronology is the key to the study of social class as of virtually all else in Shakespeare. One can never discard the great achievement of Victorian scholarship, a reasonably reliable ordering of the plays. Shakespeare never stopped developing, and that should qualify generalizations based on his practice at any one time. For example, Muriel St. Clare Byrne offers what looks like a useful distinction between characters and stock types:

If his dramatic purpose simply required persons occupying a recognized position in the social scheme, we get such sketches as Lucetta, waiting-gentlewoman to Julia; Margaret and Ursula; Lady Macbeth's gentlewoman, and the Queen's woman in *Richard II*. Being first and foremost stock utilities they are true to type. They know their place, because they *are* their place.[15]

I agree that Lucetta, the pert lady's maid, is stock; but what of the others? Margaret (in *Much Ado*) betrays Hero, on whom she attends. This is a character who does not "know her place." What is her motive—resentment, or infatuation for Borachio? The actress will have to decide,

but "stock type" will not resolve the question. Similarly, the Gentlewoman who stands her ground against the Doctor in Lady Macbeth's
sleepwalking scene is also something more than "stock." She reflects a
whole hinterland of communal response to the great crime on which the
ruling house is founded. Or take the Soldier in *Antony and Cleopatra*: his
familiar way with his General is the sign of a long relationship and of the
sort of man Antony is with his troops. Even those transparent necessities,
Messengers, can transmit something individual. They are not there
merely to deliver oral telegrams. The usefulness of the character/stock
type distinction fades, to my mind, as one leaves the early Shakespeare
behind. In the mature Shakespeare, all but the smallest spear-carrying
parts have something beyond the routine. They are miniature versions of
the larger roles, rather than distinct species.

   Again, one has to know the phases of Shakespeare's career to identify
his sense of social order. The societies of the early plays are composed of
stable relationships (between classes and groups) and fixed counters.
There is, of course, contention. Young gentlemen fall out over young
ladies. Peers quarrel with one another over precedence. Revolutionary
mobs exact class revenges, before being quelled. Servants have to be
thumped. The inferior orders are sometimes saucy, but the servants are,
after all, thumped by their masters. And there is no doubt as to the
relative standing of Costard and the visitors from France, or of Speed and
Valentine. We know where we are. All this certainty shifts, however, with
the more dynamic, difficult, and unstable world of the middle comedies.
We cannot be sure of the standing of Gratiano (gentleman, social
climber?) or Malvolio (upstart bureaucrat, wronged gentleman?). We
cannot be sure of the values with which we are invited to contemplate
these people. The skeptical and problem-racked essays of the early seventeenth century—*King Lear* and *Measure for Measure* are the representative
plays—bring all social values into question. Things have stabilized by the
final romances, and one has a sense of ordered placing (which does not
preclude such transformations as the Shepherd of *The Winter's Tale* into a
"gentleman born"). At all times, one needs to have some idea of the play's
approximate position in Shakespeare's career.

   I have arranged this book, then, into chapters which correspond
broadly with a phase of Shakespeare's work. There is no schema that
really works; Shakespeare resists organization. Still, the solutions I have
adopted are reasonably close to those of other writers faced with dividing
up Shakespeare's output. The Roman plays are a special problem. The
series, if it is that, begins early with *Titus Andronicus* and ends late with

Antony and Cleopatra and *Coriolanus*: there are perhaps fifteen years between first and last. Yet I share the general view that the Roman plays are a distinct subspecies, comment on which can be concentrated. *Timon of Athens* is always a problem, and I have preferred to slip it in at the end of the chapter on the Roman plays. "Shakespeare's Classical Tragedies," though, is too guiltily strained a chapter heading for my taste. The other plays can reasonably be nudged into groupings that combine genre and chronology. These are matters of persuasive convenience, however. At all times, the unit that matters is the play.

The basis of this book is linguistic. The text is what I work from. Even so, I have on occasion appealed to the stage as a record of how problems have been solved and options chosen. For the play, one needs players. It seems to me absurd to ignore the contributions that the stage has made to the presentation of Shakespeare. Shakespeare left a set of possibilities to be rendered in performance, not a documentary record of types and classes. And after all, a certain ambiguity cannot be filtered out of questions of social class. As Lawrence Stone has said, "A class is not a finite group of families, but rather a bus or a hotel, always full but always filled with different people."[16] The stage knows how to present shifting views of these different people.

Moreover, through the stage one grasps some sense of dramatic values, without which an accurate judgment would be impossible. For instance, Jack Cade in *Henry VI* is a brute and a dangerous demagogue. Yet his last scene is ambivalent. He is a fugitive and starving, and he tells us so. Then Iden comes into his orchard and tells the audience in eight complacent lines how well content he is with his lot. At him, Cade jerks his head, and to the audience confides "Here's the lord of the soil, come to seize me for a stray" (4.10. 24–25). Whatever the audience remembers about Cade, whatever its views on social order, they will at that moment side with the man on the run, not the man of property. In the same play, the Duke of Suffolk is an extraordinarily objectionable aristocrat. But he dies game, and will capture some sympathy. Social values, like human values generally, cannot be pinned down to stereotypes of being or audience response.

In brief, here are the main periods and emphases of Shakespeare's work as they bear upon social class:

1. The early history plays are dominated by a single order, the nobility, who are characteristically willful, self-assertive, and unable to make the adjustments necessary for the peaceful evolution of social life. In themselves, these nobles cause the outbreak of the Wars of the Roses.

2. The early comedies offer a straightforward, stable account of the

social classes. The ranks are fixed with precision and interesting detail. The implied need is simply for the classes to get along with each other. *Love's Labor's Lost*, though disturbed at the end, offers for the most part a model of communal harmony and *A Midsummer Night's Dream* leads to a harmonious encounter of court and mechanicals.

3. The middle comedies are altogether more complex and dynamic. Far more information is built into the key personages: we know far more about Portia and Bassanio than any previous aristocrat in the canon. *The Merry Wives of Windsor*, the only "English" comedy, is based on the idea that society is competitive, not stable. It is a middle-class, not a court/ mechanicals play. Resentments, frictions, and competition for social reward drive the action of *Twelfth Night*.

4. The second tetralogy offers, in the *Henry* plays, a panorama of English society. That society is examined under the extreme pressures of war in *Henry V*, while the class tensions of the battlefield, at Harfleur and Agincourt, are detailed with great acuity.

5. The four major tragedies show class as completely assimilated into character and motivation. Hamlet, Lear, and Macbeth hold a particular rank in a particular society, and Iago's hatred of Othello (and Cassio) is rooted in class resentment.

6. The problem plays show social class in relation to sex. *All's Well That Ends Well* rests on an aristocrat's repugnance to a physician's daughter. *Troilus and Cressida* deals with an affair, from which marriage appears excluded, between members of different social classes. *Measure for Measure* represents the sexual problem of a society as it bears upon the gentry and, in the end, upon the Duke.

7. The Roman plays are not, I think, a single arc of thought. They are, however, a separate issue. The four Roman tragedies differ from other plays set abroad because the playwright was expected to offer a respectful and well-informed imitation of Roman society; he was tied to authenticity. But analogues emerge from time to time; no society is totally unlike another society, and there are glimpses of England in Rome. The Roman patricians are obviously not mirror-images of the Elizabethan nobility. But the audience is not prevented from identifying a certain cast of mind in the Roman fascination with "nobility" as appears in Antony's Forum speech and Brutus's behavior at all times. These analogies are most strongly and provocatively pressed in *Coriolanus*, that bleak and unyielding analysis of the class struggle.

8. The final romances show, on the whole, a diminished interest in class orderings. It is as though Shakespeare was beginning to take social class

for granted as the carbon to which the human species is reduced. But there are many telling cameos of class exchange, and some good jokes, as in *The Winter's Tale*. The core relationship of *The Tempest* is that of master and man, with the play ending in freedom for the men and freedom for the master. *Henry VIII* closes in social accord, as all classes rejoice in the birth of a princess.

CHAPTER ONE

The Early Histories

HENRY VI

*H*enry VI is a story of civil war and national disaster. *Part One* is a stately contention among nobles, *Part Two* an explosion into class warfare, and *Part Three* a human cataclysm, in which the English are reduced to warring animality. The roots of this disaster, as Shakespeare shows, are nourished by class feeling, and not even in *Coriolanus* is there a more intense opposition between the aristocratic and popular principle. *Henry VI* is an unflinching account of class pride and class resistance.

The general problem in England is, of course, a weak king and a willful, self-assertive aristocracy. The breakdown of order is clear from the opening, as the nobles quarrel and the Messenger charges "that here you maintain several factions" (1.1. 71). It is a matter of class pride, linked with class contempt. The good Duke Humphrey of Gloucester, backed by his Bluecoats, finds his way to the Tower barred: "Shall I be flouted thus by dunghill grooms?" (1.3. 14). Hotheadedness is the endemic failing of the nobility. Almost everyone has it—Winchester, Somerset, Plantagenet. A man who can control his passions, as Warwick can, stands head and shoulders above the rest. And the audience is not asked to admire these mettlesome patricians. Nothing is more interesting than the wink and nudge of complicity with which the Mayor of London buttonholes his audience:

> Good God, these nobles should such stomachs bear!
> I myself fight not once in forty year.
>
> (1.4.89–90)

That is the scene's end, a summing up by a burgher and a survivor. He has just, with great difficulty, parted the fray. For a moment, but it is a long one, he is the adult of sense and good humor who has kept quarrelsome children from doing real damage.

The Temple Garden encounter is the big scene, and the formal origin of England's troubles. At bottom, the quarrel is a refusal of arbitration. The aristocratic cynicism of Suffolk's "Faith, I have been a truant in the law/And never yet could frame my will to it;/And therefore frame the law unto my will" (2.4. 7–9) says it all. For the contestants, the issue is one of will and pride, and Plantagenet makes his claim through the rhetoric of class:

> Let him that is a true-born gentleman
> And stands upon the honor of his birth,
> If he supposes that I have pleaded truth,
> From off this brier pluck a white rose with me.
>
> (2.4.27–30)

Which is as much as to say that anyone disagreeing with him can scarcely be "a true-born gentleman." Predictably, the temperature rises, and soon Somerset addresses the fatal word to Plantagenet: "We grace the yeoman by conversing with him" (2.4. 81). "Yeoman": that is much like addressing Coriolanus as "boy." The scene degenerates into name-calling, with fierce assertions of paternal guilt and paternal innocence.

> *Somerset*:   Was not thy father, Richard Earl of Cambridge,
>   For treason executed in our late king's days? (2.4.
>   90–91)
> *Plantagenet*: My father was *attached*, not attainted [that is,
>   arrested, not convicted, 2.4. 96].

The nobles compete in a kind of snakes-and-ladders game of language. To lose one's nobility, to become a yeoman, is to start all over again.

Title is the obsessive concern of the nobles. Mortimer, in the scene that follows (2.5), expends his final breath in relating the family history. The rapt genealogy of the dying Mortimer, his passionate interest in "pedigree," signals a kind of occupational disease. Robert Speaight, of the parallel scene in *Part Two* (2.2), remarks wearily that York retails his claim to the throne "at great length to Warwick and Salisbury who know it by heart already, and to an audience of amateur genealogists who apparently cannot hear it too often."[1] The audience must have liked it, too.

If title is everything, then "bastard" is the supreme insult. It has in this society an explosive force. Thus Gloucester's "Thou bastard of my grandfather!" (3.1. 42) is the key to the deep antagonism between the two. There's a strong vein of the "bastard" motivation in Winchester, the evil genius of *Part One*. Historically, he is ancestor to Edmund and Don John. Dramatically, he embodies the principle of force creating an equal and opposite counterforce. In the world of title, illegitimacy is the deepest stigma.

Talbot used to be thought of as the hero of *Part One*; so it is worth noting that when John Barton and Peter Hall cut the part completely from the version of *Henry VI* that they staged as *The Wars of the Roses* in 1964, he was not greatly missed. In fact, Talbot seems to epitomize qualities on view elsewhere in the play. The aristocrat as warrior, that is his role; and it is legitimized dramatically by the need to fight the French, efficiently and successfully. Again, this is as much a social as a nationalist trait. Talbot's jeer at the "base muleteers of France" is that

> Like peasant foot-boys do they keep the walls,
> And dare not take up arms like gentlemen.
>
> (3.2.68–70)

And it is agreed by all that Sir John Falstaff (the most distant cousin here of the great Sir John) has disgraced his class by his conduct at the battle of Patay. As Gloucester puts it:

> To say the truth, this fact was infamous
> And ill beseeming any common man,
> Much more a knight, a captain, and a leader.
>
> (4.1.30–32)

Falstaff should, says Talbot, "Be quite degraded, like a hedge-born swain/That doth presume to boast of gentle blood" (4.1. 43–44). Even the mild Henry concurs. Theirs is a warrior caste, distinguished from all others by its superior fighting qualities, where cowardice and rank are incompatible, indeed mutually exclusive.

As the supreme representative of the warrior caste, Talbot is permitted the valiant and moving death that befits his life. Even so, the play does not endorse Talbot's code of values, which are challenged by Joan La Pucelle herself. To Lucy's ringing declamation

> But where's the great Alcides of the field,
> Valiant Lord Talbot, Earl of Shrewsbury,
> Created for his rare success in arms
> Great Earl of Washford, Waterford, and Valence,
> Lord Talbot of Goodrig and Urchinfield,
> Lord Strange of Blackmere, Lord Verdun of Alton,
> Lord Cromwell of Wingfield, Lord Furnival of Sheffield,
> The thrice victorious Lord of Faulconbridge,
> Knight of the noble order of Saint George,
> Worthy Saint Michael, and the Golden Fleece,
> Great Marshal to Henry the Sixth
> Of all his wars within the realm of France?
>
> (4.7.60–71)

Pucelle answers:

> Here's a silly-stately style indeed!
> The Turk, that two and fifty kingdoms hath,
> Writes not so tedious a style as this.
> Him that thou magnifi'st with all these titles,
> Stinking and fly-blown lies here at our feet.
>
> (4.7.72–76)

It is an amazing moment. The "hero" of *Part One* is eulogized with all the panoply of rank and chivalry. No title is omitted. The words that might be inscribed by his tomb, a roll call of achievement and honor, are sonorously declaimed by the English herald. And Pucelle destroys them. *That*, the play insinuates, was posturing and unreality, for all its glamor; *this* is the reality: a dead man at our feet. It is the play's reduction of "title."

After this, the play naturally backs away from identifying itself with Pucelle's subversive commentary. Pucelle herself, it turns out, is not above claiming "noble birth" to save her life from the English, even if it means disavowing her father:

> I am descended of a gentler blood;
> Thou art no father nor no friend of mine.
>
> (5.4.8–9)

Shakespeare makes heartless fun of Pucelle's late conversion to title, and of the English nobles' reaction to her multiple paternity order. "A married man! That's most intolerable" (5.4.79). This is black humor, and it goes some way toward effacing the questions that have been raised.

Still, the strong, coarse class interest of *Part One* has left certain propositions on the table. This play is not merely a contention among nobles; it is about people who contend because they *are* noble. England is shown as saddled with a quarrelsome and ungovernable aristocracy, with a bent for martial action at which their own divisions render them incompetent. Other classes are a gauge of unworthiness. The class pride is all. The fall is to come.

2 HENRY VI

The social convulsions of *Part Two* are instigated by the nobles, the Duke of Suffolk and the Duke of York. More than anyone else, Suffolk strikes the tuning fork of class pride that vibrates throughout the play. When Salisbury enters with the news that the Commons are after Suffolk's blood, his response is

> 'Tis like the Commons, rude unpolish'd hinds,
> Could send such message to their sovereign;
> But you, my lord, were glad to be employ'd,
> To show how quaint an orator you are.
> But all the honor Salisbury hath won
> Is that he was the lord ambassador
> Sent from a sort of tinkers to the King.
>
> (3.2.271–77)

Unsurprisingly, the tinkers get him. The class revenge exacted on the Kentish sands is his personal nemesis, presented with a brutal immediacy. Two nameless Gentlemen save their lives by paying their ransom. Suffolk is different. His attempt at brazening things out, "Look on my George, I am a gentleman" (4.1.29), soon leads to his unmasking. In character to the end, Suffolk defies his captors in the old vein:

> Obscure and lowly swain, King Henry's blood,
> The honorable blood of Lancaster,
> Must not be shed by such a jaded groom.
> Hast thou not kiss'd my hand and held my stirrup,
> Bareheaded plodded by my foot-cloth mule,
> And thought thee happy when I shook my head?
>
> (4.1.50–56)

It meets only Whitmore's "Speak, Captain, shall I stab the forlorn swain?" (4.1.65) and the Lieutenant's brutal dismissal, "Convey him hence, and on our longboat's side/Strike off his head" (4.1.68). But this is more than a bloody scuffle over a longboat. Suffolk is to be arraigned, not merely extinguished. The Lieutenant now speaks for England, and in the long speech "Poole! . . . /Ay, kennel, puddle, sink, whose filth and dirt/ Troubles the silver spring where England drinks" (4.1.70–103) delivers the charge, the verdict, and the sentence. It is a judge who speaks. The verse has the solemnity and elevation of a great formal indictment, and the catalogue of national disaster comes down to "And all by thee. Away! Convey him hence" (4.1.103). It is unanswerable; and Suffolk, who insists that "true nobility is exempt from fear" (4.1.129), dies game to the last.

All this is a preview. The major class conflict begins with the Cade forces in action at Blackheath. The rebellion is the work of a maverick nobleman, York, who has "seduc'd a headstrong Kentishman, /John Cade of Ashford, /To make commotion as full well he can" (3.1.356–58). It is not a spontaneous uprising, ignited by a sense of social wrongs. The mob's personality is rendered through its leader, and Cade turns out to be an engaging enough brute. He is found claiming a distinguished genealogy, just like his social betters:

> *Cade*: My father was a Mortimer—
> *Dick*: [*aside*] He was an honest man and a good bricklayer.
> *Cade*: My mother a Plantagenet—
> *Dick*: [*aside*] I knew her well; she was a midwife.
> *Cade*: My wife descended of the Lacies—
> *Dick*: [*aside*] She was, indeed, a pedlar's daughter, and
>   sold many laces.
> *Smith*: [*aside*] But now of late, not able to travel with
>   with her furr'd pack, she washes bucks here at home.
> *Cade*: Therefore am I of an honorable house.
>
> (4.2.37–47)

Having already seen one Mortimer, the audience now encounters a cadet branch of the same distinguished house. Good fun in itself, this is a wicked parody of the upmarket claims.

The radical program that Cade advances in his election addresses resembles later essays in the genre. Items in the radical program come and go, of course. But bread subsidies are always there in some form: "There shall be in England seven halfpenny loaves sold for a penny"

(4.2.62–64). The aversion from grammar schools, which has reemerged in the later twentieth century, has its *locus classicus* in Cade's charge against Lord Say: "Thou hast most traitorously corrupted the youth of the realm in erecting a grammar school" (4.7.30–32). The "felony to drink small beer," which Cade proposes (4.2.64–65), might seem of antique interest. In fact, Cade is alert to that grave class offense, Watering the Workers' Beer. Small beer was the weakest and cheapest beer. Mindful of the need to expand his constituency, Cade proposes as his first act, "sitting upon London Stone," to "charge and command that, of the city's cost, the pissing-conduit run nothing but claret wine this first year of our reign" (4.6.1–4). Add to this glimpse of social democracy in action, "The first thing that we do, let's kill all the lawyers" (4.2.73), and we have the elements of a genuine popular program. There is even a foreign policy, based on a rough nationalism of the anti-French order. The program is one to appeal to, if not unite, all audiences.

Unluckily for Cade, the forces of the Establishment take over precisely that part of his program with most enduring popular appeal—hatred of the French combined with profitable looting at their expense. "To France, to France, and get what you have lost! /Spare England, for it is your native coast" (4.8.48–49). This is the Henry V card, as Cade well realizes. "Was feather ever so lightly blown to and fro as this multitude? The name of Henry the Fifth hales them to an hundred mischiefs, and makes them leave me desolate" (4.8.54–57). The game is up. Shakespeare describes a proto-election in Act 4 (just as he describes a real election in *Coriolanus*), with Clifford and Buckingham the successful politicians of the Establishment. It is a kind of medieval Eatanswill.

The funny-horrible tone of all this has to accommodate the killings. Shakespeare is unsparing in his account of a dangerous demagogue on the rampage. Yet the audience's sympathy is invited. Take the confrontation between Sir Humphrey Stafford and Cade. Sir Humphrey has a wooden charmlessness: "Rebellious hinds, the filth and scum of Kent, /Mark'd for the gallows, lay your weapons down" (4.2.117–18). Cade, after responding in verse—not very well, it is not his métier—soon reverts to his habitual prose. The real man comes through after a brief attempt to ape the speech ways of the gentry. Cade has the bounce and vitality of a Card. Insidiously, the power of dramatic suggestion shapes the audience response. Of course he has to be stopped. But not too many will rejoice at his fall.

It is the middle classes who dispatch Cade. Iden, "Esquire of Kent," has had a generally good press. He is widely seen as a symbol of order, as when he says: "This small inheritance my father left me/Contenteth me, and worth a monarchy" (4.10.18–19). Does Shakespeare side with the man of property? Not if the actor playing Cade is up to it. He can destroy Iden with an inflection and a jerk of his head: "Here's the lord of the soil come to seize me for a stray, for entering his fee-simple without leave." Besides, it's a rule of escape drama that the audience always sides with the man on the run. In sporting terms, the combat that follows is a mismatch, since Cade is much smaller and weakened with hunger, as the dialogue emphasizes. More, for all the sanctimonious "I seek not to wax great by others' waning," Iden hastens to claim his reward. He bears Cade's head to the King, and Buckingham prompts Henry to do the politic thing: "So please it you, my lord, 'twere not amiss/He were created knight for his good service" (5.1.76–77). A moment later he is Sir Alexander Iden and a thousand marks richer. I cannot see that Shakespeare invests this transaction with a moral nimbus.

Part Two, then, ends with the rebellion crushed and the warring nobles able to revert to their own contention. I agree with John Palmer's assessment: "This episode of Cade's rebellion, cited as a supreme example of Shakespeare's anti-democratic spirit, turns out . . . to be an interlude graced with touches of humanity and humor for which we shall look in vain on the aristocratic fields of Towton or Tewkesbury."[2] Put more simply, Cade has the best lines.

3 HENRY VI

Part Three tells of England's descent into the pit. The tragedies of King Henry, and England, merge, and the outcome is the rise of the sinister Gloucester. It is a play virtually confined to the nobility, Lancastrian and Yorkist, and of class interest there is little. King Edward's marriage to Lady Elizabeth Grey is seen primarily as a political blunder, rather than as a social mésalliance, though this aspect is registered. Civil war itself, rather than the jarring of classes, is the matter of *Part Three*, and Shakespeare condenses the story into two unforgettable stage directions:

Enter a Son that hath kill'd his Father, with the body in his arms.
Enter a Father that hath kill'd his Son, with the body in his arms.

The human, not class, aspect is what Shakespeare now depicts. In this drama of bloodshed and suffering, the common people, to the fore in *Part*

Two, are merely props in the nobles' contention. Edward's dismissal of the army after the battle of Tewkesbury has, in its laconic way, the sense of *Part Three*:

> Now march we hence. Discharge the common sort
> With pay and thanks; and let's away to London
> And see our gentle queen how well she fares.
>
> (5.5.87–89)

Not even a full sentence is devoted to the rank and file!

RICHARD III

The class issues of *Richard III* are complex and of a different order from the simplicities of *Henry VI*. In the *Henry VI* trilogy, the many nobles on view are clearly representative of their social class. The points are established through weight of repetition. In *Richard III*, everything depends on the title part. And he is not at all presented in straightforward class terms.

Richard of Gloucester is an aristocrat. And some of his lines have the aristocrat's pride of family and class: "Unmanner'd dog! Stand thou when I command" (1.2.39); "Ay, and much more; but I was born so high" (1.3.263); "Madam, I have a touch of your condition, /That cannot brook the accent of reproof" (4.4.157–58). This is not, however, his norm. Of those sayings, Olivier in his film cut the third and gave away the second to Buckingham. In this he showed a fine instinct for the main lines of the part, which is not at all modeled on the testy Junkers of *Henry VI*. The key to *Richard III* is audience rapport between star and audience, from the early to the middle stages of the play. Anything that threatens this rapport is to be eliminated or circumvented. The audience will reject Richard ultimately, but not before Act 5.

It follows that the hauteur of Somerset, Suffolk, and company is to be replaced by a more winning manner. Richard's language is colloquial, proverbial, uncourtly. It could fairly be termed *bourgeois* as an approximation of style with, for example, its "pack horse," "post horse" references, and "But yet I run before my horse to market" (1.1.160). Some of his lines have a rustic quality: "He is frank'd up to fatting for his pains" (1.3.314); "Small herbs have grace, great weeds do grow apace" (2.4.13); "Short summers lightly have a forward spring" (3.1.94). Often jocular and ingratiating, these sayings reach out to the concerns of the general audience. Richard's is the language of the common man, rather than the grand seigneur.

Moreover, Richard the actor delights in various personae: pious contemplative (the scene before the citizens, Act 3, scene 7), ardent lover (the scene with Lady Anne, Act 1, scene 2), unworldly innocent and country boy (Act 1 generally). None of these roles calls for a specifically aristocratic idiom. On the contrary, the strawberries episode, say, suggests a man more at home in a garden than the court. More subtly, Richard's roles promote a vein of popular morality, citizens' morality. He ridicules it, of course, but he still strikes a chord. For instance, of Edward's dalliance with Jane Shore, he says:

> Now by St. Paul, that news is bad indeed!
> O, he hath kept an evil diet long,
> And overmuch consum'd his royal person.
>
> (1.1.138–40)

And before the citizens he exclaims, "O, do not *swear*, my Lord of Buckingham" (3.7.220). Buckingham has just said "Zounds" ("God's Wounds"), the strongest available stage oath. Richard, as Buckingham remarks, "is not an Edward! /He is not lolling on a lewd love-bed . . . Not dallying with a brace of courtesans" (3.7.71–74). Act 3, scene 7, is recognizably the Draft Richard Convention, founded on the proposition that Richard speaks the language and thinks the thoughts of the people. He will initiate a reformist regime, dedicated to restoring standards of civic morality that have so sadly lapsed during the reign of Edward the Lustful.

Richard is a citizen, one of us. He doesn't believe it, we don't believe it, but that is the subliminal appeal on which the Convention is founded. And it works. The citizens do not exactly endorse Richard, but they allow Buckingham to stage matters without uproar. If you take the citizen-crowd of Act 3, scene 7 as the stage analogue to the theater audience, they assent—grudgingly, no doubt—to the view of Richard that he himself promotes.

But what has happened to class consciousness in its usual sense? Richard has exported it and fastened the blame on the wretched Woodvilles! It is his strategy in the early scenes for stirring up resentment in the court. Richard's constant theme is the unworthiness of Edward's marriage and the evil consequences that must flow from this violation of the natural order. "My Lady Grey, his wife" (in other words, the *Queen*) is the main target of scorn:

> The jealous o'erworn widow and herself,
> Since that our brother dubb'd them gentlewomen,
> Are mighty gossips in our monarchy.
>
> (1.1.81–83)

The charge is that "the Queen's kindred are made gentlefolks" (1.1.95). And the attack is kept up in the general court scene of 1.3: "Since every Jack became a gentleman, /There's many a gentle person made a jack" (72–73). This is subtler than it looks, because there is nothing in stage terms to counter Richard's view of the Woodvilles. Dorset, Rivers, and Grey are ciphers. They are alleged to be, and presumably are, the lucky beneficiaries of Lady Grey's rise to fame. Thus the Woodvilles focus whatever class resentment is in the audience: they are jumped-up gentry, a category that by definition no one (noble, popular, established gentry, bourgeois) cares for. So Richard succeeds in rallying the audience behind him.

These are very amazing tricks to play with class. The Richard of the first three acts carries out a tightrope performance with audience rapport, now getting on well with the Murderers—"I like you, lads, about your business straight" (1.3.355)—now patronizing the entire court, with the ironic descending arpeggio of "Dukes, earls, lords, gentlemen" (2.1.68). Whatever he does, he takes the audience with him. Even the Murderers come in two dimensions. They appear first as honest professionals getting on with the job, delivering a solid product no matter what the difficulties. Later they assume the role of judge before Clarence's death, rebuking and condemning him for his crimes. Somehow the sheer squalor of Richard's drive to power is shielded from us for half the play.

But of course the people know him. There is a Chorus of sorts in Act 2, scene 3, and the Third Citizen has Richard's number:

> All may be well; but if God sort it so,
> 'Tis more than we deserve or I expect.
>
> (2.3.36–37)

The nameless Scrivener, laboring over Hastings' indictment for hours before Hastings' charge, is undeceived. The four women—Elizabeth,

Anne, Margaret, Richard's own mother—see through him. The consciousness of this drama, which is a popular consciousness, knows
Richard and judges him. At the last, Richard attempts to rally his
audience with an appeal to the sexual and racial instincts of the soldiery:

> Remember whom you are to cope withal—
> A sort of vagabonds, rascals, and runaways,
> A scum of Bretons, and base lackey peasants,
> Whom their o'er-cloyed country vomits forth
> To desperate adventures and assur'd destruction.
> You having lands, and bless'd with beauteous wives,
> They would restrain the one, distain the other.
>
> . . .
>
> If we be conquer'd, let men conquer us,
> And not these bastard Bretons, whom our fathers
> Have in their own land beaten, bobb'd, and thump'd,
> And, in record, left them the heirs of shame.
> Shall these enjoy our lands? lie with our wives,
> Ravish our daughters?
>
> (5.3.315–37)

The rhetoric has a cracked ring. The soldiery/audience rejects the appeal,
and the army simply refuses to fight. Richard's last lines, to Catesby, tell a
final truth. "*Slave*, I have set my life upon a cast" (5.4.9). Catesby, once a
person, has become an object. All classes have now abandoned Richard,
and he re-assumes the state of *3 Henry VI*: "I am myself alone" (5.6.83).

KING JOHN

We move from one outsider to another. *King John*, like *Richard III*, is
built on a star role outside the regular social structures. An actor might
see things differently, and reckon King John quite as good a part as
Faulconbridge. But from an audience's viewpoint, there's no competition.
This is the Bastard's play, and an actor worth his salt can take it over.
   Why should this be? Faulconbridge must have had a special kind of
direct access to a portion of the audience, those knowing themselves to be
illegitimate. This could not have been a substantial number, however.

Peter Laslett gives a table with the ratios of illegitimacy in English parishes for the period beginning 1581. In the first decade, the percentage of registered baptisms marked illegitimate reached 2.9. In the following decade, the percentage rose to 3.9.[3] In a simple and direct way, Philip the Bastard would have been a spokesman for a sector of the audience. But of course, illegitimacy is more than a literal. It becomes a metaphor for the man in the outside lane, the New Man, the one who, without conforming to Establishment standards, makes his way through the system and arrives rapidly at the top. And Philip achieves this without the taint of the parvenu (that, say, Wolsey has). He is of royal blood, and his stigma is overborne by Coeur-de-Lion's paternity. That is the view the play takes, to which the audience assents. Faulconbridge is a composite figure, a folk hero who combines illegitimacy with immediate descent from a legendary hero of the realm.

Into this composite the audience can happily fit its dreams, desires, hopes. Legitimacy is guyed in the unimpressive figure of Sir Robert, whom the audience can dismiss as the Bastard does:

> Brother, adieu. Good fortune come to thee!
> For thou wast got i'th'way of honesty.

> (1.1.180–1)

Legitimacy is for the mediocre, and the Bastard offers a more exciting model. The folk hero comes out in the rough-hewn rhymes in which he tells how his father got there:

> Something about, a little from the right,
>   In at the window, or else o'er the hatch;
> Who dares not stir by day must walk by night;
>   And have is have, however men do catch.
> Near or far off, well won is well shot;
> And I am I, howe'er I was begot.

> (1.1.170–5)

"And I am I" is the exultant obverse of Gloucester's "I am myself alone." Philip's words are not those of an aristocrat, nor a Prince of the blood, but of an engaging, thrusting young man on the make. Gordon Crosse has a useful discrimination. Commending a performance of Ralph Richardson's, he remarks that Richardson "rightly made Faulconbridge not much more than a country lout who developed gradually into what he later becomes. Some actors make him turn miraculously into a *preux chevalier* the moment the king's sword touches his shoulder."[4] The Bastard not only gets on, he grows.

The social comedy of his first soliloquy is exactly placed:

> Well, now can I make any Joan a lady.
> "Good den, Sir Richard!"—"God-a-mercy, fellow!"
> And if his name be George, I'll call him Peter;
> For new-made honor doth forget men's names:
> 'Tis too respective and too sociable
> For your conversion. Now your traveller,
> He and his toothpick at my worship's mess—
> And when my knightly stomach is suffic'd,
> Why then I suck my teeth and catechize
> My picked man of countries: "My dear sir,"
> Thus leaning on my elbow I begin
> "I shall beseech you"—that is question now;
> And then comes answer like an Absey book:
> "O sir," says answer, "at your best command,
> At your employment, at your service, sir!"
> "No, sir," says question, "I, sweet sir, at yours."
> And so, ere answer knows what question would,
> Saving in dialogue of compliment,
> And talking of the Alps and Apennines,
> The Pyrenean and the river Po—
> It draws toward supper in conclusion so.
>
> (1.1.184–204)

Sir Richard (as the King has now dubbed him) reflects on the fun he will have rehearsing his new role. And he catches nicely the ambivalence of the audience:

> For this is worshipful society,
> And fits the mounting spirit like myself.
>
> (1.1.205–6)

"Worshipful society": there's an edge to that, as the outsider contemplates life on the inside. But Sir Richard means to get on. The message sent out in Act 1 makes two points: blood counts; merit and push will find a way. The combination is irresistible, and the audience should succumb to the Bastard's charm.

The "mounting spirit" continues to ascend. Faulconbridge in the great world develops two qualities beyond what we have already seen: patriotism, and an openmouthed astonishment at the way governments behave. The deal agreed on by France and England leaves him aghast: "Mad world! mad kings! mad composition!" (2.1.561). Direct address to the audience, naturally. This is no time for reflective, voice-over soliloquies. Faulconbridge has just learned what Count Oxenstierna told his son, "Dost thou not see, my son, with what unwisdom this world is governed?" and wants to tell the audience the way the world really works. The outsider, propelled to a close view of the mighty, signifies that he finds it unbelievable. In the same speech he discovers "commodity" (self-interest, gain) to be the principle on which the world rotates. It is drama as naiveté—and none the worse for that.

Underneath is a subtler modulation of "legitimacy." Time and again this play uses legitimacy as a metaphor for *right* (legal and moral). The connections are pointed up by the Bastard:

> *K. John*: Doth not the crown of England prove the king?
>   And if not that, I bring you witnesses:
>   Twice fifteen thousand hearts of England's breed—
> *Bastard*: Bastards and else.
> *K. John*: To verify our title with their lives.
> *K. Phil.*: As many and as well-born bloods as those—
> *Bastard*: Some bastards too.
> *K. Phil.*: Stand in his face to contradict his claim.
>
> (2.1.273–80)

Which is to say, legal claims will have to be backed up with force—a portion of which will be, well, extra-legal. In these part-asides, part-interruptions, Faulconbridge is the *raisonneur* of *King John*, as much as in his major soliloquies.

Still, *King John* does not remain in this early-Brecht vein. Faulconbridge, like the play, has to get on with it. King John makes money the old-fashioned way: he expropriates it, and Faulconbridge is ordered to "shake the bags/Of hoarding abbots" (3.3.7–8). This task he happily executes, leaving John to channel his more sinister commissions to Hubert. To Hubert also falls the class rancor in the suspicious circumstances of Arthur's death. Defending himself against the Earl of Salisbury's accusation, he remarks:

> I would not have you, lord, forget yourself,
> Nor tempt the danger of my true defence;
> Lest I, by marking of your rage, forget
> Your worth, your greatness, and nobility.

(4.3.83–86)

To this, the imaginatively named Bigot replies, "Out, dunghill! Dar'st thou brave a nobleman?" (4.3.87). We have seen this before, and Shakespeare does not lengthen the cameo of middle-class respectfulness in conflict with aristocratic hauteur. But he lets Hubert win the point.

The Bastard now continues his progress from personal opportunism to the voice of England. England, not self, governs his meditation on Arthur's body: "How easy dost thou take all England up!" (4.3.142). If there is personal ambition here, as some have thought, it's buried in a larger commitment. His actions throughout Act 5 are those of a sturdy patriot, maintaining his allegiance to a King who is not personally worth it but who is nevertheless England. At the end he has become the foremost adviser to Prince Henry, and the play's spokesman for England. The ringing affirmation of the curtain speech brings together the submerged aspirations of the individual, the audience, and the nation: "Naught shall make us rue, /If England to itself do rest but true" (5.7.117–18). Nationalism is the true legitimacy of the play's hero.

CHAPTER TWO

The Early Comedies and Romeo and Juliet

THE TWO GENTLEMEN OF VERONA

" ' All that was mine in Silvia I give thee'—one's impulse, upon this declaration, is to remark that there are, by this time, *no* gentlemen in Verona."[1] Quiller-Couch's celebrated *mot* on the play's climax—Valentine has just handed over his betrothed, Silvia, to her would-be rapist, Proteus—is, I think, the correct starting point for an assessment of this play. Unusually for Shakespeare, he offers in his title a social category for which the closest parallel is *The Merchant of Venice*. Both titles raise questions. "Which is the merchant here, and which the Jew?" asks Portia (4.1.169). In *Two Gentlemen*, it is what sort of gentlemen flourish in Verona? As we experience the title of *Two Gentlemen*, it moves from the blandly factual, to the teasing, to the hilariously provocative.

Having raised the issue, Quiller-Couch proceeds to resolved it, trenchantly. The later stages of *Two Gentlemen* contain, he says, unmistakable traces of "some interposing hand," a "faker,"[2] and he finds proof of this in the conduct of Sir Eglamour:

He is just an honest, simple, gentleman on whose chivalry Silvia makes claim for help in a most difficult adventure.

> O Eglamour, thou art a gentleman, . . .
> Upon whose faith and honor I repose.

His answer is prompt, as his service is punctual. Without warning or excuse he is reported to have taken to his heels like the veriest poltroon![3]

Can one be a gentleman and a poltroon? The Outlaws think so:

> *1 Out*: Where is the gentleman that was with her?

17

3 Out: Being nimble-footed, he hath outrun us.

                                                            (5.3.6–7)

Either Shakespeare wrote these lines, in which case Sir Eglamour stands
condemned, or "some interposing hand" has besmirched the stainless
reputation of Sir Eglamour. Later editors have been unwilling to join in
Quiller-Couch's cover-up operation. The consensus is that Shakespeare
did it, and that Sir Eglamour did it.

   If we accept this, and I see no reason why we should not, the play falls
into place. Shakespeare intends a pleasant trifle with some girds at the
eponymous heroes, Valentine and Proteus. Since the comedy owes much
to the romance tradition, events must on occasion take precedence over
psychological likelihood. In ridding himself of the unwanted Sir Eglamour, Shakespeare lays himself open to the charge of inconsistency. Or he
might be overbrusque, as E. M. Forster was with his singular dismissal, in
The Longest Journey, of an unwanted character: "He was broken up in the
football match." Or he might intend another flout at "gentleman." It
would hardly violate the comedy's strategy. Speed, the page, and Launce,
a clownish servant, are unimpressed with their masters. Often, as in the
dialogue between Lucetta and Julia, Speed and Valentine, the servants
hold a clear advantage over the master and mistress. The flavor is
agreeably tart, a Cox's Pippin to the palate.

   But what is the standing of these gentlemen? In the Folio's dramatis
personae they are listed by name only: Proteus, Eglamour, Thurio, and so
on. In the play, they are often given the "Sir" prefix. The Duke refers to
"Sir Valentine" in Act 2, scene 4, who at that point (though not earlier)
becomes the son of "Don" Antonio. We hear of Sir Proteus, Sir Thurio,
Sir Eglamour, and these terms of address are general. The play's convention, it would seem, is to present the "Sir" prefix as a general indicator of
standing: the Duke, in particular, is punctilious about addressing his
subjects as "Sir." It is used especially in formal address and in respectful
reference, whereas the simple "Valentine" and "Proteus" are a form of
tutoyer. "Sir" seems a formal term of respect and standing, rather than a
precise signification of rank. And of course the play's ambience includes
Italy and Spain, together with England. *The Two Gentlemen of Verona* is an
early, and extreme, instance of Shakespeare's playing very freely with
time and place: he plays with rank, too, seeming to create a convention
confined to this play. It may be true that the text represents several strata
of composition. Still, Shakespeare habitually avoids a system of direct
correspondences with English social orderings. The vagueness, inconsis-

tency, and oddity of *Two Gentlemen* are not so far from his preferred mode.

The key to this piece is Valentine. His dominant trait is role-playing. From his earliest stereotyping ("Home-keeping youths have ever homely wits" [1.1.2]) he moves to the appreciation of self as engaged in an intense, romantic drama of love, a role pursued with Stanislavskian thoroughness. The props include the indispensable glove ("Sweet ornament, that decks a thing divine!"[2.1.4]) and the letter whose delivery costs him such pains. Valentine's conduct is disciplined by the demands of the mode. "For love, thou know'st, is full of jealousy," he explains to Proteus (2.4.173), as he moves to cut out Thurio. He is not himself jealous, *entendu*, but the mode demands it. A moment later he can say, "I must climb her window, /The ladder made of cords" (2.4.177–78). He is exposed by the Duke. Despair! Exile! No matter, the Outlaws quickly take him to their bosom. He has only to relate his colorful past

> I kill'd a man, whose death I much repent;
> But yet I slew him manfully in fight,
> Without false vanity or base treachery
>
> (4.1.27–29)

and they at once, with a sure instinct, make him their leader. He has to listen to their tales of parallel misfortune: "Myself was from Verona banished/For practising to steal away a lady" (4.1.47–48); "And I from Mantua, for a gentleman/Who, in my mood, I stabb'd unto the heart" (1.1.50–51). (Can this same Outlaw, one wonders, have seen a performance of *Richard III*, where Gloucester cries, "Stabb'd in my angry mood at Tewkesbury" [1.2.241]? A taste for quoting Shakespeare's lines is the basis for some classic comedies, including O'Keeffe's *Wild Oats* and Sheridan's *The Critic*. The desperadoes of the forest, and their leader, pave the way for *The Pirates of Penzance*.)

The Two Gentlemen of Verona, it is clear by Act 4, aspires to the condition of operetta. Still, a certain social interest remains under the comic light. "Know, then, that *some* of us are gentlemen" is the 3rd Outlaw's haughty induction to the story of his life (4.1.44). One would like to know more about class tensions in the forest, but Shakespeare saves this material for *As You Like It*. In the final scene, the spotlight falls on the big production of Valentine's renunciation of Julia. Only Holman Hunt could take it seriously, as his painting in the Birmingham Art Gallery reminds us.[4] But no one on stage calls Valentine's bluff. Silvia, who could, says nothing. The Duke, escorted in by the Outlaws, moves astutely from "Sir Valentine!" to "I do applaud thy spirit, Valentine." This is no time for censoriousness. The dropping of the "Sir" marks the closing of distance, mental and physical, between the two. Amity is restored. The Duke's speech can now end on a note both formal and intimate:

> Sir Valentine,
> *Thou art a gentleman*, and well deriv'd:
> Take thou thy Silvia, for thou hast deserv'd her.
>
> (5.4.145–47)

After this it remains only to get people off the stage rapidly, before the audience can ask awkward questions.

The problem with *The Two Gentlemen of Verona* is that Shakespeare has not formulated clearly the play's attitude toward its title heroes. The leading characters are allowed to present themselves at their own valuation, while being sent up by their own lines. Like the rest of us, Shakespeare cannot take the young gentlemen seriously. Later, he became more professional.

THE COMEDY OF ERRORS

"Universal, immutable, impartial," said de Gaulle of gold. It is the international currency of drama, too, and is everywhere in *The Comedy of Errors*. The chain, the ring, five hundred ducats, a thousand marks, guilders, angels—*gold* pieces are the props of this play. And they define the play's society. *The Comedy of Errors* is above all a play of the merchant class. Our impressions of Ephesus may be hazy—it is a Mediterranean commercial seaport, characteristically studded with English taverns such as the Tiger, Centaur, Phoenix, and Porpentine—but our sense of its inhabitants is sharp. Topped by the Duke, tailed by the servants, Ephesan society is focused on its merchant class.

The businessmen, Antipholus of Ephesus, Balthazar, Angelo (a goldsmith), the First and Second Merchant, set the tone of the town. Ephesus is an international trading center, and like Venice, it is founded on political stability, the free movement of capital, reliable and equitable laws that the local judiciary may not adjust at whim. "Now trust me, were it not against our laws,/ . . . Which Princes, would they, may not disannul" is Solinus's apology to Aegeon (1.1.143–45). Venice, a greater city-state, has the same problem, for as Antonio says:

> The Duke cannot deny the course of law;
> For the commodity that strangers have
> With us in Venice, if it be denied,
> Will much impeach the justice of the state,
> Since that the trade and profit of the city
> Consisteth of all nations.
>
>   (3.3.26–31)

Note too the alacrity with which the Ephesan gendarmerie backs up complaints of improper trading practices. Ephesus, when running smoothly, is designed for the frictionless accumulation of wealth. Its character-note is the First Merchant, regretfully declining a dinner invitation on the grounds that "I am invited, sir, to certain merchants, /Of whom I hope to make much benefit" (1.2.24–25). A business engagement takes precedence over a purely social one, unless, like the Courtesan, who is able to diversify her business into supplying Antipholus with a diamond ring, one can happily combine the two. The action of *The Comedy of Errors* could not take place other than in a town whose business is business.

Nor could the comedy. The Ephesan merchants have to adjust to shock, dislocation of good business, repudiation of debt, and solid citizens behaving erratically. The Rotarians see a fellow member in good standing break out, and know not what to make of it. Much of the fun comes from seeing primal fears crowd in upon the merchants, when, for example, the Syracusan Antipholus cries at curtain: "I greatly fear my money is *not safe!*" (1.2.105) and his Ephesan brother realizes: "This jest shall cost me some expense" (3.1.123). This is the curtain line that Komisarjevsky made into a Handelian glee song. "My gold!" the repeated heart cry of the Syracusan (as reported by Dromio in 2.1) becomes the play's refrain. The shadow that falls over the merchant class is the settlement of accounts: "You know since Pentecost the sum is due" is the Second Merchant's tuning fork opening to Act 4, just as Act 5 opens with a credit investigation:

> *Second Merchant*: How is the man esteem'd here in the city?
> *Angelo*:   Of very reverent reputation, sir,
>   Of credit infinite, highly belov'd,
>   Second to none that lives here in the city;
>   His name might bear my wealth at any time.

Normality violated by the bizarre is the formula for comedy here. Shakespeare has little interest in investigating the merchant class beyond the limits of the dramatically feasible. There is a domestic drama, certainly, in the tensions between Adriana and her husband, and Luciana and Adriana debate the issues of womanly compliance and assertion. More interesting, perhaps, is the master and servant relationship. Indeed, the dark side of the comedy coincides with a principle of farce: that much of the action, if taken at all seriously, is simple cruelty. *The Comedy of Errors* is regularly punctuated by the cries of the Dromios as their masters (and Adriana) beat them up. They seem used to it, and I don't intend to invoke later standards. It is a given of the play that the beating-up of servants is funny; and so it is, if you take the Dromios as mere dramatic fictions, two-dimensional cartoon figures. But once, a Dromio is given a longer speech to mark his sense of things:

I am an ass indeed; you may prove it by my long ears. I have served him from the hour of my nativity to this instant, and have nothing at his hands for my service but blows. When I am cold he heats me with beating; when I am warm he cools me with beating. I am wak'd with it when I sleep; rais'd with it when I sit; driven out of doors with it when I go from home; welcom'd home with it when I return; nay, I bear it on my shoulders as a beggar doth her brat; and I think, when he hath lam'd me, I shall beg with it from door to door.

(4.4.27–37)

It is a disturbing reminder of the human being behind the cartoon. Being sane in a mad world bears hard upon servants, the shock absorbers of the social system. It is a glimpse, which this play offers frequently, of the pain involved in farce. On the evidence of *The Comedy of Errors*, the worst masters in the canon are merchants.

THE TAMING OF THE SHREW

"Altogether disgusting to modern sensibility" was Shaw's verdict on the final scene, and here we are, ninety years later, with our no less modern sensibilities no less disgusted. "No man with any decency of feeling can sit it out in the company of a woman without being extremely ashamed of the lord-of-creation moral implied in the wager and the speech put into the woman's own mouth."[5] Shaw's sentiments are close to those of the latest New Cambridge editor of *The Taming of the Shrew*, who sees it as an early Problem Play and hints that it might be vulnerable to censorship today.[6] Still, the relations between the sexes have somewhat adjusted since Shaw's day, and the comedy continues to attract large mixed audiences, at what cost to decency of feeling it is impossible to hazard. In practice, there are various strategies by which a director can refine the excesses of Katherina's final speech. He or she can have the actress play it in tones of accusing irony, all out, as Michael Bogdanov did in his Royal Shakespeare Company production of 1977. Or the speech can be rapt affirmation of a great truth, one understood by the parties. Petruchio can be shown as undertaking the reeducation of Katherina, in what can be termed the social worker approach. Or the speech can be the last phase in a covert game played by the principals, in which they combine to despoil the neighbors. The New Oxford editor is convinced that Katherina's final speech is the only possible climax to the *farce*;[7] the New Arden editor believes "that any actor striving to represent Petruchio's feelings at this moment in the play [at 'Come on, and kiss me, Kate'] should show him as perilously close to tears, tears of pride, and gratitude, and love."[8] Shaw would not be the only one to doubt a Petruchio ready to blub at this point. Still, the psychology of the closing lines is open to varying interpretations, which reflect back on the entire play. We can now set them aside.

The final scene, whatever accounts are given of it, concludes a study in bourgeois realism. The play rests on the marriage arrangements characteristic of the Padua/Verona gentry, which were strikingly similar to those of Elizabethan England. It is this aspect of *The Shrew* that Shaw, who hated the conclusion, warmly applauded:

Petruchio is worth fifty Orlandos as a human study. The preliminary scenes in which he shews his character by pricking up his ears at the news that there is a fortune to be got by any man who will take an ugly and ill-tempered woman off her father's hands, and hurrying off to strike the bargain before somebody else picks it up, are not romantic; but they give an honest and masterly account of a real man, whose like we have all met.[9]

Not *all*, perhaps, but the discriminating praise of the realism is well founded. As G. R. Hibbard has emphasized, *The Shrew* is about marriage, and about marriage in Elizabethan England.[10] The actuality of the marriage arrangements—dowries, contracts, widowhood contingencies, wedding gowns, pots and pans—is the vital tissue of *The Shrew*. And yet the play follows an Induction that is largely given over to fantasizing.

If the play proper is about minor gentry, the Induction is about the framing classes. The two roles that matter are Sly's and the Lord's, behind whom is a sensed hinterland of low life and high life. Clearly, there are strong elements of realism in this, yet the note of fantasizing is struck right away. Sly comes on protesting his ancestry, for all the world like one of the nobles in *Henry VI*, insisting "the Slys are no rogues. Look in the chronicles: we came in with Richard the Conqueror." Refusing to pay for breakages, insensible to the threat of calling in the constabulary, Sly falls asleep. The Lord creates for him a waking dream; he inhabits a fantasy:

> Carry him gently to my fairest chamber,
> And hang it round with all my wanton pictures.
>
> (Ind.1.44–45)

All the props are there. Music, a silver basin full of rose water, sweet wood to be burned, servants, a gracious lady wife!

> I long to hear him call the drunkard "husband";
> And how my men will stay themselves from laughter
> When they do homage to this simple peasant.
>
> (Ind.131–33)

That is the Lord defining the experience at the scene's close, and it gives the formula for the Induction as a whole. It is a dual perception: low life, as viewed by the Lord and his followers; high life, as seen by Christopher Sly. Each class is perceived from the vantage of the other.

Between these poles the dramatic charge flickers. At one extreme is the earthy reality of "Marian Hacket, the fat ale-wife of Wincot." At the other, there is Sly wondering "Am I a lord and have I such a lady?" The lord becomes a prototype of Sir Epicure Mammon, listing the worldly delights of his house:

> We'll have thee to a couch
> Softer and sweeter than the lustful bed
> On purpose trimm'd up for Semiramis.
>
> (Ind.2.35–37)

Pictures of Adonis and Cytherea are to be provided; pornography for the quality is at hand. Moreover, Sly responds to these thrilling images: he speaks verse! "Upon my life, I am a lord indeed" (1.2.70), and he keeps it up until his request, "Madam, undress you, and come now to bed" (115). There is instruction, too, in how Sly should comport himself in his newfound splendor:

> *Sly*:   What must I call her?
> *Lord*:   Madam.
> *Sly*:   Al'ce madam, or Joan madam?
> *Lord*: Madam, and nothing else; so lords call ladies.
>
> (1.2.106–9)

The comedy has become a dramatized etiquette book, a glamorized version of the lives lords lead. It can't go on. The Messenger who enters with the tidings that "Your honor's players . . . Are come to play a pleasant comedy" brings Sly to earth, for he now relapses into prose. He is prepared to watch the play, with, as it seems, diminishing pleasure. "'Tis a very excellent piece of work, madam lady. Would 'twere done!" The main action of *The Shrew* is Sly's decompression chamber. It is an account of an Elizabethan marriage, as negotiated by a pair of tough-minded practitioners. After the fantasies of the Induction, this is the real thing.

As always, one needs to place the characters socially. The New Arden wrongly described Baptista as "a rich merchant." He is in fact, as Hortensio says, "an affable and courteous gentleman" and as Tranio confirms, "a noble gentleman." Baptista's sole reference to the merchant class indicates that he is not of it:

> Faith, gentlemen, now I play the merchant's part,
> And venture madly on a desperate mart.
>
> (2.1.318–19)

Note the value system: a merchant is one who takes risks. A well-founded gentleman, as Baptista is, has got where he is by the certainties of family merger and marriage contracts. *The Shrew* is about people who know a better way of thriving than the merchant's way, and to take it otherwise is to misunderstand the play's assumptions. Marriage is *serious*.

A single term covers the male actors who control this play: *gentleman*. It's given that Baptista, Hortensio, Gremio, and Petruchio are of the same class; it is sufficient among them to establish a personal connection. "I know him well," says Baptista, using the same phrase for Lucentio's father and Petruchio's father. With the connection established, they proceed directly to business, and it is as brisk an affair as one could wish. Petruchio, having informed Baptista that he has somewhat improved on his inheritance, asks, "What dowry shall I have with her to wife?" (2.1.119), and he receives a prompt answer: "After my death the one half

of my lands, /And in possession twenty thousand crowns" (2.1.120–21).
Good enough: Petruchio immediately closes the deal:

> And for that dowry, I'll assure her of
> Her widowhood, be it that she survive me,
> In all my lands and leases whatsoever.
> Let specialties be therefore drawn between us,
> That covenants may be kept on either hand.
>
> (2.1.122–26)

We can now turn to "the special thing" that has to be negotiated between
Katherina and Petruchio.

Katherina's position is easily legible. She stands to lose if her minx
sister is married first, an outcome that would leave her alone with a father
and fewer options. By playing the terrorist card, she blocks any agreement. It is successful, naturally. All members of the near community
combine in what is seen as the first priority, to get Katherina married to
someone, anyone. Only then can other interests be served.

Katherina's strategy works, and the interview with Petruchio she
conducts in Act 2, scene 1 is essentially to her satisfaction. The actors will
determine the sexual attraction and rapport that is developed between
them. The key passage is actually a redefinition of class, the "wasp"
dialogue leading to this:

> *Petruchio*: Who knows not where a wasp does wear his sting?
>   In his tail.
> *Katherina*:   In his tongue.
> *Petruchio*: Whose tongue?
> *Katherina*: Yours, if you talk of tails; and so farewell.
> *Petruchio*: What, with my tongue in your tail? Nay, come again,
>   Good Kate; I *am* a gentleman.
>
> (2.1.212–16)

Trivial in substance, the badinage escalates to what is not trivial, Petruchio's obscene jest in line 215. The speed of the exchange has betrayed
him into error. He knows it immediately, and "Good Kate, I am a
gentleman" attempts to put things right. The line means "I am not the oaf
you take me for." So "gentleman" is advanced as a measure of conduct,
not merely (as previously in the play) a statement of rank. Petruchio's
part assertion, part apology is at once tested:

Katherina: [That I'll try. [*She strikes him.*]
Petruchio: I swear I'll cuff you, if you strike again.
Katherina: So may you lose your arms.
If you strike me, you are no gentleman;
And if no gentleman, why then no arms.

(2.1.216–20)

Fixed! And Petruchio good-humoredly acknowledges it. The rest of the scene backs away from confrontation, whatever physical by-play the actors bring to it. But the assumptions governing the muffled explosion are interesting. Katherina has said in effect: You have gone too far, I am entitled to strike you, and I do. Petruchio says: Very well, I did. But don't ever do that to me again. Guidelines have been laid down. And are respected. After this, Petruchio does *not* go too far, and Katherina does *not* strike him. There is essential agreement here, and I side with those who hold that it is ratified at the scene's end. After Kate's (surely) part-amused, part-incredulous "I'll see thee hang'd on Sunday first" (2.1.291) she has nothing at all to say during the twenty-five lines of the scene that are played out during her presence. Surely a shrew worthy the name could announce in twenty-five lines her unyielding objection to Petruchio? And when Baptista says, "I know not what to say, but *give me your hands*. /God send you joy, Petruchio, 'tis a match" (2.1.310–11), there has evidently been a joining of hands, whatever the degree of ostensible reluctance on Katherina's part. *Hands*: everything is in that plural. This is now, as Hibbard says, a brief ceremony constituting a "pre-contract."[11] Katherina's silence can be taken both as acquiescence and as a prudent reservation from which later objections can be lodged. "A flaw in the procedure may be useful later on," as the Inquisitor in *Saint Joan* says. But the main thing is the agreement.

A robust materialism is never far away. The auction for Bianca, conducted by Gremio and Tranio (standing in for Lucentio), is explicit: the highest bid wins, and the auctioneer, Baptista, has nothing to say concerning the age of the competitors. They say it for themselves, and Baptista has only to confirm the outcome:

I must confess your offer is the best;
And let your father make her the assurance,
She is your own.

(2.1.378–80)

Nothing in this denies the existence of romance, to which the play is evidently addressed. It merely elaborates the system within which the principals negotiate. What is shown is a union of hearts and minds, attained after certain legal and financial steps.

The premises of the comedy are in a manner confirmed by its later stages, which include the painfully accurate picture of Elizabethan travel and the sense of a genuine Elizabethan household created in Act 4, scene 1. There are boisterous exchanges between Petruchio and his servants, and once again one sees that servant in this society is not the most glamorous of occupations. The account of the master treating them roughly seems closer to dramatic intensification than to caricature. As for Katherina, she, like her husband, learns another aspect of *gentle*: her appointment with the haberdasher focuses on a velvet cap. When she says, "This doth fit the time/And gentlewomen wear such caps as these," Petruchio has a smart counter: "When you are *gentle*, you shall have one too" (4.3.69–71). Gradually the behavior of both is encased within a class formation. Petruchio and Katherina are learning to live as a gentleman and a gentlewoman.

Their accord is illustrated, rather than sealed, in Katherina's great set piece on the duties of wife and husband. The passage that precedes it is significant, perhaps decisive:

> *Lucentio*: The wisdom of your duty, fair Bianca, Hath cost me a
> hundred crowns since supper-time.
> *Bianca*:   The more fool you, for laying on my duty.

So Katherina knows that Petruchio has already won a handsome bet on her. Who knows what more is to come, after she has responded to Petruchio's "Katherine, I charge thee, tell these headstrong women/What duty they do owe their lords and husbands?" (5.2.127–31). I see no reason why Katherina alone in Padua and Verona should be untouched by the economic drives that sustain those communities. Two views of marriage, a spiritual union and a business arrangement, meet in the accord between Petruchio and Katherina. Hearts and minds concur on sound commercial practices. The outcome is a partnership that seems set to continue its competitive and successful ways.

LOVE'S LABOR'S LOST

"Then for the place where?" as Armado asks. That country of the mind, Navarre, makes a few gestures toward France, Brabant, and Aquitaine.

Its dwellers may sometimes cry "Allons!" But this is England, all the same. The setting has the density and solidity of a rural English community centering on the great house. Of the house itself we see nothing: Armado's more specific question, "Now for the ground which? which, I mean, I walked upon: it is yclept thy park" (1.1.232–34) gives us all we are going to get. As Granville-Barker explains,

The convention of place involved is "about Navarre's Court"; outdoors, it seems to be, nothing more definite. The recluse King may walk there, the Princess may be met there . . . a pricket may be driven near for shooting, a pageant be shown there, a measure trod on the grass.[12]

It is the deer park of an English country house, not a world away from Charlecote, I dare say. But this makes its owner something other than a King. It is, of course, a matter of dramatic scale, and this is not a play where we need to think of the King of Navarre as the stage equivalent of a king offstage. He is a minor Elizabethan nobleman living on his estate.

Socially, therefore, this play is a glamorized rendering of domestic Elizabethan realities. The Lords attending on the King are evidently three young gentlemen. With Don Armado, they are all of Navarre's court that we see. The Princess is of the same social standing as Navarre, or perhaps marginally higher, reflecting the relationship of France to Navarre. Royalty translates into aristocracy, and the retinue of Ladies-in-waiting observes the same principle of scale. It is curious how the sense of all this coincides with the country-house theatricals into which the last act evolves. This is a play of "dressing up," and its charm owes something to its subliminal fusion of rank and mode.

With the rest of the community, no translation is needed. The curate, the schoolmaster, the constable are themselves. The rustics are literal. Don Armado gives us some problems, though. How Spanish is he? Actors don't usually give him a Spanish accent, and his lines contain few opportunities for the rasping Spanish aspirate (which Shakespeare would presumably know as the easy way of getting across national flavor). His mode of speech is spoof Lyly, an unusual accomplishment for a visiting Spaniard. Robert Speaight is surely right when he argues that

the schoolmaster's strictures on Don Armado suggest that upper class Englishmen in Shakespeare's time made a point of their mis-pronunciations, as they do in ours. The Don says "cauf" for "calf", "hauf" for "half", and "nebour" for "neigh-bour". No doubt he also said "wescot" for "waistcoat", and "orffer" for "offer."[13]

It seems best to take Don Armado as a dodo Englishman, a soldier, an antiquary, and a man of honor. The name "Don Armado" conveys nobility, and a certain Hispanic excess (hence the attraction of Quixote for the actors), and not, in a strict sense, Spain. Spain is the metaphor, not the literal.

Love's Labor's Lost frames an idyll, an Eden within a park. And its social relations are, if not Edenic, a reasonable earthly approximation. The classes rub along well enough, with an endearing mixture of definition, mingling, containable friction, and acceptance of each other. Costard continually interrupts the King, in the opening scene, and is allowed to get away with it. The suggestion is of a hardened petty offender, up again before a young and tolerant Justice of the Peace. The same Costard later elbows his way into a passage of badinage among the gentry, meeting only a rebuke from Margaret: "Come, come, you talk greasily; your lips grow foul" (4.1.130). Sex crosses the class lines, as it would in this setting: Jaquenetta and Armado find a way.

Again, take the Holofernes/Sir Nathaniel/Dull triangle, a grouping with its own social dynamics. Sir Nathaniel (the title was conventional for an ordinary priest) is audience to Holofernes, and Dull is audience to them both. Holofernes, the group leader, is the eternal prep-school master, whose existence owes everything to his scraps of Latin and his entries in literary magazine competitions. (Actors have sometimes found additional life in Sir Nathaniel's innocent tribute, "their daughters profit very greatly under you.") A natural follower, Sir Nathaniel founds a later school of fictional curates. When Costard says of him, "He is a marvellous good neighbour, faith, and a very good bowler" (5.2.576), the reference must be to bowls; but many a member of the audience must have taken away the image of the traditional curate's leg-break bowling. I always think of Richard Goolden at Regent's Park, scurrying after the bowl to side-foot it in the right direction, which is quite in keeping with the values of *Love's Labor's Lost*, too: people are allowed to get away with things; it's their natural right. Dull has to put up with the linguistic brilliance of his betters; he is their audience, without whom their education would be null. But he stands up for himself, with his insistence that a pricket is not a haud credo. He even has the audacity to try an ancient riddle on the two savants. And he gets included in a dinner invitation. Schoolmasters have some pull with parents, and Holofernes is resolved that his current credit shall extend to his friends:

I do dine today at the father's of a certain pupil of mine; where, if before repast, it shall please you to gratify the table with a grace, I will, on my privilege I have with the parents of the foresaid child or pupil, undertake your *ben venuto*.

(4.2.144–47)

Not only Sir Nathaniel, but Dull must come too: "Sir, I do invite you too: you shall not say me nay: *pauca verba*" (4.2.154–55). There is more tact and good feeling in Holofernes than at first appears. But it is evidently that kind of community. Indeed, much of *Love's Labor's Lost* appears as a sketch for Shakespeare's *Our Village*.

For four acts and more, the easy class relations within Navarre make the dominant impression. Typical of the easygoing local style is Holofernes's dismissal of Jaquenetta: "Trip and go, my sweet; deliver this paper into the royal hand of the king; it may concern much. Stay not thy compliment; I forgive thy duty. Adieu" (4.2.132–35). Jaquenetta is excused a curtsy. Boyet, the visiting *chef-de-protocole*, raises an eyebrow at the inclusiveness of Navarre: "Here comes a member of the commonwealth" is his announcement of Costard (4.1.41)—a hint, perhaps, that social matters are ordered more stringently in France. Boyet is, however, the agent of the Princess, whose graciousness colors so many of the transactions. She is on good terms, for example, with the gentlemanly Forester ("Forester, my friend"), who speaks blank verse and is permitted to pay her a compliment in that form: "Nothing but fair is that which you inherit" (4.1.20). Through the Princess the tone of the exchanges is controlled, and the eventual standards are set.

Love's Labor's Lost is an encounter between two teams, the Locals and the Visitors, which the pageant of the Worthies brings together. It is here that the host community should show itself at its best. That it does not is the fault of the young lords (and implicitly Navarre, for not controlling his friends and followers). The psychological context is clear. The young men have been put down badly by the ladies in their own pageant, the Muscovite dance. They are in no mood to give quarter to the village efforts. Berowne, in particular, has come some way from "Did not I dance with you in Brabant once?" (2.1.113), the archetypal line of the young blood opening his campaign. And it is Berowne who sets the increasingly disagreeable tone of the theatricals.

Some indication of what is to come occurs early, as the King and Berowne read the program together. Somewhat distrait, the King miscounts the numbers in the first show—four instead of five—and Berowne, who puts him right, is set in a mood of superior correction. There follows Berowne's summary of the cast: "The pedant, the braggart, the hedge-priest, the fool, and the boy" (5.2.538–39). Whatever may be said of this play's debt to the stylized characters of the *commedia dell'arte*, the terms here in English are contemptuous and dismissive. No character in the play has been referred to like this before. Berowne is obviously out for blood. When the pageant begins, Costard is allowed to get out three words before the barracking starts:

> *Costard*: I Pompey am—
> *Berowne*:   You lie, you are not he.
>
>   (5.2.543)

And, since no check is forthcoming, others join in. Boyet is tempted by a rhyming witticism:

> *Costard*: I Pompey am—
> *Boyet*:   With libbard's head on knee.
>
>   (5.2.544)

Dumain cannot miss the chance to put Costard right at "Pompey surnam'd the big." The Princess does what she can to soften matters, with "Great thanks, great Pompey" and a prompt "Proceed, good Alexander!" when the unfortunate Sir Nathaniel dries. Holofernes is too tempting a target and runs into a barrage of merciless ragging. Even so, he has one of the play's best lines to exit on: "This is not generous, not gentle, not humble" (5.2.621). *Not gentle*: the rebuke is a reminder that they are letting down themselves, and their class.

The darkness falling on the park is real now. "A light for Monsieur Judas! It grows dark, he may stumble" (5.2.622). Boyet's mockery gives way to the Princess's balm: "Alas! Poor Maccabeus [and not 'Judas'], how he hath been baited" (5.2.623). Armado, as Hector, comes on to face the barrage and to conclude the first show. His method is to absorb things with his exquisite, archaic courtesy: "Sweet Lord Longaville, rein thy tongue" (5.2.648). It has little effect, and Armado expands his appeal into a statement of values; the comic Spaniard has become the spirit of chivalry incarnate: "The sweet war-man is dead and rotten; sweet chucks, beat not the bones of the buried; when he breathed, he was a man" (5.2.652–54). "Sweet royalty, bestow on me the sense of hearing"— presumably this is an appeal to the Princess to interrupt her conversation and attend to the performance, and with words of rapidly escalating sexual import—"love," "yard," "surmounted," "the party is gone" — the show explodes into Costard's challenge and Armado's acceptance of combat. Still the hysteria mounts, until quelled by the most somberly powerful of all entrances in Shakespeare: *Enter as messenger, Monsieur Marcade.*

This last episode in *Love's Labor's Lost* is all about *manners*, about going too far, then farther still, and encountering checks. The brutal high spirits of the young men, abetted by Boyet, cannot be reined by the courtesy of Armado and the Princess, well as they try, much less by the open rebuke of Holofernes. In the end, it is Marcade who stills the clamor. His presence is a reminder of mortality, a rebuke administered by the forces governing the pageant. An offense has been committed. It must be purged.

When the King launches his gracelessly strained plea to the Princess, "The extreme parts of time extremely forms" (5.2.728–39), it is an uncomfortable, even embarrassing moment. Navarre has got his timing wrong, as usual; and the Princess fixes the mistake with "I understand you not; my griefs are double" (5.2.740). Berowne, as a gentleman and an aide, comes well to the support of his leader: "Honest plain words best pierce the ear of grief; /And by these badges understand the King" (5.2.741). But it is too late for wooing. The penance imposed on the young men, a year's retreat—for Berowne, a year's social work in a hospital—is more than a betrothal test. It is a punishment imposed on them for criminal frivolity and for the excesses of the pageant. And we feel, obscurely but unmistakably, that the sentence is correct. They are to be put on a year's probation. What could be more apt?

The resonances of the final stages go beyond a brief recital of categories, but we could get at them through another question of Armado's, "the time when?" This play has always to be staged, and the period setting shapes its meaning. In my experience, the remoter eras do little for *Love's Labor's Lost*, nor do the most recent. I have seen the play lie inert at the Old Vic under the medieval trappings of *Les Très Riches Heures du Duc de Berri*, and remain as unresponsive to an injection of 1960s hormones at Stratford, Connecticut. Peter Brook, famously, found in the *fête champêtre* of Watteau and Lancret the analogue to the idyll in the park. The play also vibrates, I find, to a pre-1914 setting, and recent productions of the Royal Shakespeare Company (Stratford-upon-Avon, 1984) and of the Stratford Festival (Ontario, 1979 and 1984) have made the connections. *Belle époque* works well for obvious decorative reasons and also because it reflects the last great era of class distinctions in the West. Moreover, the text has hints of a latent time-leap. "A set of wit well played" (5.2.29) catches the country house, tennis party atmosphere that seems to belong to an Edwardian lawn. Michael Langham, directing the play at Stratford, Ontario, says that he was put on to *belle époque* by Lady Diana Cooper's celebrated memoirs: she relates how Duff Cooper wooed her with sonnets, a form of courtship scarcely conceivable after the early Georgian years. For Langham, the frame was a reading party of young men down from Zuleika Dobson's Oxford. For his Stratford colleague, Robin Phillips, the setting was a chateau, as it might be near the cavalry school of Saumur, in the summer of 1914. At the end, Navarre led his guests from the park at the line, "The words of Mercury are harsh after the songs of Apollo." A low rumbling sound was heard in the distance. The guests paused, looking at each other. Was it thunder? Or gunfire? The guns of the Marne ended the revels of *belle époque*, just as the entrance of Marcade had stilled the pageant of the Worthies. This lurch into history, like the tumbrils at the end of the RSC's *Les Liaisons Dangéreuses*, is a surfacing of the inner forces in *Love's Labor's Lost*. The analogues are all there, waiting to be drawn.

A MIDSUMMER NIGHT'S DREAM

For all its magical tonalities, *A Midsummer Night's Dream* is a four-square construction consisting of court, lovers, fairies, and mechanicals. The class structure is shaped with equally decisive strokes. There is the Duke and his bride-to-be, the courtiers, and the mechanicals. A shadowy court-in-exile is visible in fairyland, one which, like the moon, reflects its counterpart: it, too, is composed of a King and Queen (whose disputes realize the tensions between Theseus and Hippolyta), an agent to the King, and Lords and Ladies in waiting (the fairies attending on Titania). Since Peter Brook's production (RSC, 1970), the vogue for doubling the major parts has brought out strongly the psychic relations between Titania and Hippolyta and between Oberon and Theseus. There are deep layers of longing and antipathy, appeasement and hostility. But socially, all is ordered with a perfect gyroscope of stability and propriety.

The strategy emerges early, in the contention between Lysander and Demetrius for Hermia. "Demetrius is a worthy gentleman," says Theseus (1.1.52), echoing Egeus's reference to "this gentleman." Lysander's response is

I am, my lord, as well deriv'd as he,
As well possess'd; my love is more than his;

> My fortunes every way as fairly rank'd,
> If not with vantage, as Demetrius.
>
> (1.1.99–102)

This is a symmetrical dispute within a class. The young gentlemen are virtually identical in standing, and the reasons for preferring one to the other must be subjective. I confess I always have difficulty in telling them apart. Nor is there the kind of social interest in their wooing that abounds in *The Merchant of Venice.* Lysander's "I have a widow aunt, a dowager/Of great revenue, and she hath no child" (1.1.157–58) momentarily suggests a comedy of manners, but nothing comes of it. As for Helena and Hermia, they have evidently been quarreling ever since they were at school together. For all the physical and mental differences between them, they are coevals and coequals. In this square dance of changing partners, there is no room for individual movement outside the choreography. *A Midsummer Night's Dream* contains levels rather than slopes, equivalences rather than asymmetries.

The social interest in the play is, I think, largely confined to the relations between the artificers and the court. Quince and company are a solidly defined stratum of Athens. Of their working practices we learn little. The play their scenes compose is, essentially, *The Artificers' Holiday,* complete, as Bottom puts it, with "good strings to your beards, new ribbons to your pumps" (4.2.32–33). They seem entirely loyal to, but apprehensive of, "the Duke and the Duchess." (Hippolyta is only so called by the mechanicals.) To frighten the ladies "were enough to hang us all," at which all chorus "That would hang us, every mother's son!" (1.2.69). The matter preys on their minds during the rehearsal scene, too, and affects some of their staging plans. Not till 4.2. does an economic motive for their production emerge. There has been speculation on what the company's star would have received by way of pension. Flute rates it high: "O sweet bully Bottom! Thus hath he lost sixpence a day during his life; he could not have' scaped sixpence a day" (4.2.18–20). That was more than the earnings of an Elizabethan master carpenter, a handsome pension indeed. However, we learn nothing of the outcome. Only the play is presented along with Theseus's reasons for receiving it.

Theseus governs the social style of *A Midsummer Night's Dream.* His model of princely courtesy and accomplishment controls the framing acts, 1 and 5. He discharges all his roles with distinction: conqueror, judge, lover; he travels on progresses, rides to hounds (of which he keeps an excellent pack) and is both a patron and connoisseur of the arts. If

Shakespeare's ideal ruler exists, it is here and not in *Henry V* that one should look for him.

Theseus's salient trait, however, is his unfailing tact. Whether cajoling Egeus and Demetrius into good sense ("I have some private schooling for you both" [1.1.116]), or registering ironic surprise at the sleeping lovers ("No doubt they rose up early to observe/The rite of May" [4.1.129–30]), he seems always to be handling affairs with a man-of-the-world's balance and discretion. His handling of the mechanicals is exemplary. "What are they that do play it?" asks Theseus, and Philostrate's class judgment is uncompromising:

> Hard-handed men that work in Athens here,
> Which never labor'd in their minds till now.
>
> (5.1.72–73)

It is pointless to hear their play, says Philostrate, "Unless you can find sport in their intent." "Sport"—that is, the kind of reception the young gentlemen gave to the Worthies' pageant in *Love's Labor's Lost*. Theseus at once makes up his mind:

> I will hear that play;
> For never anything can be amiss
> When simpleness and duty tender it.
>
> (5.1.81–83)

He also explains his intentions.

> *Our sport* shall be to take what they mistake;
> And what poor duty cannot do, noble respect
> Takes it in might, not merit.
>
> (5.1.90–92)

"Noble respect," the noble way of looking at things, is the value projected in what follows.

The mechanicals' production is a replay of the Worthies' pageant (perhaps a year or two later), with one essential difference: the audience shows due courtesy and never lets its amusement get out of hand. The great point about the courtiers' running commentary is that it is *to one*

another, semi-private, and not hurled at the actors. Shakespeare is extraordinarily skilled at writing dialogue that is also a set of stage directions.
They are the instructions of *the director*. Theseus is made to set the
standards with his comment on the prologue, *"This fellow* doth not stand
upon points" (5.1.118), a remark that cannot be addressed to Quince.
(Compare Berowne's opening shot, *"You lie, you are not he."*) And Lysander's reply accepts the form: "A good moral, my lord" (5.1.120). There's a
deal of "my lord" in the ensuing dialogue that is not to be written off as
obsequiousness or formula writing. It means that the young men are
addressing Theseus, not putting off the actors, a point registered half a
dozen times. Not till line 226 does either gentleman speak without
addressing Theseus, and not till line 249 is there a direct address to an
actor. "Proceed, Moon." There are other controls. At the entrance of
Pyramus, Theseus warns, "Pyramus draws near the wall; *silence,"* and a
few minutes later Demetrius picks up the word as a courtier should: *"But
silence*; here comes Thisby." In between *silences*, Hippolyta grows mutinous, but her grumble "This is the silliest stuff that ever I heard" occurs
during a cleared stage.

The courtly audience is not, of course, oppressively decorous. There are
some cheerful audience reactions with "Well roared, Lion!" and "Well
moused, Lion!" but only during and after the exits of Thisby and Lion.
After this, the comments are within the court circle. Finally, Theseus finds
an excuse for getting out of the Epilogue, but permits the dance to go
forward. One joke slips out, "Marry, if he that writ it had played
Pyramus, and hang'd himself in Thisby's garter, it would have been a fine
tragedy." Then, picking himself up, he adds, "And so it is, truly; and very
notably discharg'd" (5.1.348–51). The actors have perhaps looked a trifle
downcast. But the dance salves all, and the deep harmonies of the close
mark the spiritual and social accord of *A Midsummer's Night Dream*.

I have labored the points of the final scene because it shows Shakespeare the director keeping a firm grip on events. Shakespeare becomes
Theseus, so to speak. At all points Theseus is in charge, imposing his
princely courtesy upon a stage audience that could easily get out of hand,
as Navarre's court did. The play offers a model of the class extremes
meeting with civility, good will, and harmony. It is not a model that can
be adjusted to all circumstances, and it may look primitive when set
against Shakespeare's later work. Within its own terms, the play's statement of relations between rulers and ruled is wholly satisfying. And that
ideal, of course, is presented within a *Dream*.

ROMEO AND JULIET

Romeo and Juliet, half comedy, half tragedy, is the natural terminus to the comedies Shakespeare wrote in the early 1590s, for his method here recapitulates the earlier plays. He presents a closed community that is socially fixed, where all the energies of this drama flow into contention, or to love that crosses the barrier of feud, not class. "Two noble households, *both alike in dignity*" is the Chorus's opening line; socially there is nothing to choose between Montagues and Capulets, two distinguished and well-founded families. The keynote image is the opening brawl, as Montagues and Capulets encounter each other (presumably from different doors), fight, and are quelled by the Prince, who in the early productions would speak from the upper stage/balcony. Diagrammatically, the forces are represented by strong horizontal and contending arrows, with the firm vertical strokes of authority pressing down upon the combatants. This is another four-square construction.

The Veronese community is an affair of families, of *houses*. The servants back their masters. Their masters back the extended family, a network of alliances that means everyone among the Veronese gentry knows or is related to someone else. The guest list for Capulet's party, which Romeo reads, must be a fair cross section of Veronese society. In it Mercutio's name is included, so a good friend of Romeo's is invited to a Capulet function. Granville-Barker is a little unfair in terming the young gentlemen "gatecrashers";[14] Mercutio has brought in some friends on his ticket. Anyway, if the servant bearing the list can issue a casual invitation to a gentlemanly passerby, the affair cannot be overwhelmingly formal. ("A trifling foolish banquet" means light refreshments on the sideboard, not a grand sit-down dinner.) Capulet, in refusing to have Romeo thrown out, combines civic and class consciousness:

> 'A bears him like a portly gentleman;
> And, to say truth, Verona brags of him
> To be a virtuous and well-govern'd youth.

(1.5.64–66)

It will never do to make a scene over Romeo. The phrase with which the Nurse ends the evening gives the true sense of the occasion: "Come, let's away; the strangers all are gone" (1.5.142). "Strangers"—there are none. Only in a closed community could "Signor Martino and his wife and daughters" be rendered so, even figuratively. Verona, everywhere one touches it, is a close-knit and stable community, for all its brawls.

Its leading personages are placed with that crafty vagueness that is by now Shakespeare's settled form, solidity of impression allied to inaccuracy of reference. Capulet appears not as a nobleman but, as Muriel St. Clare Byrne considers, a burgess.[15] Granville-Barker thought him "the portrait of a very English old gentleman . . . a familiar figure in many a home; the complete gentleman, the genial host, the kindliest of men—as long as no one crosses him."[16] Robert Speaight was categoric: "Capulet is a lively portrait of a Warwickshire squire, though not of an Italian nobleman . . . but Lady Capulet is good for nothing better than to open the local flower show."[17] Paris is regularly referred to as "County," an obsolete form of an un-English title; he is also "this noble earl" to Capulet (3.4.21). One gathers that Capulet has secured in him an excellent match, which in part accounts for Capulet's rage over Juliet's recalcitrance:

> And having now provided
> A gentleman of noble parentage,
> Of fair demesnes, youthful and nobly lign'd . . .
>
> (3.5.179–81)

It is the classic trade-off between wealth and rank, and Friar Laurence's reproach is unequivocal: "The most you sought was her promotion" (4.5.71). Paris, while clearly taken with Juliet's charms, has a solid sense of the "honorable reckoning" of the Capulets, and the need to negotiate decorously. Romeo shows no interest in these matters and once only refers to "the fair daughter of rich Capulet" (2.3.58). This is not a play about economic motives, but one needs to know that they are there, proportionately reduced from their position in the *The Taming of the Shrew*.

Kinship is everything. At one level we see it in Capulet's insistence on a quiet wedding:

> For, hark you, Tybalt being slain so late,
> It may be thought we held him carelessly,
> *Being our kinsman*, if we revel much;
> Therefore we'll have some half-a-dozen friends,
> And there an end.
>
> (3.4.24–28)

What people think matters. (Even so, Capulet changes his mind later, demanding "Sirrah, go hire me some twenty cunning cooks" [4.2.2]. As usual, the guest list is getting out of hand. The caterers will have to be called in.) At another level, consider the Nurse's standing as faithful retainer. She cannot be disciplined, and she cannot be fired. The comedy of Act 1, scene 3 rests on her tyranny over her employers and family. One and a half lines from Lady Capulet says it all: "Nurse, give leave awhile, /We must talk in secret. Nurse, come back again" (1.3.8–9). One look, one offended move toward the exit, has broken Lady Capulet. The cost of a private conversation will be too high. So the Nurse is licensed to repeat her favorite recital of Juliet's precocity. It is hardly a demonstration of brutal class domination.

The Nurse places the transactions around her with great accuracy. She is concerned to check that Romeo is making "a gentlemanlike" offer (that is, marriage) to Juliet, and accepts, with becoming protests, a tip from Romeo. With Mercutio she is all outraged respectability (which does not contradict a current of appreciative lubricity). Linguistically she is interesting. Shakespeare experiments with her speech in 1.3, when she joins in the conversation with Lady Capulet and Juliet. The outcome is passable, if unstately, blank verse. "Blank verse has shed its corsets, as it were," says G. R. Hibbard, "like the Nurse itself it is loose, free, and ample."[18] Her lamentation in 4.5 is all but a parody of her employers. And there's an early malapropism at "I desire some confidence with you" (2.4.126), naughtily underlined by Benvolio: "She will *endite* him to some supper." This trait will flower into Dogberry. Shakespeare, as I take it, is becoming more interested in the borderlines of class activity. It is in the shadings that virtuosity shows.

Still, the servants generally give the sense of the extended family. Sampson and Gregory have no doubt of their duty, which is to fight Montagues upon advantage. The upstairs-downstairs cutting of the domestic scenes in the Capulet household offers a rich, two-tiered view. Below stairs the pretense that the setting of this play is Italian, is dropped; Potpan, Simon Catling, and James Soundpost make no disguise of their national origin. Making the servants overtly English is standard Shakespearean practice, but there is also more than a trace of Englishness upstairs.

"Very much the young John Bull of his time" was Granville-Barker's view of Mercutio.[19] His high spirits and quarrelsomeness might be taken for granted. There's a strong vein of resistance to foreign importations, however, which comes out in his ridicule of Tybalt. For Mercutio, Tybalt is an affected ass who has learned only the dancing-master tricks of a fencing school:

> O, he's the courageous captain of compliments. He fights as you sing prick-song: keeps time, distance, and proportion; he rests his minim rests, one, two, and the third in your bosom; the very butcher of a silk button, a duellist; a gentleman of the very first house, of the first and second cause. Ah, the immortal passado! the punto reverso! the hay!
>
> (2.4.18–26)

Mercutio enters Tybalt for Pseuds Corner, 1595. Several fencing schools existed in London at that time, the most famous being Rocco Bonetti's in Blackfriars. Scholars have found traces of French, Italian, and Spanish usages in Mercutio's lines: he dislikes them all. This robust contempt for foreigners presupposes, naturally, an English temperament and perspective that the audience is invited to share. It makes little sense to purvey Italo-Spanish tensions on the English stage. So Mercutio's derision of Tybalt's affectations, "O their bones [*bons*], their bones!" aligns the audience with resistance to Gallicisms. An additional possibility in "a gentleman of the very first house," is as the New Arden editor suggests, that Mercutio is not only mocking fashionable foreign teachers, but implying "that Tybalt pretends to a higher social rank than he actually holds; the only first house he belongs to being a fencing school."[20] As one of "these new tuners of accent," Tybalt stands condemned for affected speech anyway. In all, Mercutio–Tybalt is a conflict based on much more than simple human distaste for each other. It is the Englishman against the foreigner (and one infatuated with foreign ways); the provincial against the metropolitan (or would-be sophisticate); the amateur against the pseudo-professional; the gentleman against the pretender or aspirant to higher rank. And there are some class tensions inherent in fencing, as emerges with Hamlet and Laertes: it is a gentlemanly exercise that one cannot afford to ignore, however irritating its stylistic tricks may be.

Hence the explosion of Act 3, scene 1 converts great dramatic energy, far more than mere physical violence. Observe how the conflict between Mercutio and Tybalt shapes up. Tybalt, very punctilious, is in the mode of duellist, all according to the prescribed rules. He has come to fight Romeo, not Mercutio, and has no intention of losing his temper with the wrong man. But this makes him even more intolerable to Mercutio. He speaks blank verse, naturally: "Gentlemen, good e'en: a word with one of you." Mercutio—the stage convention of having him lying on his back through the early dialogue is perfectly in keeping—prefers, as usual, prose. It is not for him to accept Tybalt's terms of encounter. But the fatal word "consortest" provokes him, and he slips, dangerously, into blank verse after Benvolio's (characteristically) blank verse intervention. Blank verse is both control of passion and acquiescence in Tybalt's mode. When Romeo refuses to ignite at Tybalt's insult, Mercutio knows his cue:

> O calm, dishonorable, vile submission!
> Alla stoccata carries it away!
> Tybalt, you rat-catcher, will you walk?

> (3.1.71–73)

A moment later it is the prose that he knows best and that he dies in.

The personal styles of Tybalt and Mercutio fight against each other at all points. The fascination lies in the extraordinary range with which Shakespeare depicts two young men, of the same social class and background, as inevitably drawn to conflict as Romeo and Juliet to love. The entire action is presented through the class register. Tybalt, for example, enters the play on a class note, "What, art thou drawn among these heartless hinds?" (1.1.64), and leaves it on a sneer of the same order, "Thou wretched boy, that didst consort with him here, /Shalt with him hence" (3.1.127–28). In between he has received some rough handling from his host at the party: Capulet's address turns rapidly from "gentle coz" to "goodman boy" (which places him below a yeoman) and "saucy boy." In choler, these people reach first for the epithet of class disdain.

Fittingly, the last stages take place at the Capulets' monument. The family tomb is the symbol of their standing, as well as the container for their victims. Sepulchral statues in gold will be added: the families, united in grief, will make public tokens of reconciliation. In the end, these people are, as their monument attests, pillars of the community.

CHAPTER THREE

The Middle Comedies

THE MERCHANT OF VENICE

The new phase begins with *The Merchant of Venice*. Class as a patent fact is integral to the early plays. In *The Merchant of Venice*, Shakespeare goes much further, treating class in its relation to money. The tabu is brilliantly violated. Shakespeare proposes two ways of making money, Shylock's and Antonio's, and he places them in relation to money as it already exists, the inherited wealth of Portia. He also shows how this wealth dominates all relationships, and he indicates, on an internal scale of the finest calibration, the social standing of all the characters. It will not do to start with fixed social standings as givens. The business of this play is to establish the rankings after an internal auditing. One should hold one's judgments until the conclusion of *The Merchant of Venice*, not begin with them.

The convenient place to begin is Act 1, scene 3, since it is a debate on money. The encounter takes place somewhere in the business sector of Venice. Its opening line, Shylock's "Three thousand ducats," touches on everything: how much, under what security, and what order of satisfaction may money buy? It emerges that Antonio and Bassanio are highly embarrassed at the need to borrow from Shylock—moneylending was an altogether more personal affair in the past—and therefore they overcompensate. This leads to the crucial exchange, Shylock's deliberately long-winded account of how Jacob overreached Laban. It is interrupted by Antonio's question, "And what of him? Did he take interest?" to which Shylock delivers his elegantly killing riposte: "No, not take interest; not, as you would say, /Directly int'rest" (1.3.71–72). "Directly int'rest": that is the play. What is "direct interest" and what are the alternatives?

"Direct interest" is to us a straightforward recognition of a natural law, that capital must increase. It is morally neutral, however much one complains of high interest rates. But *The Merchant of Venice* comes at the tail end of an ancient tradition, in which usury was regarded as sinful and unnatural. The commentaries on *The Merchant of Venice* make too much of this tradition, as though the England of 1596 were populated with fundamentalists all expecting interest-free loans from their friends. It makes more sense to go forward ten years to 1606, when Bacon published—we do not know when he wrote—his essay "Of Usury." In it, his very cool and sophisticated treatment takes it for granted that usury is a fact of life and will remain so.

It is a vanity to conceive that there would be ordinary borrowing without profit; and it is impossible to conceive the number of inconveniences that will ensue if borrowing be cramped. Therefore to speak of the abolishing of usury is idle. All states have ever had it, in one kind or rate or other. So as that opinion must be sent to Utopia.

Usury, for Bacon, is obviously necessary, and the problem is primarily one of regulation, for preference through a two-tier rate system. Bacon makes Antonio's doctrine look archaic, which it was. Historically, usury had begun by *The Merchant of Venice* to acquire its tension between two major senses: the taking of interest, and the taking of excessive interest.

It is this tension that Antonio and Shylock dramatize. Shylock makes his living by lending money. We would today call him a banker. His complaint against Antonio is that "He lends out money gratis, and brings down/The rate of usance here with us in Venice" (1.3.39–40). Antonio's position is that "I neither lend nor borrow/By taking nor by giving of excess" (56–57), which is not the same thing: Antonio says he is against *excessive* interest rates. Naturally one would like to know how much, but Shakespeare never specifies the rates. What is cardinal is Antonio's claim that moneylending is morally inferior to his own line of business.

Antonio is a merchant. That word, in itself, does not tell us very much. It emerges that Antonio trades in high-risk overseas commodities, including voyages to Tripoli, Mexico, and the Indies. These, to an English audience, would suggest the high-risk/high-profit ventures common in the era. (At one extreme, Drake's *Golden Hind* voyage, which paid out £47 for every pound invested: at the other extreme, Raleigh and the block.) These speculative ventures came with a moral justification that Antonio cites when linking Jacob's methods with his own:

> This was a *venture*, sir, that Jacob serv'd for;
> A thing not in his power to bring to pass,
> But sway'd and fashion'd by the hand of heaven.
>
> (1.3.86–88)

The argument seems spurious to us and might well have seemed so to Shakespeare's own audience.

The encounter between Shylock and Antonio is taxing for us. The extraordinary difficulties that confront a modern audience stem primarily from the Holocaust. But they stem in part also from the revolution in banking since Shakespeare's day. Shakespeare conflates the Jew and the Banker, imposing upon the audience the need to separate out the elements. Banking now is perfectly respectable, but so is anti-banking sentiment. It is normal for respectable citizens to inveigh against high interest rates in terms similar to those denouncing usury in the Middle Ages, especially if, in the last few years, they happen to have taken out a mortgage at around 20 percent. They might in that event recall, wryly, that the Elizabethans fixed a ceiling on interest rates. It was 10 percent. Resentment against banking practices is perennial, and Shakespeare taps it here. If one could distinguish between legitimate banking and the operations we attribute to loan sharks, the problem of judgment would be eased; but the interest rates are not disclosed. In sum moneylending, as practiced by Shylock, is proposed as morally dubious and socially stigmatized. High-risk overseas trading, as practiced by Antonio, has an altogether higher tone.

But what precisely is a merchant's status? The Arden edition offers, without comment, an intriguing quotation from Coryat: "The Rialto . . . is a most stately building, being the Exchange of Venice, where the Venetian gentlemen and the Merchants doe meete twice a day."[1] Gentlemen and merchants": that will do to begin with. Antonio, by the standards one habitually brings to the matter, is a gentleman. He is well respected in the business community, and Shylock's assessment "Antonio is a good [sufficient] man" is accurate. Plainly, he makes a great deal of money, and plainly, he spends it. The pattern is familiar, of a successful businessman living near the margin of a high income. He takes chances, and Shylock's early "other ventures he hath squander'd abroad" is a warning. What does he do with his gains?

We come back to Shylock's implied meaning, "indirectly interest." Antonio's money goes on Bassanio. "To you, Antonio, /I owe the most, in money and in love" (1.1.130–31). "Love" is the interest paid on the loans. What the play offers, with uninflected candor, is a relationship between two men—Antonio is always taken as the elder—in which one regularly benefits from interest-free loans. These loans are unsecured and unredeemed. They are, in effect, gifts between friends of unequal social rank.

The play is exact about this. There's an early hint when Solanio announces "Here comes Bassanio, your most noble kinsman" (1.1.57). This exploits the ambiguity of the superlative; that is, "most noble" can mean "very noble" or "the most noble you have got." When Bassanio enters, accompanied by Lorenzo and Gratiano, Salerio greets them with "Good morrow, *my good lords.*" "Lords," it emerges, refers primarily to Bassanio; the other two are included by courtesy. Bassanio returns the greeting (necessarily confined to Salerio and Solanio) as *"Good signiors both."* So we have lords and signiors, and a moment later, the major standings are confirmed, with Lorenzo addressing "My Lord Bassanio" and Gratiano "Signior Antonio." Bassanio, we learn, first visited Belmont "in company of the Marquis of Montferrat" (1.2.102). In Belmont, he is always "Lord Bassanio." Bassanio and Antonio come from the nobility and the merchant class; their relationship is founded on inequality and compensation.

Bassanio is a perfectly shaded portrait. He is an aristocrat using his charm and social connections as a form of credit, which he converts into the capture of an heiress. As Lady Bracknell observed of Algernon Moncrieff, "He has nothing, and he looks everything." When he has a problem, which is often, he immediately appeals for help, and his friends or betrothed hasten to bail him out. It is a way to thrive, and he is blest. Nobody in the play calls him a fortune-hunter, and we are not coerced into that simple, brutal formulation. It is merely an available conclusion.

The same order of judgment is available on the distressing Gratiano. Muriel St. Clare Byrne is suggestive about his development. She regards him as Bassanio's equal in the first scene. "After this, however, he slides rapidly down the social scale," she argues, "and by the end of Act 4 is obviously nothing more than a gentleman-in-waiting to Bassanio."[2] The impression undoubtedly shifts, but I don't accept that Gratiano "is obviously conceived first as a character, and only afterwards as someone in a certain social position."[3] This begs the question. Why is Gratiano not conceived as "a character" who is "in a certain social position"? Why should the terms exclude each other? In my reading, Gratiano—who is merely a noisy hanger-on in scene one—slides rapidly *up* the social scale by ruthlessly attaching himself to Bassanio. "You must not deny me, I must go with you to Belmont" (2.2.164). Shakespeare has moved on to the technique of his great period. Instead of having characters declare themselves ("I am determined to prove a villain") and then go on to illustrate themselves, he depicts characters who reveal themselves, but do not declare themselves, through five acts. Only at the end can one put together a retrospective judgment. Gratiano, I think, can adequately be characterized as a determined social climber, intent on getting an invitation to the great house and exploiting what must seem to Nerissa his sexual charm so as to remain there. Opportunism is its own reward, as it should be. But this conclusion is not pressed upon the audience, and anyone who wants to take Gratiano as loud but good-hearted, one who just happens to strike it lucky in Belmont, is free to do so.

Lorenzo is also worth a glance. He has the Venetian knack of coupling his emotions to his interests, and his pairing with Jessica turns out to be on traditional Venetian lines. The elopement is preceded by a dowry arrangement as explicit as the one in *The Taming of the Shrew*; they merely leave Shylock out of the discussion. Lorenzo, in advance, knows all about "what gold and jewels she is furnish'd with" (2.4.31), and Jessica, in advance, pays her way: "Here catch this casket, it is worth the pains," she tells him. "I will make fast the doors, and gild myself/With some more ducats" (2.6.33, 49–50). They run through it all in Genoa, apparently. But Lorenzo arrives in Belmont to be offered by Portia "the husbandry and manage of my house" (3.4.25), which makes him the estate manager or steward. Whether or not he is given tenure in this position, while he waits for Shylock to die off, the ending leaves unclear. He will certainly make himself useful in the great house, if only as the exponent of a philosophy agreeable to its owner: harmony, the theme of his Act 5 musings, is the musical equivalent of social hierarchy. And hierarchy, like everything else in this play, is dominated by Portia.

Portia, the actor-manager of the trial scene, stars in the play's climax. This is fitting, for the trial compresses all the explosive energies of *The Merchant of Venice*, and no part of the action is uninfluenced by Portia. This is a study in patrician poise, a great lady accommodating herself to the heterodox social problems of Nerissa's engagement (about which she has *not* been consulted), which include a trio of wooers, two of them totally unsuitable, the lumpish manners of Gratiano, and the swarm of hangers-on that Bassanio has picked up and who hopefully deposit themselves upon Belmont. There are human difficulties to be overcome, and Portia overcomes them, but nobody challenges her. Great possessions and great qualities combine in her; aristocracy and wealth unite.

What can wealth buy? First of all, silence about its origins. Shylock and Antonio bicker over their ways of thriving, which the play offers as an interesting issue. But before Portia's wealth, the play draws back. She inherits it, that is all. No speculation is admitted about the source of father's wealth. He is not even named. This silence makes its own point, contributing to Belmont's image of great wealth as being, not becoming.

Second, wealth governs all relations. Belmont is a magnet to the Venetians, who once there are compliant to the chatelaine's will. The Venetians do not fall under Portia's spell, they define its existence. From Jessica comes the clearest statement of the awe that Portia inspires:

> It is very meet
> The Lord Bassanio live an upright life,
> For having such a blessing in his lady,
> He finds the joys of heaven here on earth.
>
> (3.5.64–67)

It is like the admiring glance the equerry lifts up to the King, in Van Dyck's equestrian portrait of Charles I. The respect which Portia exacts from all is achieved without her raising her voice. One has to look twice at the passage, for example, to realize that "fare you well, Jessica" (3.4.44) is a dismissal of Jessica, not a personal leave-taking. Bassanio, equally under her spell, is no exception to the rule. The adventurer of Act 1 becomes the subdued husband of Act 5. As so often, personal insecurity comes out in variation in mode of address; and in the final scene, Bassanio addresses Portia in six different ways—"Madam," "sweet Portia," "sweet lady," "good lady," "Portia," and "sweet Doctor." That is the measure of Portia's patrician dominance.

It would be a crudity, and a distortion, to say simply: wealth buys people. What *The Merchant of Venice* shows is allegiance, respect, and love as they are directed toward human sources of wealth. Wealth is a precondition, not a guarantor, of their existence. This is all in that most delicately balanced of lines, when Portia says to Bassanio, "Since you are dear bought, I will love you dear" (3.2.315), that comes at the end of the speech in which Portia pledges all necessary sums to deal with the Shylock problem. Everything is in the inflection. At one extreme the line suggests a hardheaded heiress, coolly shopping for a husband and letting him know the score. At the other it suggests a lady consciously distancing herself from the apparent commercialism of the sentiment, an intelligent woman playing with crassness, knowing it will be understood. In the middle range of tones, there is a slight edge to her mild joke, but Bassanio is made to feel it. "Dear" embraces much.

Third, wealth governs the means of solving problems as they occur. Portia's first reaction to the Shylock difficulty is, buy the man out:

What no more?
Pay him six thousand, and deface the bond:
Double six thousand, and then treble that,
Before a friend of this description
Shall lose a hair through Bassanio's fault.

(3.2.300–4)

This is a lady who means what she says; her offer of 36,000 ducats is not empty rhetoric. The point is that she has the ducats. She is also in a position to buy the best legal advice, from Doctor Bellario ("And look what notes and garments he doth give thee," [3.4.51]). With resources like that, intelligence and good will ought to prevail. This is a play, not a thesis, and the dramatic possibilities of failure are necessarily present. Certainly there is a will whose terms have to be negotiated. The wishes of dead custodians of wealth are not lightly set aside, for there is posthumous directional power to wealth. But there is no real chance that Morocco or Arragon will be the successful suitor, and the teasing hints of "bred" and "lead" point the way for Bassanio. The outcome of the trial does seem finely poised, and one can conclude that Bellario has earned his retainer. Again, Gratiano is a cause of social friction, and Portia will have to take in hand his propensity for vulgar jests. She can, and she will. To the steely will of the chatelaine, all Belmont's problems yield: she has the will, the intelligence, and the means.

Act 5 renders the accounts. It is the world as seen from Belmont. From it Shylock is excluded, even by name, but proper arrangements are made for the transference of his estate to his daughter and son-in-law. Jessica will be treated with the icy courtesy due to Lorenzo's wife, and Lorenzo's future will be ordained by Portia. He will accept it, as the house ideologue, and so will others within Portia's orbit. Antonio's standing is as Bassanio's friend, and he will always be welcomed. He is also defeated, and the restoratives offered cannot bring him back to full life: "I am the tainted wether of the flock" (4.1.114) is as close to a confession of personal and financial sterility as the play can get. By the end, he has lost Bassanio and regained half his ships. That seems about right.

And finally, the social relations in this play are absorbed into the larger relation of Venice to Belmont. Venice is a city much like London, the workshop of wealth. Venice is to Belmont as the city is to the home counties: Shakespeare holds in balance the means of gaining wealth, and wealth in triumphant being. Belmont is an image of the Earthly Paradise, depicted with a dispassionate accuracy of control that Shakespeare shares with its chatelaine.

THE MERRY WIVES OF WINDSOR

At the core of *The Merry Wives of Windsor* is a conflict between the metropolis and the provinces, between city and town. Falstaff brings his city sophistication and rank to Windsor, hoping to make a killing on the local exchange. The Wives, bridling, affirm middle-class morality against the blandishments of the knighthood. This is the only play in the canon grounded in the middle classes, and it presents a collision of values and rank in which Falstaff comes off badly worsted.

Dating this play is, therefore, more important than it first seems. It has been pretty well established that *The Merry Wives* was written in 1597. But there are still questions about its internal setting. Since this play is tied to Falstaff, and Falstaff is tied to the reigns of Henry IV and Henry V, *The Merry Wives* is apparently set in the Middle Ages. But no one thinks of it that way, and it is rare for directors to choose a medieval mise-en-scène. By common consent, this is an Elizabethan play, and more often than not an Elizabethan setting is chosen. I add that a slightly later period flavor works well, with Falstaff and company appearing as Cavaliers (rather bedraggled) encountering a solid Puritan/bourgeois resistance. The point is that this citizen comedy picks up what was socially in the air in the late sixteenth and early seventeenth centuries. It is in essence a contemporary play. I prefer then, like Robert Speaight, to see *The Merry Wives* "as a parenthesis rather than a sequel" to the *Henry IV* plays.[4] Indeed, it is almost a parenthesis to the canon, for this panorama of the middle classes is not on view elsewhere. They need no translation in this English comedy. Windsor is its burghers.

The character-note is struck at once by Shallow: "Sir Hugh, persuade me not: I will make a Star Chamber matter of it; if he were twenty Sir John Falstaffs, he shall not abuse Robert Shallow, esquire" (1.1.1–4). Expressing wounded pride, resentment against knights pulling rank, and determination that Falstaff shall not get away with it, Shallow offers a prologue to the Wives and announces their song. If there were a chorus, he would present in more temperate language the same catalogue of Shallow's wrongs and of his armigerous ancestors. "Esquire," one rank below the knighthood, meant more than it does today. And Shallow is "a gentleman born," a pleasant touch from the author, who happened to become a gentleman born in the previous year, 1596. The affronted Justice of the Peace needs to be talked out of his plan to take the matter to the highest court in the land. But Falstaff plainly has behaved badly. "Knight, you have beaten my men, kill'd my deer, and broke open my lodge," complains Shallow (1.1.100–1). It looks a bad case of metropolitan arrogance and of Falstaff's regular assumption that laws are framed around his wishes. Falstaff, facing Shallow down, gets away with it for the moment, and Page mediates with "a hot venison pasty." The local resentments, however, are not to be treated thus cavalierly.

Revenge is an important concept for Shakespeare. Excepting *Love's Labor's Lost*, each of his plays contains at least one instance, sometimes many, of revenge or revenger. Shakespeare sees it as a recurring human motive. And observe that here the Wives burn for revenge *before* finding that the other has been written to in identical terms. "How shall I be reveng'd on him? for reveng'd I will be," asks Mistress Page. "How shall I be reveng'd on him?" wonders Mistress Ford (2.1.24; 57). After exchanging letters, they unite operatically in "Let's be reveng'd on him!" (2.1.82). Mistress Ford is scathing in dismissing the "honor" that Falstaff would bring her. It comes down to "What doth he think of us?" (2.1.80), which translates easily as, Who does he think we are? The Wives are far less flattered than resentful at Falstaff's assumption that they will be easy game. His assumption reduces them, and their resentments parallel Shallow's.

Does this discussion of revenge seem excessive, leaving something perhaps not quite accounted for in the play? Not, I think, if we take aboard Mistress Quickly's report to Falstaff on Mistress Ford's reaction. Mistress Quickly is not the most accurate of reporters, but neither is she a total liar:

The best courtier of them all, when the court lay at Windsor, could never have brought her to such a canary. Yet there has been knights, and lords, and gentlemen, with their coaches; I warrant you, coach after coach, letter after letter, gift after gift; smelling so sweetly, all musk , and so rushling, I warrant you, in silk and gold; and in such alligant terms; and in such wine and sugar of the best and fairest, that would have won any woman's heart; and, I warrant you, they could never get an eye-wink of her. I had myself twenty angels given me this morning; but I defy all angels, in any such sort, as they say, but in the way of honesty; and, I warrant you, they could never get her so much sip on a cup with the proudest of them all; and yet there has been earls, nay, which is more, pensioners; but, I warrant you, all is one with her.

(2.2.55–70)

Mistress Ford has been there before. As a comely matron of the town, she has been approached by various of the quality based on the castle. (Pensioners are gentlemen of the royal household there.) To all of them, she has given the same dusty answer. Hence the contempt with which she dismisses Falstaff, who is no kind of catch: "What doth he think of us?"

He thinks, naturally, that a line that worked so well at the Boar's Head will serve in Windsor: "I would thy husband were dead; I'll speak it before the best lord, I would make thee my lady" (3.3.42–44). One has to applaud the Falstaffian gall as he defies class ("I'll speak it before the best lord") in order to exploit it. But now the line that used to work no longer functions in the same way. Perhaps Hamlet can offer a clue: "By the Lord, Horatio, this three years I have took note of it: the age is grown so picked that the toe of the peasant comes so near the heel of the courtier, he galls his kibe" (5.1.133–36). With *Hamlet* at around 1600, that fixes *The Merry Wives of Windsor* nicely. There is social change in the air, and Hamlet senses it as a shortage of deference. So could Falstaff.

The Windsor that Shakespeare constructs rests squarely on the Pages and Fords, with the attendant figures of a Welsh parson, a French physician, the Host of the Garter, and others. Socially, there are many hints of bourgeois comfort and recreation—fowling, drinking sack, and grey-hound racing. The play's key word is "master," which occurs an astonishing 174 times. It is almost always the polite mode of address to a citizen, "Master Brook," "Master Page." Linguistically the play is a Dickensian medley, as assorted individualists mangle the tongue their way: the comic Frenchman and Welshman, Nym with his "humors" catchphrase, mine Host with his "bully-rook," Quickly with her early malapropisms. These linguistic oddities will be milked by the actors according to their skills. (I have known the loudest laugh of the evening to be drawn by "I 'ave married *un garçon!*") And the teeming sub-class gives the comedy its gamey flavor. But in terms of dramatic energies, the action owes everything to two factors: the revenge of the Wives and the standing of their husbands. Page and Ford matter because they have some property. Ford, it appears, has £20 to disburse on his private detective agency, and Page, additionally, has a daughter, Anne, whose "goot gifts" drive the citizens of Windsor to a collective frenzy.

For one with so small a speaking part, Anne Page exercises a remarkable influence over *The Merry Wives of Windsor*. Shakespeare has, of course, no interest in her personally. He has examined dowries at some length in *The Taming of the Shrew* and *The Merchant of Venice*, and will do so again in *Much Ado About Nothing*. He needs Anne, though, as the agent who distracts an entire community. After all, she divides the Windsorites into groups: one that wishes to marry her (Dr. Caius, Slender, and Fenton); another that wishes to promote the candidate of their choice (Page, Mistress Page, Sir Hugh Evans, and Shallow); a third, consisting of Mistress Quickly, that intends to collect from the winning candidate, whatever happens ("I will do what I can for them all three" [3.4.103–4]). Of the three candidates, the visiting Frenchman can safely be ruled out. It is true that Mistress Page favors him:

> I'll to the Doctor; he hath my good will,
> And none but he, to marry with Nan Page.
> That Slender, though well landed, is an idiot;
> And he my husband best affects.
> The Doctor is well money'd, and his friends
> Potent at court; he, none but he, shall have her
>
> (4.4.83–88)

But this is not the assessment anyone else would make. The Frenchman has presumably talked up his connections, and Mistress Page is overly impressed with his propaganda. Slender, after his abysmal courtship (3.4) is clearly not going to catch the selector's eye. There remains Fenton. How does he do it?

The Bassanio of this play enters on a high line, "How now, good woman, how dost thou?" (1.4.121), in response to which Mistress Quickly at once meets the deference quota. "The better that it pleases your good worship to ask" (1.4.122). But it is not quite like that. The conversation soon settles into a deal negotiated between two sharp-eyed business operators. I translate:

> *Fenton*: Shall I do any good, think'st thou?
> Shall I not lose my suit?
> [Is it worth my while, and your while, to keep this going?]
>
> *Quickly*: Troth, sir, all is in His hands above; but notwithstanding, Master Fenton, I'll be sworn on a book she loves you. Have not your worship a wart above your eye?
> [You stand a chance. But there is this problem of your wart. It could tell against you, especially if I mention it.]

Fenton: Yes, marry, have I; what of that? [True.]
Quickly: Well, thereby hangs a tale; good faith, it
            is such another Nan; but, I detest, an honest
            maid as ever broke bread. We had an hour's
            talk of that wart; I shall never laugh but
            in that maid's company! But indeed, she is
            given too much to allicholy and musing; but
            for you—well, go to.
            [You need a friend at Court with that wart, especially
            one prepared to stop talking about it. Draw your own
            conclusions.]
Fenton: Well, I shall see her today. Hold, there's money
            for thee; let me have thy voice in my behalf.
            If thou seest her before me, commend me.
            [I'm going to take a chance on you. Don't let me
            down.]

                                              (1.4.128–42)

And Fenton exits in haste. Mistress Quickly thinks little of his chances—
"Truly, an honest gentleman, but Anne loves him not"—but takes his
money anyway. She underestimates the resourceful Fenton, who shows
even better in his next scene:

Fenton: I see I cannot get thy father's love;
           Therefore no more turn me to him, sweet Nan.
Anne: Alas, how then?
Fenton: Why, thou must be thyself.
           He doth object I am too great of birth;
           And that, my state being gall'd with my expense,
           I seek to heal it only by his wealth.
           Besides these, other bars he lays before me,
           My riots past, my wild societies;
           And tells me 'tis a thing impossible
           I should love thee but as a property.
Anne: May be he tells you true.
Fenton: No, heaven so speed me in my time to come!
           Albeit I will confess thy father's wealth
           Was the first motive that I woo'd thee, Anne;
           Yet, wooing thee, I found thee of more value
           Than stamps in gold, or sums in sealed bags;

> And 'tis the very riches of thyself
> That now I aim at.
>
> (3.4.1–18)

He handsomely confesses to a sordid motive, only to claim moral points for rising above it. He has still to overcome Page's suspicions, but does not neglect to pay his agent ("There's for thy pains" [3.4.98]). When mine host has to be squared, Fenton raises the stakes: "Assist me in my purpose, /And, as I am a gentleman, I'll give thee/A hundred pound in gold more than your loss" (4.6.3–5). This is an offer the host cannot refuse, especially after the promise, "Besides, I'll make a present recompense" (4.6.55).

The last scene is the apotheosis of Fenton. Speaking in the blank verse that is his trademark, distinguishing him from the habitual Windsor prose, Fenton reveals to an amazed world the outcome of his wooing:

> Hear the truth of it.
> You would have married her most shamefully,
> Where there was no proportion held in love.
> The truth is, she and I, long since contracted,
> Are now so sure that nothing can dissolve us.
> Th'offense is holy that she hath committed;
> And this deceit loses the name of craft,
> Of disobedience, or unduteous title,
> Since therein she doth evitate and shun
> A thousand irreligious cursed hours,
> Which forced marriage would have brought upon her.
>
> (5.5.207–17)

The Miseries of Enforced Marriage—Fenton has saved Anne from all this! Love, and not crass commercialism, has conquered all! The lofty moral tone of Fenton's rebuke to his parents-in-law is what registers here, not the lie ("long since contracted"). Ford's response is as good as any, "Money buys lands, and wives are sold by fate," which declines further inquiry. For the audience, no problem arises. Anne has evitated, and indeed shunned, the horrors of marriage to Slender or Caius. The victor is the sanctimonious Fenton, and no one can say he has not laid out his money to good effect.

The plot of *The Merry Wives* brings together two class formulas. Sir John, trying his luck with the local matrons, is rebuffed by a combination of morality and social resentment. Fenton, who moves in high circles, has to overcome suspicions within the bourgeois alliance he seeks. He succeeds through an astute crossing of subordinate palms and by taking a high moral line with his principal and her family. He will go far, that one.

But what of Windsor? For the most part, its inhabitants are stereotypes limited by name and humor. Their behavior is obviously class-based, yet volatile and random in effect. No general principle seems to be illustrated. Instead of iron laws crushing individuals to a set pattern, we see people on the make, plotting wildly, failing ludicrously to reach their goals, exercising their economic and social freedoms in all directions and with all results. They scheme marriage, and find themselves betrayed by love. They plot amours, and find themselves betrayed by class. Slender cannot decide whether he should follow or precede Anne Page indoors, and Ford has no idea if fidelity is within his wife's vision of things. People cannot arrange an elopement or a duel or an ambush without getting it wrong. Windsor is openly, cheerfully incompetent in the pursuit of its ends. We are left with a composite image of a large group rushing after whatever false assignation or botched prospectus has most recently caught its attention. If Windsor is a microcosm of the great world, this comedy has some of the most interesting social comment in the canon.

The ending of the play has its ambivalences, however, despite all the rush of high spirits and surprise dénouements. The Windsorites unite to defeat Falstaff in a fine show of local solidarity. For that reason, the audience may begin to detach itself from the burghers' triumph. Everything depends on performance, naturally, and on the text played, but one can become very conscious of Ford's unpleasant insistence on getting his money back, coupled with the outrageous claim that Falstaff cozened him of it. Ford looks like a man refusing to pay the private detective agency, now that his wife is proven honest after all. One sides with Falstaff against the pack. Hence the disclosure of Anne Page's marriage comes congenially to the audience; it is good to see the burghers lose one. The invitation to "laugh this sport off by a country fire, /Sir John and all" (5.5.229–30) is perhaps best not taken up. We shall not, after all, be staying too long in Windsor.

MUCH ADO ABOUT NOTHING

The plot line is the impact of the visitors upon the locals, and the outcome is wooing, misunderstanding, marriage. *Much Ado* is usually played as a straightforward mingling of ladies and gentlemen, essentially of the same rank, with the main interest attaching to the performance of the two star parts. The signals in the text are more complex than that, however. Not only is there a certain amount of class gradation, but class values also play a part in the Act 4 explosion. Moreover, there is some delicate subversion of values here, and Shaw's questioning of "Shakespeare's Merry Gentlemen" still lies unresolved. But of that, more later.

First, the rankings. Leonato, as the opening stage direction (but nothing in the text) tells us, is Governor of Messina, although at times he seems more like a Mayor than a Governor, and in his dealings with Dogberry he obviously acts as an English Justice of the Peace. He appears generally as a prosperous burgher, who can contemplate the enormous expenses of having soldiers billeted upon him for a month without apparent qualm. His only daughter, Hero, is seen as a prize by Claudio. Beatrice, Leonato's niece, must come from the same social background. Of Leonato's wife, the phantom Innogen who appears in two stage directions only, one can say no more than E. K. Chambers: "A Lady, whose daughter is successively betrothed, defamed, repudiated before the altar, taken for dead, and restored to life, ought not to be a mute. It is not motherly."[5]

The visitors are of markedly higher rank. Don Pedro is Prince of Arragon, and while he is most affable in his demeanor (addressing Leonato as "my dear friend"), there is no doubt of his standing. Leonato and Benedick, for example, address him as "Your Grace," which in England would make him a Duke. At an important moment, Claudio addresses him as "My liege, your Highness" (1.1.252). Don Pedro is also a military leader, and there are passages when he appears to be a Colonel of the Regiment, benignly expediting the affairs of the young officers of the garrison. They usually call him "my Lord," which corresponds to the routine "Sir." His brother, "John the Bastard," is still a Count, and treated with appropriate respect by all. *Don* Pedro is, by right and by name, the social arbiter of the play.

His young officers are *not* of equal standing, even though the dramatis personae (in the New Arden and other editions) lists both as "a young lord." It is true that Don Pedro addresses them early as "Signior Claudio and Signior Benedick" (1.1.126), but that is no more than a tactful evening of mode (with perhaps a further nuance, that the younger man comes first, making it a reverse bid). Benedick, as the play proceeds, is always "Signior Benedick." He is a gentleman. Claudio is "Count Claudio," a usage introduced by Benedick with mock formality (1.1.180) and confirmed elsewhere later. The Messenger has hinted at the disparity of rank, when he says, "He [Benedick] is most in the company of the right noble Claudio" (1.1.69). It's an early sketch for a formation more familiar in the relationship between Parolles and Bertram.

The wooing of the visiting soldiers proceeds on markedly dissimilar lines, though each has a class component. Claudio, the more conventional, begins his with an interview—with his commanding officer. It is amusingly done, the dialogue stiffening at 1.1.252 (the exit of Benedick) into blank verse: "My liege, your Highness now may do me good." The switch from prose to verse is mentally a move from the mess to the C.O.'s office. "Permission to marry, Sir." All turns on that most artfully compressed of lines, "Hath Leonato any son, my lord?" And Don Pedro, who understands perfectly that this is not a casual inquiry, answers to the point: "No child but Hero; she's his only heir." We are back in dowryland, fixed here as the coming together of the nobility and the haute bourgeoisie. And that is part of Claudio's anger at Don John's revelation. He has entered into an arrangement under certain assurances, virginity among them, and feels his honor to be betrayed. Broadly, Claudio is a portrait of an insecure young man who enters into marriage for reasons of part-liking, part-calculation: he knows Hero very little, and is not well placed to resist calumnies. He is morally overborne by Don John of the blood royal. Claudio and Hero are such an obvious good match that nobody troubles to explore it. The personal weakness of Claudio reflects the social arrangements that bring him and Hero together.

Beatrice and Benedick go at things differently. Their relationship is one of psychological maneuvering, and everything leads to and from the emotional hurdle which Benedick has to overcome—and it takes a shared crisis for him to do it—"I do love nothing in the world so well as you. Is not that strange?" (4.1.266–7). The extraordinary interest and enduring stage popularity of their encounter comes down, I think, to this: it is a model relationship, worked out between equals, and there is nothing to touch it on the English stage until Millamant and Mirabel negotiate their accord in *The Way of the World*. It is this sense of a proposed model that communicates with an audience (and makes Claudio and Hero seem, by contrast, woodenly conventional). Three features stand out. One, it is between people of equal social rank—a lady and gentleman, simply. Two, no dowry is mentioned. Benedick theorizes of his ideal woman, "Rich she shall be, that's certain" (2.3.30), but that is before he learns about Beatrice. He makes no inquiry about her dowry, if any, and the general implication of the badinage in Act 2, scene 1 is that if Beatrice is to be "one day fitted with a husband," she will have to manage it through her own charms, without fiscal additives. And three, their betrothal is secured after an intense and emotionally exacting courtship, with the tests following the initial declaration. For all the social help given them, Benedick and Beatrice have to explore matters on their own. These three elements impress on us their encounter as disturbingly vital. Stage history and audiences look back on them with good reason.

A microcourtship remains, that of Don Pedro with Beatrice. His passage with Beatrice in 2.1 is a fascinating vignette. The engagement of Hero and Claudio has just been announced, and Beatrice laments her single state: "I may sit in a corner and cry 'Heigh-ho for a husband!'" (2.1.288), to which Don Pedro responds, "Lady Beatrice, I will get you one." How is this staged? There is general company on stage, but it is natural for Claudio, Hero, and Leonato to be busy with their affairs. If so, with Don Pedro and Beatrice a little apart from the main group, their conversation assumes a different tone. Beatrice, perhaps a trifle nervously, essays a joke on the husbands Don Pedro's father got. Then he asks, "Will you have me, lady?" She backs off with another joke, a gracious compliment follows, and Leonato comes unwittingly to Beatrice's rescue with "Niece, will you look to those things I told you of?" The moment is over. Were the others in earshot, or not? If they were, then "Will you have me, lady?" is heavy, public flirtatiousness, harmless because public. If not, then Don Pedro is making a sexual inquiry. Tone is everything, and only the actor can suggest how serious, if at all, the speaker is. What is behind the way Don Pedro tests the resistance, only to be so easily rebuffed? Is that what he wants? He *says*, in the first eavesdrop scene, "I would she had bestowed her dotage on me. I would have daff'd *all other respects* and made her half myself" (2.3.154–56). Whether it is encouragement or not, that is a handsome compliment, and an admission that Don Pedro is prepared to close the social gap. Around him forms an aura of solitude, which he bequeaths to the play in its final lines.

The Act 4 explosion is, technically, the weak point in the play. It is inherently unlikely that the charge against Hero should be accepted. Shakespeare has therefore to strengthen the factors that make the outcome credible. He does this by making the event a collision between two parties, the locals and the nobility, and by making Leonato the key figure. Leonato fails to support his daughter as he should, the crux being "Would the two princes lie?" (4.1.152). At this point the underlying forces surface for inspection. The affair becomes one of class deference, Leonato being unable to conceive of the princes lying or being in error. And it is precisely this aspect that Beatrice rages against: "Princes and counties! Surely, a princely testimony, a goodly count, Count Comfect; a sweet gallant, surely!" (311–13). The rank-words are fairly spat out, releasing a targeted rage. Benedick gives the impression of being a floating voter, as it were. He pointedly fails to exit with the Prince and his entourage, and he is won over by Beatrice's passion and conviction. The audience, knowing the truth of the matter, will judge Beatrice and Benedick to have been right and Leonato to have failed.

Much Ado cannot, however, be reduced to an ambush of the aristocracy. Its subversions are distributed more widely than that. One can say, for example, that Dogberry and company show up their betters. They have to endure the malaprop jokes, and the distinction of founding the school of comic constabulary that lasts so long in English fiction and folklore. But they get things right, and their "Softly, softly" methods do lead to the apprehension and conviction of the villains. Leonato, for all his Justice of the Peace urbanity ("Drink some wine ere you go" [2.5.48]), is not well advised to leave the examination to Dogberry. Still, Dogberry, with intelligent help from the Sexton, pulls things through. The Watch compares well for honesty and all-around efficiency with others on view here.

The larger questions relate to the leading personages, and they have been incisively registered by Shaw:

The main pretension in *Much Ado* is that Benedick and Beatrice are exquisitely witty and amusing persons. Benedick's pleasantries might pass at a sing-song in a public-house parlour; but a gentleman rash enough to venture on them in even the very mildest £52-a-year suburban imitation of polite society today would assuredly never be invited again. From his first joke, "Were you in doubt, sir, that you asked her?" to his last, "There is no staff more reverend than one tipped with horn," he is not a wit, but a blackguard.[6]

This is true enough, save Shaw's final exaggeration, but why pick on Benedick? He's close to Gratiano and Lucio in his manners. Still, Shaw is right. It is not enough to say that Elizabethan England is not Victorian suburbia. I cannot believe that it has ever been usual, in the opening words of a reunion, to cast public doubt on the legitimacy of the host's daughter. Psychologically, there is an explanation: Benedick is stuck with the role of "Prince's jester," which he plays in and out of season. (This may also be one reason why he needs Beatrice, who is also burdened with a jarring role.) He is not, in fact, very funny—true of Shakespeare's clowns so often, alas—save in the two great soliloquies of 2.3, when he should pillage the audience. Similarly, Beatrice's hard, forced witticisms are not in themselves attractive, save as an indicator of a more vulnerable person underneath. The masks of Beatrice and Benedick (2.1) are their emblems. But the question of Benedick's behavior remains. It can be met with a generalization: Shakespeare is disposed to reveal, in a range of plays, gentlemen behaving in an ungentlemanly way. The point is that they know better and can prove it. Take, as a single example, the iron self-discipline and schooled propriety of Benedick's challenge to Claudio, coupled with his leave-taking of the Prince. The alternating current, good/dubious behavior, electrifies what would otherwise be inert figures. To explore the frontiers of bad taste is to open up inviting territory. Even so, there is a subacid quality to Shakespeare's social reportage of this period; one cannot say with certainty that he likes what he sees. The upper-range social comedy is detailed with something other than syco-phancy, and something harder than acquiescence.

AS YOU LIKE IT

Arden: the great image of escape from the workaday world. It is a timeless country of the mind, and no one evokes it better than Charles the Wrestler:

They say he is already in the Forest of Arden, and a many merry men with him; and there they live like the old Robin Hood of England. They say many young gentlemen flock to him every day, and fleet the time carelessly, as they did in the golden world. (1.1.105–9)

That image is probably what one retains from one's first visit to a production of *As You Like It*, a glow that lingers on the mental retina. It is meant to.

But the person who describes Arden so memorably has never been there. Charles has to rely on "they say" for his authority. The Arden we see has for all its glow some disturbing, nonescapist actualities. The most obvious is the weather, of course: Duke Senior gets over that at the beginning of Act 2. Beyond that are many other touches that link Arden with the real world, including the problems of primogeniture, labor and wages, and satisfactory ceremonies. Social distinctions don't vanish in the woods. And, as everyone notes, the Arden dwellers have no hesitation in stampeding back to the court when they get their chance. The pastoral idyll, observed at close quarters, turns out to contain its contradictions. Arden looks like a continuation of the real world by other means.

The real world is present at once in the country seat of Oliver de Boys. What galls his younger brother is the injustice of primogeniture, which leaves a man "But poor a thousand crowns." For the rest he must look to his brother. "For my part," says Orlando, "he keeps me rustically at home . . . call you that keeping for a gentleman of my birth that differs not from the stalling of an ox?" (1.1.6.–10). The grievance is that Oliver "bars me the place of a brother, and as much as in him lies, mines [undermines] my gentility with my education." This is no fiction created out of air for a fantasy-comedy. A contemporary, Thomas Wilson, makes a complaint strikingly similar to Orlando's:

My elder brother forsooth must be my master. He must have all, and all the rest that which the cat left on the malt heap, perhaps some small annuity during his life or what please our elder brother's worship to bestow upon us if we please him and my mistress his wife.[7]

That was the system, the eldest takes all: hence the reality of Orlando's plea to be given a decent education or given his portion and allowed to try his luck. And within the shadow of this injustice was the perhaps less dramatic but no less familiar one: the plight of the elderly servant who loses favor. "Get you with him, you old dog" is in effect Oliver's dismissal of Adam. The servant has saved 500 crowns and needs them. The opening scene is charged with anger and frustration, and it stems from living on terms dictated by others. "Know you where you are, sir?" "O, sir, very well; *here in your orchard*" (1.1.36–37). That is the motif, the pain of the disinherited chained to a plot he cannot own. The nearby court, a focus of fears, resentments, wrongs, is no alternative. The suspicious and hostile Duke Frederick expresses its tensions. Still, if "court" stands for "town" in the argument of this play, then Arden must surely stand for freedom and escape? Yes, but only in highly qualified ways.

The Forest of Arden is not quite what we should call a forest. Within a year of *As You Like It,* John Manwood had opened his book on forest laws with this definition: "A Forrest is a certen Territorie of woody grounds & fruitful pastures."[8] It is not a wilderness, then. Arden appears a parish of scattered sheep cotes, mostly pasture land with some wood. "You can't play Rosalind", Dame Peggy Ashcroft has said, "without a hat and a tree," but in fact few scenes call for trees. What matters in the play's ecology is the sheep cote. Arden may contain exotic suggestions of Ardennes, but the play depicts a district closer to Arden in rural Warwickshire.

The sheep matter. Shepherds and shepherdesses must look after them,

and someone owns them. Sheep link the pastoral world and the real
world. As soon as the court refugees come within the confines of Arden,
they encounter Corin, who explains his position: "But I am shepherd to
another man, /And do not sheer the fleeces that I graze" (2.4.73–74). He
is a hired laborer, whose "master is of churlish disposition." After this
understated vignette of rural life, the talk shifts to property:

> Besides, his cote, his flocks, and bounds of feed
> Are now on sale, and at our sheepcote now,
> By reason of his absence there is nothing
> That you will feed on.

>   (2.4.78–81)

Silvius, it appears, has the money to buy it, but can think of nothing
except Phebe. Rosalind—typically of the out-of-town visitor to the country—
makes a spur-of-the-moment decision to buy:

> I pray thee, if it stand with honesty,
> Buy thou the cottage, pasture, and the flock,
> And thou shalt have to pay for it of us.

>   (2.4.86–88)

"Arcadia," as Jan Kott remarks, "has been turned into real estate, into
landed property."[9] And Corin, who it seems combines part-time commission work as estate agent with his regular employment, is happy to oblige:

> Assuredly the thing is to be sold.
> Go with me; if you like upon report
> The soil, the profit, and this kind of life,
> I will your very faithful feeder be,
> And buy it with your gold right suddenly.

>   (2.4.91–95)

Highly condensed, this episode is fascinatingly specific. Real estate is
always *real*. Shakespeare is facing up to the question, how does Arden
work? (Unlike William Morris, who in his Utopian fantasy *News From
Nowhere* never explains the workings of society, so that one has no idea
how the English acquire the Bordeaux wine that graces their meals.) And
the answer is, Arden runs on money, which is capital, return, wages, and

the means of acquiring and maintaining desirable property: "the soil, the profit, and this kind of life." Corin engages to continue under the new management, upon Celia's promise "And we will mend thy wages" (2.4.89). The pocket farm will pay its way.

Shepherd is the key word, whose meaning slants two ways. One side is all pastoral allure, porcelain figures in a porcelain landscape, engaging young people draped over the greensward or leaning on crooks, while the sheep nibble away at what nature has provided for them. This is pure myth, and doesn't happen in *As You Like It*. It is still a mental presence. The other side, the muted rigors of hired labor, we have already seen. Then another dimension comes into existence with the way in which out-of-town visitors regard shepherds.

Touchstone, that prototype of the dandy, registers the point immediately:

> *Touchstone*: Holla, you clown!
> *Rosalind*: Peace, fool; he's not thy kinsman.
> *Corin*: Who calls?
> *Touchstone*: Your betters, sir.
>
> (2.4.62–63)

"*Your betters, sir,*" is uttered by the townee among the rustics. Touchstone, the lens through which so much is viewed, patronizes the locals insufferably. His scene with Corin (3.2) is the most extended instance, and the terms of address grip the relationship. Touchstone is "Master Touchstone" and Corin is (repeatedly and disdainfully) "Shepherd." Touchstone's view of Arden comes down to "Now in respect it is in the fields, it pleaseth me well; but in respect it is not in the court, it is tedious" (3.2.17–19). His wooing of Audrey is based on court superiority. From first to last, from "Ay, now am I in Arden; the more fool I" to "I press in here, sir, amongst the country copulatives," Touchstone despises the country.

Touchstone is extreme. All the same, he is not so far different from Rosalind in this. The sight of Phebe incites Rosalind to heights of denunciation, possibly because of the unfortunate parallels between Silvius and Orlando. One does not observe Rosalind on her knees, thanking God fasting for a good man's love. Rosalind's jeer

> I saw her hand; she has a leathern hand,
> A freestone color'd hand; I verily did think

> That her old gloves were on, but 'twas her hands
>
> (4.3.24–26)

is unattractive and characteristic of what the Arden dwellers have to put up with from the visitors. Corin, Silvius, Phebe, Audrey, William, and Sir Oliver Martext, all have to run the gauntlet of courtly derision. Their collective statement is unambiguous: the permanent Arden dwellers (as distinct from the refugees) are inferior to their urban visitors. But this is a commonplace of social history. A century after *As You Like It*, Millamant has her great flout at Sir Wilfull Witwoud, the country squire: "Ah rustic, ruder than gothic!" Herrick could bewail his imprisonment in "this dull Devonshire." Not till the eighteenth century did something like a balance between town and country come into sight. *As You Like It* is sharply tilted.

We can take as read, then, the great divide between Ardenites and visitors. As interesting are the social definitions within the refugee group, since they continue the forms of the outside world. The Duke's demeanor is that of a great English nobleman on a hunting party with his entourage. He rules a genially relaxed court-in-exile, whose tone is subtly modulated to a sense of informal decorum. It is not Versailles, and neither is it a mere sprawling picnic that Orlando interrupts. For disturbing the peace, Orlando is made to look something of a fool. It is worse than a threat, a *faux pas*, and the Duke fixes the offense:

> Art thou thus bolden'd, man, by thy distress?
> Or else a rude despiser of good manners,
> That in civility thou seem'st so empty?
>
> (2.7.91–93)

And Orlando, abashed, admits that he may have given the wrong impression: "yet am I inland bred, /And know some nurture" (1.2.96–97). *Inland* is opposed to our "outlandish," and means familiar with good society, not rustic. Further apologies ensue, and Orlando becomes one of the company.

The tone of this company is consistently on a higher plane than the rough textures of the stage habitually impart. The contention between Jaques and Orlando, for example, is very courtier-like:

> *Jaques*:   I thank you for your company; but good faith,
>   I had as lief have been myself alone.
> *Orlando*: And so had I; but yet, for fashion sake, I thank
>   you too for your society.

> *Jaques*: God buy you; let's meet as little as we can.
> *Orlando*: I do desire we may be better strangers.
>
> (3.2.238–43)

This is Restoration comedy, two men-about-town strolling around St. James's Park and elegantly carving each other. The note of social inquiry continues into the passage between Rosalind and Ganymede that follows; Orlando is developing rapidly in Arden:

> *Orlando*: Your accent is something finer than you could
>   purchase in so removed a dwelling.
> *Rosalind*: I have been told so of many; but indeed an old
>   religious uncle of mine taught me to speak,
>   who was in his youth an inland man . . .
>
> (3.2.318–22)

Again, that "inland": "properly brought up." As G. L. Brook observes, "We find in *As You Like It* the beginnings of a feeling for class dialect."[10] It is not possible here to gauge how regional dialect is shading into class. But a feeling for accent is part of this play's awareness of social nuance and of its understanding that the important happenings in Arden are not rustic.

Jaques and Touchstone embody all this. Their relationship is one of subdued tension based on an undeclared rivalry. Each in his own way is a court entertainer, one a professional, the other a gentleman-amateur. Consider Jaques' first account of Touchstone: "A fool, a fool! I met a fool i'th' forest, / A motley fool" (2.7.12–13). "Lack-lustre eye" does not sound much like the Touchstone we see. There is some kind of personal shadowing here, and Jaques' "O that I were a fool! I am ambitious for a motley coat" hints at a sense of self-caricature.

Jaques' impulse to assert superiority is marked in the interrupted wedding of Touchstone and Audrey. His offer to give Audrey away finds Touchstone at a disadvantage, from which he resourcefully recovers into counter-patronage:

> *Touchstone*: Good even, good Master What-ye-call't; how do you,
>   sir? You are very well met. Goddild you for your last
>   company. I am very glad to see you. Even a toy in
>   hand here, sir. Nay, pray be cover'd.
>
> (3.3.64–67)

It won't do: Jaques is on top and intends to stay there. "Will you be married, *motley?*" The inhabitants of Arden like to establish a social advantage by naming the other person's calling. Touchstone's admission, that wedlock would be nibbling, fails to deflect the next thrust: "And will you, *being a man of your breeding*, be married under a bush, like a beggar? Get you to church and have a good priest, that can tell you what marriage is." Jaques makes it sound like the Elizabethan equivalent of a registry office, which no doubt it was. Touchstone succumbs, after the face-saving formula (which may be an aside, or spoken directly to Jaques, a little apart, as a man-of-the-world's explanation) that "not being well married, it will be a good excuse for me hereafter to leave my wife" (3.3.79–81). This is bottomless cynicism or a cover-up for social embarrassment: take your choice. The nuptials are deferred either way. Once again a social *faux pas* has been put right.

The relationship between Jaques and Touchstone develops through the final scene. Jaques wants to claim credit for being a patron of Touchstone: "This is the motley-minded gentleman that I have so often met in the forest. He hath been a courtier, he swears" (5.4.39–41). Jaques is now a connoisseur of virtuosi; hence he says, "Good my lord, like this fellow." But not too much. After Touchstone has launched, with a little prompting, into his set piece on the degrees of the quarrel, Jaques' comment is, "Is not this a rare fellow, my lord? He's as good at any thing, *and yet a fool*" (5.4.98–99). Patron and virtuoso are not, after all, so close. The final stab of rancour that Jaques delivers to Touchstone has been in waiting all through: "And you to wrangling; for thy loving voyage/Is but for two months victuall'd' (5.4.185–86). It might be true, but there are things better left unsaid.

As You Like It is urban and urbane in feeling. Its perceptions are those of the visitors, not those who live permanently in Arden. The rustics are not altogether mocked; Corin, for instance, gets a fair run. But they are properties in this comedy, viewed from outside by the refugees whose sojourn in Arden is temporary. The class interest lies partly in the relations between the locals and the refugees, partly in the visitors themselves. Yet it is diffused, flaring up in odd pockets of resistance. The town, transplanted to the forest, is never absent in spirit.

At the heart of *As You Like It* is the eternal tension between the things you can only get in the country and the things you can only get in town. Many people, perhaps most, never do resolve this tension. The thing is to have somewhere else to go to. One leaves Arden with the feeling we all know so well, that four acts in the country is a little long. Duke Senior seems to have no doubts. Duke Frederick may come to regret his decision.

TWELFTH NIGHT

Twelfth Night is a feast and an end to feasting. Everything in this comedy has to express the dual values of the title, the impulse to have a good time and the awareness that this is the last party of the season. Tomorrow one goes back to work. Like *As You Like It*, which it follows closely, *Twelfth Night* is an escape comedy that nevertheless contains insistent reminders of the world to which it offers an alternative. Escape from class is impossible, and the nuanced queries of class accompany the action throughout. In no play of Shakespeare's is it more important to place the characters socially, and in none do they spend more time in pursuit of their definitions. Much of the result is a social blur. We know where we are with Orsino, Olivia, Sir Andrew, and Sir Toby. We don't have this degree of certainty with Malvolio and Maria, or with Fabian. Hence the need is to assess the characters.

Orsino gives us no trouble, even if Shakespeare cannot decide whether he is a Duke or Count. A young, handsome bachelor, he inflects the play with his character-note of bored langor: "Enough, no more, 'tis not so sweet now as it was before" (1.1.7–8). He sets the plot in motion, and to him it ultimately defers. All that is ambivalent in Orsino is his sexuality, which does not concern us. His court is drawn with the lightest of strokes, having nothing like the density of Olivia's household. Olivia may give us pause, because we are not sure of her age. Theatrical tradition cast Olivia as the elder of the company's two leading ladies, until Peter Hall's Stratford production of 1958. Robert Speaight explains that "the director was reacting against the stately contraltos whom a sudden bereavement has distracted from the organization of the Hunt Ball".[11] Still, a mature Olivia suits "For youth is bought more oft than begg'd or borrow'd" (3.4.3), a line that can be made to resonate. Today's tendency is for young, flighty Olivias. The casting is crucial in this respect, so that a mature Olivia coupled with a Malvolio who is not a buffoon might just seem a possible match.

Then there is Sir Andrew, the eternal type of the young man whose fortune is to inherit his fortune. One might come across a score of Aguecheeks, thought Granville-Barker, "in greater or less perfection, any day after a west-end London lunch, doing what I believe is called 'a slope down Bond.'"[12] Brains aside, this gallant is adequately characterized by his fashionable swearing ("slight," "od's lifelings," "nay, let me alone for swearing") and his résumé of recreations ("fencing, dancing, and bear-baiting"). Sir Andrew is not without ambition and hopes to make a brilliant marriage with the Countess Olivia. Interestingly, Sir Toby encourages him with what may be the truth: "She'll none o'th' Count; she'll not match above her degree, neither in estate, years, nor wit; I have heard her swear't" (1.3.101–4). Does Olivia plan to keep her social advantage in marriage? For she does in fact marry below her degree, Cesario being a gentleman of Orsino's court.

Sir Toby is altogether more densely characterized. His is the largest speaking part. There are two sides to him, *Belch* (with its stereotypical, humorous suggestion), and *Sir Toby*, "a knight, a gentleman, and a soldier," as in the epigraph that Elgar affixes to his *Falstaff*. In the old days, Sir Tobys were played as drunken ruffians. "By mine honor, *half* drunk" says Olivia wearily, of an early appearance (1.5.110). What was the finished product like? But it may be true that, appallingly, Sir Toby is never drunk. What we see is what he is. Tynan remarks, of Sir Cedric Hardwicke's Sir Toby, that "an impression of extreme, almost disintegrating alcoholism was perfectly conveyed," and all done without a hiccough or slur.[13] To a later age, accustomed to asking questions about alcohol addiction, Sir Toby is not too hard to read. He is a case history of unemployed, unoccupied knighthood. He has no possessions, no land or duties, but lives reasonably at ease with a wealthy kinswoman. He has rank and nothing else, hence his addiction to spectator sports, conversation, drinking, and practical jokes. The major actions of the comedy, the gulling of Malvolio and the duel between Sir Andrew and Cesario/Viola, are both products of his mind-set. His is the classic ennui of the unemployed, at all social levels. All this has to be interpreted. Shakespeare offers no speeches in which a more personal psychology is developed. He presents an apparently two-dimensional figure, set in a certain social context, and in effect says, "Use your understanding of the social context to explain the man."

The more recent stage tendency, I think rightly, is in Tynan's phrase "to restore Sir Toby to the knighthood."[14] To play Sir Toby as an intelligent and well-born failure, perfectly aware of himself, makes good sense. David Waller, for one, had no doubt that "I hate a drunken rogue" (5.1.192) was self-hatred. The main contours of the part remain clear. Illyria notwithstanding, this is an English knight, a man of education and social accomplishment. Crosse, in his meticulous way, singles out a detail in a performance that he disapproved of: "It was characteristic of the carelessness which some producers show in small things that in the kitchen scene he was allowed to say 'surgēre.'"[15] He has a point: Sir Toby would get that right.

We move to the more socially ambivalent characters, pausing at Fabian. It's a colorless part, deliberately so. But when Fabian has to make the speech for the defense in the final scene, it is in blank verse. Moreover, he speaks of "myself and Toby" (not "Sir Toby") in the presence of Orsino and Olivia. This would never do if he were not within the same social range as Sir Toby. Fabian is, therefore, a gentleman, one who can speak familiarly of Sir Toby without affronting protocol. It is a mistake, I think, to play Fabian as a stableboy or Tony Lumpkin.

With Maria lie all the problems and all the solutions of the play. How old is she? The recent RSC convention has been to make her of a certain age, who sees Sir Toby as her last chance. Yet there is nothing in the text to verify this. On the other hand, the stage tradition of the bouncy, vital soubrette is also pure convention. Maria's age is open, and so is her status. She is on the border of upstairs and downstairs, my lady's gentlewoman. To the Elizabethans, this would signify an established pattern. The daughter of a gentleman who lacked dowry potential would find her best social chances in the great house. There she would be protected, given the opportunity to meet suitable young gentlemen, and enabled to see something of the world. Her duties would be those of lady-in-waiting. Maria is correctly identified when Olivia orders "Call in my gentlewoman," and Malvolio sonorously rephrases: "Gentlewoman, my lady calls" (1.5.154).

But that is the correct, formal mode. Olivia and Malvolio are always punctilious. There is an alternative, which emerges in Sir Toby's mischievous answer to Sir Andrew's first reaction to Maria, "What's that?" "My lady's chambermaid" (1.3.46–47). Is this exchange within Maria's hearing? I think not; Sir Andrew is making a surreptitious inquiry concerning the standing of a woman unknown to him. Sir Toby's answer is meant for Sir Andrew alone. Now, in Shakespeare's time "chambermaid" did mean "lady-in-waiting," "lady's maid." But it could also mean "female servant," roughly the usage which has survived to the present day. We can read Sir Toby's response two ways. He is deliberately feeding Sir Andrew misinformation. "Chambermaid" is a malicious attempt at misleading Sir Andrew, putting him at cross purposes with Maria, which sorts well with Sir Toby's ways. Or he is casting a social slight. Sir Toby is saying, in effect, that Maria is no better than a servant. And this meaning is echoed later by Viola/Cesario. When Maria has the temerity to intervene in her parley with Olivia, she is immediately rent:

> *Maria*: Will you hoist sail, sir? Here lies your way.
> *Viola*: No, good swabber, I am to hull here a little longer.
>
> (1.5.190–91)

A "swabber" is one who swabs down the decks, with the implication that this activity is suitable for one of Maria's standing. Maria has to accept the social insult in silence, and a minute later her mistress dismisses her.

Technically, Maria is like Sir Toby. She has no soliloquy. Everything has to be inferred from her social position and her public words and actions. One thing we can be sure of: she loathes Malvolio. And what she gains is a certitude of a different order, which in retrospect colors everything that happens. Maria's conduct looks different when perceived as leading up to her post-curtain apotheosis: Lady Belch.

There are a few direct pointers. Sir Toby is evidently on good terms with her in their opening scene, and Maria has no difficulty in taking Feste's deliciously corkscrewed point: "Well, go thy way; if Sir Toby would leave drinking, thou wert as witty a piece of Eve's flesh as any in Illyria." "Peace, you rogue, no more o'that" (1.5.22–26). Sir Toby is not above dropping a gentlemanly hint to Sir Andrew. "She's a beagle true-bred, and one that adores me. What o'that?" (2.3.168–69). She is *true-bred*, of good family; one could do worse. The passage follows closely upon Maria's "if I do not gull him into a nay-word and make him a common recreation, do not think I have wit enough to lie straight in my bed" (127–29). How do we read it? Invitation or rejection? A coquette's maneuver, or the initiation of serious negotiations? Has an idea been put into Sir Toby's head, or was it already there? Things should be clearer at "Come by and by to my chamber" (4.2.69), when the director will have to determine whether Sir Toby's remark is addressed to Feste or to Maria. It matters. If the second option is taken, the complicity of the theatricals is demonstrably the antechamber to the bedroom. Overall, the pattern seems to me marked. Maria's game is to bind Sir Toby to herself via the gulling action, to make the conspiracy coalesce into betrothal.

Malvolio is the great issue, and he is artfully located across the social frontiers. *Steward*: this is a serious and responsible position. I prefer to avoid such approximations as "major-domo," which smacks of Gilbert and Sullivan, or "butler," a Victorian/Edwardian development as we receive it. "Steward" can still be an office of distinction (like the Steward of the Jockey Club). Malvolio is the house administrator, in charge of all domestic arrangements in Olivia's household and also in charge of protocol: he makes the announcements. The impression of pomposity Malvolio conveys in the early scenes is only one side of him. (Exactly the same is true of Polonius.) No fool could hold down the job he does. His aspirations of upward social mobility are patently unrealistic, but as he says, "There is example for't: the Lady of the Strachy married the yeoman of the wardrobe" (2.5.36–38). Fourteen years later, he could have added, "And the Duchess of Malfi married Antonio, her steward." A man of some education, he knows of Pythagoras's theories and is attracted to "politic authors." The nature of his position and responsibilities make him a gentleman. This is what he claims in the cell scene ("as I am a gentleman," 4.2.79), and Orsino and Olivia ratify the claim. Antonio, says the Duke, "Is now in durance, at Malvolio's suit, /A gentleman and follower of my lady's" (5.1.268–69). A moment later, Olivia refers to Malvolio as "poor gentleman." His final passionate outburst is in verse, the language of a gentleman. The later evidence is plain, that the Steward is accepted as a gentleman. The respective roles played by education, appointment, birth, and breeding are left undefined.

It is for the stage to determine these matters, and the stage history is equivocal. The record shows two major traditions of presenting Malvolio. Lamb's marvelous essay, "On Some of the Old Actors," singles out Bensley's superbly dignified Malvolio. "Bensley, accordingly, threw over the part an air of Spanish loftiness. He looked, spake, and moved like an old Castilian. He was starch, spruce, opinionated, but his superstructure of pride seemed bottomed upon a sense of worth. There was something in it beyond the coxcomb." Irving's Malvolio was in the same tradition, and so was Beerbohm Tree's. But against that tradition is the arriviste Malvolio. Olivier's vowels kept flaking away to reveal an opportunist of no exalted upbringing. Nicol Williamson (RSC, 1974) suggested a non-conformist preacher on the make. These traditions have established their legitimacy, and it is clear that Shakespeare left a major option in the text. But I personally can never forget Olivier's eyes roaming around the Stratford auditorium at "cast thy humble, er, sleouwgh? sluff?" Extremely funny, and one of those insights that make Olivier alone in his class. What is more, that interpretation creates more dramatic energy in the great confrontation with Sir Toby.

"Art any more than a steward?" is the play's crux. It is the only occasion in *Twelfth Night* when there really is a party, and someone acts to stop it. The audience, naturally, wants the party to go on. It would. Since in theater- time, it is around 8:30 of an English evening (mid-afternoon in Shakespeare's day), no audience can ever see why the fun should be closed down early by the resident bureaucrat. Hence the audience naturally lines up behind Sir Toby and his warmhearted tribute to cakes and ale. But the defense, although excellent, gets no sort of hearing. The stage time is in the small hours and Malvolio, acting on orders from Olivia, warns a set of noisy drunks to stop disturbing the household. It is pure theatrical sleight of hand to channel audience sympathies behind Sir Toby. The attitudes behind "Art any more than a steward?" remain less than universally appealing.

The clash between Sir Toby and Malvolio is not a momentary spurt of anger but a collision of types, social classes, and responsibilities. Malvolio's duty is to administer the household. This necessarily brings some kind of authority (ill-defined, no doubt) over all those dwelling there, of whatever rank. Sir Toby's view, like Richard of Gloucester's, is "but I was born so high." It is a matter of rank over ambition, birth over office, pleasure over duty, play over work, the Cavalier over the Puritan; Sir Toby and Malvolio were born to contend. Their troubles are from eternity. More than three centuries after the play was written, Radclyffe Hall remarked of a bibulous aristocratic guest, "if you want to have a properly run house, you can't have people like him around. The servants won't stand for it."

The confrontation is the flash point of a heavily charged atmosphere. The entire play is filled with frictions, ambitions, and resentments. *Twelfth Night* is an anatomy of social mobility; three of its personages marry upward (Sebastian, Viola, and Maria), and two seek to (Sir Andrew and Malvolio). The advice in the letter to Malvolio, "Be opposite with a kinsman, surly with servants; let thy tongue tang arguments of state" is a miniature handbook for getting on. Those who have, maneuver with those who desire. Identity is sometimes asserted, sometimes infringed upon. Sir Andrew knows his rank and qualifies his claim to be a connoisseur of the stage with "As any man in Illyria, whatsoever he be, under the degree of my betters" (1.3.108–9). Viola/Cesario is shocked at Olivia's attempt to tip her "I am no fee'd post, lady, keep your purse" (1.5.268), a gaffe that confuses a Duke's Messenger with a postboy. Sir Toby has an eye for the social insult, "if thou thou'st him some thrice, it shall not be amiss" (3.3.40). ("Thou," of course, is the familiar way of addressing an intimate or inferior.) In *Twelfth Night* especially, one comes to appreciate the force of A. L. Rowse's general observation: "Never can there have been more class consciousness, one feels, in any age."[16]

Finally, we come to Feste, who watches in his detached way the conflict of Malvolio and Sir Toby. (So detached, indeed, that his exit from that scene, 2.3, is not even marked in the Folio. He sidles offstage, presumably.) Feste is an entertainer. He makes his calling pay, rather well. He has been on tour, obviously ("so long absent," 1.5.15), and Maria hints that he may be "turn'd away." The immediate reply, "and for turning away, let summer bear it out" might suggest that Feste is prepared to sleep rough for a while. But it emerges that Feste lives "at my house, and my house doth stand by the church" (3.1.6–7). A certain independence here, which correlates nicely with the independence of spirit he shows elsewhere. And it is all done on regular rates of pay. Sir Toby and Sir Andrew have to come up with sixpence a head before the singing can begin (2.3). Orsino does the expected thing after "Come away, Death," "There's for thy pains." Viola senses the need to provide "expenses" (3.1.41), and so does her brother: "There's money for thee" (4.1.18). Feste's milking of the Duke in 5.1. is perfectly outrageous, and Orsino, through clenched teeth, has to stop the act: "You can fool no more money out of me at this throw" (35–36). The musicians' union has the public at its mercy and is merciless in extortion.

Feste, more than anyone else in Shakespeare, suggests the historic shift from *servant* (idealized in Adam) to today's *service industry*. Independent, detached, ruthlessly professional in his dealings, he refuses to be absorbed into the needs of his employers. He cannot be said to have a single employer, since he performs in Orsino's court as well as Olivia's household. In the institutional politics of that household, his role is ill-defined. He seems well placed at the start of the gulling action, yet by the garden scene Fabian is in the front line and Feste has prudently removed himself. Once Malvolio is down, Feste is merciless on the attack. Not a good team player, one would say. Gareth Lloyd Evans remarks that Feste is "everyone's acquaintance and no one's friend."[17] But in the casting and performance of Feste the play's keynote is always struck. He has the last word and colors the final impressions of Illyria.

If the core of *Twelfth Night* is the party scene, then Feste's final song is the party's aftermath. It is hauntingly reminiscent, a kind of broken résumé in which Feste's attempts to say something about his life collapse always into "But when" and the refrain of "For the rain it raineth every day." There are no disclosures here, only mood. The play-as-party can now be placed in retrospect. There have been some good songs, people discovering love at first sight, alcoholics refusing to go home, some frictions and some fun, presumed winners and clear losers. Whatever the play has contained of carnival has died away, and tomorrow one goes back to work. *Carnival* means farewell to the flesh.

CHAPTER FOUR

The Mature Histories

O f class interest in the usual sense, there is almost nothing in *Richard II*. The action is all but confined to the aristocracy and their followers, with a couple of modest interventions by the Gardeners and the Groom. The passion and death of Richard is the play's subject, on which Shakespeare concentrates to the exclusion of other factors. It is not an especially political play even, and the triumph of Bolingbroke is presented rather than analyzed. There are suggestions, though, that Shakespeare was not satisfied with depicting a historical pageant.

John of Gaunt can offer a hint, if we pick out a word in his great speech. The elegy on England's past kings pays tribute to them as "Renowned . . . /For Christian service and true chivalry" (2.1.54). Why "true" chivalry, unless to imply that Richard's version is ersatz? Chivalry is what we get in the opening scene and in the Coventry tournament, of a somewhat stilted kind. The encounter is full of gage throwing, "rites of knighthood," "chivalrous design of knightly trial," and at Coventry, lists, marshals, trumpets, champions, and appellants. There is no obvious irony in the costume drama, unless the actor playing Richard wants to import it, which he can well do. Even so, the anticlimactic stopping of the combat insinuates that the whole affair is a show, a piece of elaborate theater that Richard, at least, does not take seriously. That is a resource of theater, not a prescription, but the same issue returns to plague the director in Act 4, scene 1, the gage-throwing scene when actor after actor has to go through the motions of knightly tomfoolery. At Aumerle's "Who sets me else? By heaven, I'll throw at all!" (4.1.57) the actors and audience are in a quandary together: are we all supposed to laugh? Judicious cutting can help, but the Spirit Ironic does seem rampant here. More follows, in the scene when Aumerle, York, and his Duchess all kneel to Bolingbroke, reminding one of the "exit kneeling" passage in *The Critic*. It is absurd to suppose that the Shakespeare of this period (1594–96) did not know what he was doing, and had never observed the effects of repeated action on an audience. The impulse to mock the knightly rituals in *Richard II* is voiced by no man, yet is in the air.

These seem hints of another play, one that Shakespeare suppressed because it would get in the way of the play he was writing. He prefers to register Richard as an individual study, rather than one arising from a social context. The same is proportionately true of Bolingbroke. Their situations are plotted vertically, moving in mechanical counterpoise. They pass each other like men sealed in glass elevators in a public atrium, noting each other's rise and fall but unable to communicate. Loss and gain are their ways of expressing identity, and there's a certain parallelism. Bolingbroke catalogues his losses in exile:

> Eating the bitter bread of banishment,
> Whilst you have fed upon my signories,
> Dispark'd my parks and fell'd my forest woods,
> From my own windows torn my household coat,
> Raz'd out my imprese, leaving me no sign
> Save men's opinions and my living blood
> To show the world I am a gentleman
>
> (3.1.21–27)

Richard cites the tokens of his fall:

> I'll give my jewels for a set of beads,
> My gorgeous palace for a hermitage,
> My gay apparel for an almsman's gown,
> My figur'd goblets for a dish of wood,
> My sceptre for a palmer's walking staff,
> My subjects for a pair of carved saints.
>
> (3.3.147–52)

What they have is what they are. The play declines to go far beyond self as measured by possessions.

Again, the emblem scene with the Gardeners (3.4) is strictly limited in focus. They belong to the tradition of Renaissance pastoral, eyeing the failings of the great and courtly with insight but without radical questioning. For them, the matter is viewed through analogies at hand. Weeds are to be rooted up, fast-growing sprays cut back, caterpillars destroyed. The commonwealth/garden will otherwise run wild. "Great and growing men" should be wounded in season, like trees, lest they become "over-proud in sap and blood." It is wisdom from beneath; the Gardeners understand the story in a way that no one else does.

The Groom remains, offering a sympathetic devotion that is the back-projection of Richard's fall. Speaking in the blank verse that is this play's mode, the Groom seems less an individual than a voice absorbed into Richard's consciousness. Essentially, he is there to bring news—the defection of Richard's barbary horse to Bolingbroke—so that Richard can react to it. The Groom's is the last touch of the old devotion before the murderers rush in. On a miniature scale, the Groom shows the play's method, in which all other characters tend to be adjuncts to Richard's psychodrama, and the classes have no independent existence.

HENRY IV, PART ONE

All that changes in *Henry IV*, a panorama of English social life. The land is no longer defined in terms of its (ailing) ruler. Instead, the sprawling, autonomous vitality of the people is everywhere. This is epic drama, and one can do worse than touch it first at the small scene with the Carriers in the Rochester inn-yard. Here are the realities of work, early starts, the insanitary habits of the English, things going wrong, fleas, damp proven-der, livestock to be cared for, the absence of the people who used to see that things worked, the bustle and exhilaration of the early morning. The passing of Robin Ostler is lamented, no doubt as a Homeric formula: "Poor fellow never joyed since the price of oats rose, it was the death of him" (2.1.11–12). The extraordinary sense of life as it is lived, outside the subjectivities of the main personages, is everywhere. We even know the breakfast order of the travelers, who "call for eggs and butter." Can reality be more pointed than that?

The play cannot be seen simply as The Education of a Prince, or The Adventures of Jack Falstaff. The major characters grow out of the teeming life all around, who all sense this outside world of classes, types, and humanity at large. Simply to list occupations and functionaries takes a little space: burgomaster, underskinker, vintner, grandjuror, franklin, clerk, sheriff, chamberlain, hangman, drawer, weaver, factor, inn-keeper, auditor. Of this world of beings and types, Falstaff knows a great deal, and Hal picks up a great deal. The play traces Hal's learning curve.

Something of this comes out in the prologue to the tavern scene. Hal becomes a field worker specializing in language, a cultural anthropologist among a tribe virtually unknown to him. His visit to the cellar, at the invitation of the drawers, has impressed him. People are usually impressed by a tour of the cellar. Hal has encountered the drinking habits of the drawers—"when you breathe in your watering they cry 'Hem!' and bid you play it off" and concludes that "I am so good a proficient in one quarter of an hour that I can drink with any tinker in his own language during my life" (2.4.16–19). This might be an overestimate. Hal has fallen into the classic trap of the anthropologist, who contaminates the data by being there to record it. The Carriers, in the presence of nobody but each other, speak a far more vivid and resourceful language than the drawers in the presence of the Prince.

Still, they add to the Prince's experience. The prime virtue of Hal is that he is prepared to experiment with roles, while retaining his identity. This is superbly symbolized in the play scene with Falstaff, when Hal first takes on the role of the Prince, then of the King himself. That, of course, is the role that most expresses him: "*I'll play my father*" (2.4.419). But just as Hal has seemed an undergraduate learning drinking practices, he puts on years in the encounter with the Sheriff who interrupts the play world. It is a neat cameo of a police inquiry, in which the detective must enter a house of multiple repute and discreetly interrogate a highly placed individual. The dangerous tensions of the matter are scrupulously depicted: the Prince may not deal with the situation via a simple discharge of vehemence; the official does his duty, but may not press it too hard. Both men tread a fine line, as the Prince finds a formula that the Sheriff can accept:

> The man I do assure you is not here,
> For I myself at this time have employed him"
> [a pause, surely, for the following "And" is suggestive]
> And Sheriff, I will engage my word to thee,
> That I will by tomorrow dinnertime
> Send him to answer thee, or any man.
>
> (2.4.494–98)

It is an astonishingly mature performance. The ambivalent position of the Prince of Wales is turned to dramatic advantage: Shakespeare shows a young man not yet invested in the authority that will be his, having to deal with all social classes from tinkers to the Lord Chief Justice. Con men, friends, offers, criticisms, traps, he has to surmount them all. It is an education, and Hal devours it.

Hotspur, evidently, is a different story. The point about Hotspur is not that he is stupid, but that he might just as well be. There's an archaism, a resistance to learning in his mentality that makes him functionally obsolete—not to mention, dead. Dramatically, Shakespeare has solved the problem of *Henry VI*: how does one make attractive and interesting a representative of the quarrelsome nobility that swamps the dramatis personae? He creates an enormously vital, likeable young man, hotheaded to a fault, who considers his resistance to all forms of challenge as the absolute imperative of identity. The class governs the individual. There is nothing in Hotspur of the wary adaptability of Hal, evidence of a species headed for survival and progress.

The point is obvious enough, but Worcester's phrasing gives it weight:

> You must needs learn, lord, to amend this fault;
> Though sometimes it show greatness, courage, blood—
> And that's the dearest grace it renders you—
> Yet oftentimes it doth present harsh rage,
> Defect of manners, want of government,
> Pride, haughtiness, opinion, and disdain;
> The least of which, haunting a nobleman,
> Loseth men's hearts.
>
> (3.1.180–87)

That is important, coming from a member of Hotspur's own class. Arrogance, the obverse of courage, is the great defect for an aristocrat. And even Hotspur accepts that. "Well, I am school'd—good manners be your speed!" Then take the encounter with the fop at Holmedon, as reported in Act 1 scene 3. Wavell picked out this incident as the eternal conflict between the staff officer and the field officer:

> He questioned me: among the rest, demanded
> My prisoners in your Majesty's behalf.
> I then, all smarting with my wounds being cold,
> To be so pester'd with a popinjay,
> Out of my grief and my impatience
> Answer'd neglectingly I know not what—
> He should, or he should not—for he made me mad
> To see him shine so brisk, and smell so sweet,
> And talk so like a waiting-gentlewoman
> Of guns, and drums, and wounds—God save the mark!
>
> (1.3.47–56)

Men just out of the trenches do not bear easily with those who slept last
night at the chateau and will sleep there again tonight. Hotspur's reaction
is wholly understandable. The point is that he denies the category in
which matters are presented. The "certain lord," the "popinjay," is not
only a courtier, he is functionally some kind of staff officer who has every
right to know about the prisoners. (Then, of course, these prisoners were a
source less of information than of ransom money; to Hotspur they are
"his" prisoners, obviously not the category of the future.) Hotspur can
admit of no sort of relationship save that which concedes his rights of
temperament.

Again, take the passage in which he chides Lady Percy for swearing "in
good sooth":

> Not yours, in good sooth! Heart! you swear like a
> comfit-maker's wife. "Not you, in good sooth" and
> "As true as I live" and "As God shall mend me" and
> "As sure as day."
> And givest such sarcenet surety for thy oaths
> As if thou never walk'st further than Finsbury.
> Swear me, Kate, like a lady as thou art,
> A good mouth-filling oath; and leave "in sooth"
> And such protest of pepper-gingerbread
> To velvet-guards and Sunday-citizens.
>
> (3.1.248–57)

The class identification is sharply etched. "Finsbury" is code for the
citizen-classes, "suburbia" as a later age would say. What Hotspur
despises is the genteel bourgeois, with their mincing of oaths. There's a
deal of evidence, says Frances Shirley, "that more swearing was done at
the ends of the social scale than the middle."[1] Hotspur's disdain is an
early proof of the linguistic separation of the respectable classes from the
ruffians at the extremes. (Malvolio's "I protest" is a mild form of "I
swear," another clue to his social provenance.) It all points to Shakespeare's concept of Hotspur as a feudal type, whose identity comprises a
few qualities that are in no way negotiable. For Hotspur, the function of
the armigerous classes is to bear arms in battle. It is as simple as that.
"Honor," the word that summarizes his values, comes to mean never
refusing a challenge.

Hal learns; Hotspur refuses to learn; Falstaff exploits. Exploitation is
Falstaff's chief principle, vitality in action. Everything that he is, all that

he owns or can borrow, serves his gigantic appetite for continuing life and continuing pleasure. Of the composite of figures that Falstaff is—Vice, Fool, *miles gloriosus*, parasite—one aspect only concerns us, his rank. Falstaff has been born with rank, and never lets it go. It is the spine of his part, and it was well said of Ralph Richardson's Falstaff that "he was Sir John first, and Falstaff second." Given Falstaff's inclinations, his part documents the possibilities of the knighthood.

Viewed from this angle, certain passages stand out. "Perpetual gaiety," *pace* Johnson, is not Falstaff's style, and the opening of Act 3, scene 3 finds him in despondent mood. From it emerges this cameo-idyll of the gentlemanly life:

I was as virtuously given as a gentleman need to be; virtuous enough: swore little, dic'd not above seven times a week, went to a bawdy-house not above once in a quarter—of an hour, paid money that I borrowed—three or four times, lived well, and in good compass. . . .

(3.3.13–18)

A lifestyle of pleasure tempered with occasional repayments—that is Falstaff's way. It is an ideal of sorts. No need to elaborate on Falstaff's regular refusal to pay up: "Base is the slave that pays," says Pistol, echoing the table-talk of his leader. Paying up would be a betrayal of the principles Falstaff holds most dear. Other features of Falstaff's method are illustrated in the same scene. He has run up a monstrous bill at the Boar's Head: "You owe money here besides, Sir John, for your diet and by-drinking, and money lent you, four and twenty pound" (3.3.71–73). The instinctive Keynesianism of Falstaff's approach to fiscal problems is matched, logically enough, by his willingness to repudiate debt; hence the quarrel he picks up with the Hostess concerning the alleged thefts of his possessions. He has certainly been relieved (by Hal) of his bills, but not of the "Three or four bonds of forty pound a-piece" that Falstaff claims. One has to admire Falstaff's gall in converting lost bills into a complaint. Some of us will have an acquaintance who brought a recalcitrant bank manager to heel by threatening to take the overdraft elsewhere. Falstaff is the archetype.

From the lofty airs of "Hostess, I forgive thee," Falstaff turns to the next phase in his progress, the charge of foot that the Prince has procured him. It is central to Falstaff's thinking that all relationships must pay their way; there is no such thing as Platonic friendship. From the earliest scene with Hal, with Falstaff constantly boring at the heir to promise preferment once on the throne, Falstaff's doctrine is plain: something must be done for Jack. Position is all, and with the coming of the rebellion Falstaff turns position to account.

The charge of foot, even if not the charge of horse that Falstaff would have liked, is still a license to print money. And Falstaff knows it: "Well, God be thank'd for these rebels, they offend none but the virtuous; I laud them, I praise them" (3.3.189–91). The reasons are soon made clear. Falstaff catches them coming, and again going. "I have misused the King's press damnably. I have got, in exchange of a hundred and fifty soldiers, three hundred and odd pounds" (4.2.12–14). Three hundred pounds was a small fortune in an era when an artisan earned around £5 a year. Falstaff's method, as he explains, is to press the well-to-do of the community—"good householders, yeomen's sons"—and allow them to buy out of military service. This is accurate reportage of Elizabethan practices. Later on, Falstaff would profit from the dead of his company. The phantom muster-roll was a notorious abuse, as Elizabethan officers continued to draw the pay and allowances of those slain in battle. As Jorgensen remarks, "In recruiting his men he had been richly bribed; in losing them, he found solace in collecting their pay."[2]

Behind the attractive rogue is a real rogue, and the play's business is to keep these alternating images before us. It is so with the war itself. Sir Richard Vernon sees a war poster, the Household Cavalry on parade to "witch the world with noble horsemanship" (4.1.110). Falstaff, in the scene that follows, offers something akin to a war correspondent's view. Who will do the fighting? He answers, " . . . such as indeed were never soldiers, but discarded unjust serving-men, younger sons to younger brothers, revolted tapsters, and ostlers trade-fall'n" (4.2.26–29). War, as Falstaff presents it, is an affair of the poor, the unemployed, criminals, and dropouts. Those who can afford to, pay to dodge the draft. This bleak and patently accurate analysis of the social formations used by the military comes from one who is himself something of a dropout from the knight-hood. "This entire scene," as Jan Kott says, "might have been put, as it stands, into a play by Brecht."[3]

The tone has shifted from the early scenes, but the Falstaffian principle remains: the first necessity of a life-force is to remain alive. This is accomplished through Falstaff's resourceful conduct at Shrewsbury, though, as he admits, his company is badly cut up: "I have led my ragamuffins to where they are pepper'd" (5.3.35–36). The heroic, or dastardly, implications of "led . . . to" are not clarified. The knight's survival rests on the paradox, that "honor is a mere scutcheon" (5.1.140). Scutcheons are the product of battle honors; Falstaff's line is the repudiation of honor, though not of its benefits. Honor is a kind of debt, if you like. Trust Falstaff to repudiate it. The life-force takes on the look of severe rationalism. It's no accident that Shaw recycled the joke with the bottle of sack in Falstaff's case in *Arms and the Man*. There it comes out as Bluntschli's "You can always tell an old soldier by the inside of his holster and cartridge boxes. The young ones carry pistols and cartridges: the old ones, grub."

Once the military dangers are skirted, the life-force drives on for social promotion. "If your father will do me any honor, so: if not, let him kill the next Sir Percy himself. I look to be either earl or duke, I can assure you" (5.4.139–41). A typical overbid, this, but Falstaff knows the value of an inflated claim. And he does get something out of it, if only a lenient line from the Lord Chief Justice and a license to print more money in *Part Two*. At the end of *Part One*, there is an hallucinatory moment when Falstaff contemplates the life of a lord: "If I do grow great, I'll grow less; for I'll purge, and live cleanly, as a nobleman should do" (5.4.162–64). Inside a fat knight, a slim nobleman is trying to get out.

HENRY IV, PART TWO

In terms of camera work, *Part Two* calls for more close-up shots than *Part One*. It seems closer to reality, more intimate, more uncompromising. It also calls for different lenses. There is a degree of soft-focus work involving Falstaff in *Part One*. The images are slightly romanticized, presented with a lighting scheme that, in the first three acts at least, makes the best of its subjects. But now the graininess isn't filtered out with clever lens work. In his film *Chimes at Midnight*, Orson Welles shot both parts in black and white, holding to the convention that black and white is the mode of realism. The case for doing that looks stronger as *Henry IV* proceeds. *Part Two* makes the statement: This is what *Part One means*.

This comes out all the time. Falstaff has an emblematic first entrance, calling for the doctor's report on his water, although one would as soon not get that close to Falstaff's medical problems. Similarly, the Chekhovian scene at the Boar's Head is tonally leagues away from its *Part One* equivalent: "Peace, good Doll, do not speak like a death's head, do not bid me remember mine end" (2.4.224–25). And Prince John's *Realpolitik* tastes in the mouth like iron filings. There is something peculiarly offensive in the sanctimonious casuistry of his dealings with the rebels. Nor does Falstaff come out of the encounter much better. His joke at Colevile's expense, "I know not how they sold themselves, but thou like a kind fellow gavest thyself away gratis, and I thank thee for thee" (4.3.67–69), is the *something for nothing* on which his life is founded. Colevile goes to the block, and Falstaff claims his credit: it is perfectly value-free. The prisoners stood a better chance at Shrewsbury.

Then again, the dialogue between Hal and Poins in Act 2, scene 2 is disturbingly intimate. The self-disgust of the Prince flows into his disgust with Poins, and their resentments charge a tense and revealing scene. Hal's discontent is at once colored by Poins's, "I had thought weariness durst not have attach'd one of so high blood." This might be an ill-timed jest or an intended sneer. Hal takes it the second way, and answers in kind. Poins, cast among the *irregular Humorists* of the Folio's dramatis personae, has his limited wardrobe made the subject of the Prince's wit. The needling leads to

> *Prince*: Shall I tell thee one thing, Poins?
> *Poins*: Yes, and let it be an excellent good thing.
> *Prince*: It shall serve, among wits of no higher breeding than
> thine.
>
> (2.2.31–34)

Poins does not like this, and he is not meant to. He likes even less the "keeping such vile company as thou art" that the Prince offers as the reason for not showing concern at the King's illness. Hence the bluntness of his response to the key question:

> *Prince*: What wouldst thou think of me if I should weep?
> *Poins*: I would think thee a most princely hypocrite.
>
> (2.2.49–51)

The relationship is on the rocks, of course. It stands no chance of surviving the reefs of class. Hal, if he showed grief, would be to Poins and to everyone else "a most princely hypocrite." And that, says Poins, is "because you have been so lewd, and so engraffed to Falstaff." "*And*," the Prince reminds him, "*to thee* (2.2.58–60). Quite so. This is a "no-exit" relationship—from which, naturally, one exits. We hear no more of Hal and Poins after the Boar's Head scene of Act 2, scene 4.

Just as the play lengthens out *Part One*, so it extends Falstaff's credit line. Falstaff must always create new markets, the old ones being exhausted, fished out. The tradespeople have had enough already, and as his Page informs him, Master Dommelton the tailor will give no more credit: "He said, sir, you should procure him better assurance than Bardolph. He would not take his bond and yours, he liked not the security" (1.2.29–31). This is to Falstaff what a challenge is to Hotspur, and his reaction is not dissimilar: "A rascally yea-forsooth knave, to bear a gentleman in hand and stand upon security!" (1.2.35–36). Servile he may be, but Master Dommelton knows better than to work for Falstaff and for nothing. There is always "old mistress Ursula," and to her and others more begging letters are sent. But aid comes from only two sources: the Boar's Head people, and those new to Falstaff. Justice Shallow is Falstaff's line of extended credit.

The marvelous scenes in the Cotswolds are Falstaff's apotheosis, the late afternoon sun slanting down at him before his twilight. It is the audience's solace, as it is Falstaff's—a fair field and another gull! Shallow is placed with affectionate accuracy. An esquire (that is, a gentleman just below the order of knighthood), well founded in land and money, overwhelmed by the glamor of the famous Sir John, Shallow is enchanted to recover with Falstaff the youth that (according to Falstaff) he never had. Bardolph, who cannot overcome Master Dommelton, at once dazzles Shallow with his lofty mien and command of metropolitan phrases: "Sir, pardon: a soldier is better accommodated than with a wife" (3.2.65–66). "'Accommodated'—it comes of 'accommodo'; very good, a good phrase" (3.2.70–71). Thus softened up, Shallow is in no case to withstand the great man himself: "Look, here comes good Sir John. Give me your worship's good hand. By my troth, you like well, and bear your years very well. Welcome, good Sir John" (3.2.82–86). Falstaff has found a place on the provincial circuit where he can play better than in London.

The recruiting scene that follows illustrates the procedures that in *Part One* are only mentioned. It is a shameless affair. Bullcalf and Mouldy make their representations to Bardolph, their bids totaling some £4; Bardolph discreetly notifies his commanding officer that £3 is set aside to free Mouldy and Bullcalf; Falstaff acts on information received. Then the recruiting officers split the proceeds three to one, and Mouldy and Bullcalf stand aside, while Feeble and company march off to the wars. Shallow remains: "Peradventure I will with ye to the court." "'Fore God, I wish you would, Master Shallow," says Falstaff. Falstaff's assessment of his chances is shrewd enough; Shallow was something of a butt in his youth, "and now has he land and beefs . . . If the young dace may be a bait for the old pike, I see no reason in the law of nature but I may snap at him"

(3.3.327, 330–33). Or, as Kipling phrased it: "Take the money, my son, praising Allah; /This kid was ordained to be sold."

Shallow is destined to be remembered as the man who lent Falstaff £1000, but he also functions as the focus of a perfectly realized household. The opening of Act 5 looks like the diary of a country squire, with Shallow giving directions on sowing hade land (with red wheat), on accepting a blacksmith's work estimate, on stopping a servant's wages for losing a sack, and on setting up a dinner menu. Davy, Shallow's servant, enters a plea for a disreputable friend, William Visor: "If I cannot once or twice in a quarter bear out a knave against an honest man, I have very little credit with your worship." Like Falstaff, Davy thinks credit is important, and he secures it too. It is an extraordinarily dense evocation of a rural community, yet Falstaff views this picture of social cohesion with some reserve, saying of Shallow's men

They, by observing of him, do bear themselves like foolish justices; he, by conversing with them, is turned into a justice-like serving-man. Their spirits are so married in conjunction, with the participation of society, that they flock together in consent like so many wild geese.

(5.1.63–68).

For one who insists on class differentiation, as Falstaff does, the Cotswolds hold little appeal. Once again, the principle of social organization in Shakespeare turns out to be town versus country.

It is the country that is celebrated here. We do not see Shallow's feast, but we catch the aftermath in Shallow's orchard, as the diners sit down to aid digestion with a dish of caraways, some more sack, and, astonishingly, songs of Silence. It is a rural idyll, and yet the country folk think of London: "I hope," says Davy, "to see London ere I die" (5.3.59). Pistol erupts, and the idyll fragments. At once, the future takes on the forms of class elevation. "Sweet knight, thou art now one of the greatest men in this realm . . . Sir John, I am thy Pistol and thy friend." "Pistol, I will double-charge thee with dignities." As for Bardolph, he insists, "O joyful day! I would not take a knighthood for my fortune." But the most fortunate is the host, to whom Falstaff exclaims, "Master Robert Shallow, choose what office thou wilt in the land, 'tis thine . . . Master Shallow, my Lord Shallow, be what thou wilt—I am Fortune's steward" (5.3.83 ff.). Fantasy rules, and the sound of hubris is audible in Falstaff's pronouncement, "the laws of England are at my commandment. Blessed are they that have been my friends, and woe to my Lord Chief Justice!" (5.3.91–143 ff.). Decidedly, Falstaff is funnier out of power than in.

The climax to the two parts of *Henry IV* comes as a great public occasion, with cheering crowds lining the streets as Henry V and his train leave Westminster Abbey and the Coronation. What follows is the first public act of the new reign. Falstaff, so acute in his judgment of Shallow, knows nothing of Hal and has picked the worst conceivable moment to claim spiritual paternity: "God save thee, *my sweet boy!*" (5.5.44). "Boy," as elsewhere in Shakespeare, is a trigger word. The King does his best to to deal with the problem at one remove: "My Lord Chief Justice, speak to that vain man" (5.5.45). What are his emotions? Anger, irritation, embarrassment? Nobody should be put to the test like this. But he is, and the thing has to be faced. For the last time, Falstaff ignores the signal: "My King! My Jove! I speak to thee, my heart!" (5.5.47). And now comes the reply that has been waiting ever since the "I know you all" of *Part One*: "I know thee not, old man" (5.5.48). The line falls with the iron weight and rigor of a great proposition in logic. It is really beyond argument: *know* is the twin pillar of a giant suspension bridge spanning the first and tenth acts of the drama. The senses of *connaître* and *savoir* echo across the space.

The King's rebuke transmits something new to Falstaff. One could call it knowledge; nothing like that has ever been heard from him before, or ever will be again. "Master Shallow, I owe you a thousand pound." It passes, and a moment later Falstaff's himself again, putting off a creditor and confident that he will be sent for soon. Let us leave Sir John there. Falstaff has acknowledged a debt, and the King is rescheduling his. He will do what he can for Falstaff, necessarily in private. "A State," said de Gaulle, "is the coldest of cold monsters," and Hal has become the State.

HENRY V

Henry IV ends with the entrance of Henry V, who goes on to command the play bearing his name. The actor Lewis Waller used to prepare for his entrances as Henry by leaning on the back stage-wall, then thrusting himself off so as to propel himself on to the stage, and the play has that same vehement, decisive quality. It is the official record of a dazzling success, a condensed account of a meteor reign. That success tends in stage terms to overbear all reservations and doubts that the reader may lodge. Contemporary distaste for war plays has to influence the tone of productions. Directors and actors must not appear to be enjoying themselves too much at the expense of the French, and the chorus himself may appear to have doubts about it all. In fact, there is a long line of ironic Choruses in recent stage history. Still, the general impression the play makes in performance is not in doubt. I stress it here because I want to look at the smaller print in the great passages.

This is a war play, with social class transferred to military rank. Its most revealing episodes occur under combat conditions. Act 1 is pure politics; Act 2 contains the genre scenes of Pistol and company; Act 5 is the court wooing of Henry and Katherine. In these scenes the interest is defined by location—court, tavern, court. It is during the Harfleur and Agincourt operations that the class referents of men under fire take form. These matters concern primarily the English. The French, by extension and by implication, make a different point. They are confined dramatically to the court, to the nobility. All we see are the Constable, Dauphin, and so on. There are no officers and no men. Since they lose the battle, the French leave on the table an obvious suggestion: an organism that consists solely of the higher command (here, the mounted aristocracy) is vulnerable because limited. The English consist of officers—some of whom are not English—men, some of whom are not especially keen on fighting, and the higher command, which is not confined to Henry. The strength of the invading army lies in the vitality and independent strength of its parts. It is an army that composes its differences in creating a single fighting unit.

The officers are collectively an innovation in stage history. An Englishman, an Irishman, a Welshman, a Scot: nothing like this has been seen on stage before. Their origin lies, I think, in an observation Bacon makes in his essay "Of the True Greatness of Kingdoms" (published in 1596, three years before *Henry V*). Bacon believes that England is especially fortunate in her middle classess:

This . . . hath been no better seen than by comparing of England and France, whereof England, though far less in territory and population, hath been nevertheless an overmatch: in regard the middle people of England make good soldiers, which the peasants of France do not.

The "middle people" is a broad category, and there is a certain roughness of texture about Fluellen (whose classical education is not too securely based), Captain Macmorris, and Captain Jamy. But this fact makes its own point: war is an imperfect form of meritocracy, but a meritocracy it is; the Celtic captains must have some qualities to hold down their positions. They have work to do and do it.

Perhaps the most interesting of the quartet is Captain Macmorris, the Irish explosives expert in charge of mining the Harfleur fortifications. His fellow officers are more inclined to praise him for valor than learning, and this impression of his parts is supported by his reaction to the truce. It is one of deep grief. "By Chrish, la, tish ill done! I would have blowed up the town, so Chrish save me, la, in an hour . . . And there is throats to be cut, and works to be done, and there is nothing done" (3.2.81–106). The Hitchcock-like refusal of Shakespeare to set off the mines reflects the needs of the play; Agincourt, not Harfleur, is the big show. But Macmorris's lamentation allows the author to sketch in a major recess of background and psychology. Fluellen starts to put a thought to Macmorris. It is cautiously phrased, yet has explosive effect: "Captain Macmorris, I think, look you, under your correction, there is not many of your nation . . ." "Of my nation? What *ish* my nation?" Macmorris would like to know (3.2.113–16). It is a good question and somewhat canvassed during 1599, when Elizabeth's troops were again engaged in a campaign to subdue the Irish rebels. In that year Elizabeth ordered Mountjoy, the English commander, to raise no more Irish captains of companies. An oft-cited case is that of St. Laurence, an Irish captain much aware of his ambivalent situation:

I am sorry that when I am in England, I should be esteemed an Irishman, and in Ireland, an Englishman. I have spent my blood, engaged and endangered my life often to do her Majesty service, and do now beseech to have it so regarded.[4]

This complaint has the ring of historic truth. Hence Paul Jorgensen's speculation is plausible, that Fluellen's interrupted thought was "not many of your nation [who is one of his Majesty's captains]." In 1599, says Jorgensen, "Elizabethans might well have found his rank to be the most noteworthy thing about Macmorris."[5]

The grouping of the four nations by captains is schematic, if unequally proportioned. The Folio indeed gives the speakers' names simply as "Welch," "Irish." Fluellen's is the best part, a perennially attractive portrait of a valorous and determined Welshman. "Though it appear a little out of fashion, there is much care and valour in this Welshman" (4.1.83–84). If there is an element of condescension in his presentation, one really cannot expect playwrights to illustrate the social ideals of four centuries later. There is not much in Captain Jamy's part beyond the Scots accent. Gower, the torpid Englishman, has the air of placidly encompassing the volatilities of his excitable Celtic comrades. "Gentlemen both, you will mistake each other" (3.2.127) is his character note, and he has a social address not present in the other three.

The overall statement is clear: the whole is greater than the sum of its parts. If one considers the role of the four nations in these Histories, the unity achieved under Henry is amazing. At the beginning of *Henry IV*, the Welsh are in arms under "the irregular and wild Glendower." The "weasel Scot" is seen, at the beginning of *Henry V*, as a major threat to be neutralized before the invasion of France. The Chorus of *Henry V* makes what is the plainest topical allusion in all Shakespeare, the reference to Essex's Irish campaign:

> Were now the General of our gracious Empress—
> As in good time he may—from Ireland coming,
> Bringing rebellion broached on his sword,
> How many would the peaceful city quit
> To welcome him!
>
>   (Prologue 30–34)

Upon "As in good time he may" history casts a long sigh. Scotland, Wales, and Ireland are all threats to England. Yet the English army cannot function without the tough-minded professionals from those lands, who are absorbed into the matter of England. The implied subtitle of *Henry V* is *The Making of Britain*.

Upon the Anglo-Welsh leader of the army—born in Monmouth, as Fluellen emphasizes—the duty falls of uniting his men. He learns on the job, and the touchstones of his progress are the two great battle orations at Harfleur and Agincourt. These are often thought of as virtually identical in tone and import. On the contrary, they are markedly different, and the Agincourt speech is altogether superior in tone and understanding. And at the heart of each oration is the question of social class.

> Once more unto the breach, dear friends, once more;
> Or close the wall up with our English dead.
> In peace there's nothing so becomes a man
> As modest stillness and humility;
> But when the blast of war blows in our ears,
> Then imitate the action of the tiger:
> Then lend the eye a terrible aspect;
> Let it pry through the portage of the head
> Like the brass cannon; let the brow o'erwhelm it
> As fearfully doth a galled rock
> O'erhang and jutty his confounded base,
> Swill'd with the wild and wasteful ocean.

Now set the teeth and stretch the nostril wide;
Hold hard the breath, and bend up every spirit
To his full height. On, on, you noblest English,
Whose blood is fet from fathers of war-proof—
Fathers that like so many Alexanders
Have in these parts from morn till even fought,
And sheath'd their swords for lack of argument.
Dishonor not your mothers; now attest
That those whom you call'd fathers did beget you.
Be copy now to men of grosser blood,
And teach them how to war. And you, good yeomen,
Whose limbs were made in England, show us here
The mettle of your pasture; let us swear
That you are worth your breeding—which I doubt not;
For there is none of you so mean and base
That hath not noble lustre in your eyes.
I see you stand like greyhounds in the slips,
Straining upon the start. The game's afoot:
Follow your spirit; and upon this charge
Cry "God for Harry, England, and Saint George!"

(3.1.1–34)

This speech is formally a failure, for all the brilliance of its individual lines. It opens with an admission of failure, "Once more unto the breach" (the English soldiers have recoiled from the gap in the Harfleur fortifications, several times), and it ends in failure. Since the speech is the whole of a small scene, the immediate outcome is not shown, but it emerges from the episodes that follow that Harfleur is to be taken by prolonged siege. In the end, the besieged French are starved out, and not until "Our expectation hath this day an end" do they admit defeat. The heroics at the breach mark only a costly repulse.

Why does Henry's oration achieve so little? Under scrutiny, the speech itself comes apart. The "imitate the action of the tiger" passage says, in effect, "if you don't *feel* fierce, at least look the part." This is not the stuff to rally disheartened troops, who have already been knocked about by the skeptical French. And it gets worse. "On, on, you noblest English" seems to sound the right note. The King is exploiting the eternal ambivalence of "noble"—of noble descent, behaving nobly. So the message appears to be that all the troops are noble, by virtue of being English. That sense evaporates. "Dishonor not your mothers" holds up, but "Be copy now to

men of grosser blood" is a gaffe supreme. *Most of the men are of grosser blood.*
The error crystallizes in "And you, good yeomen," which is to say that
Henry was not addressing that group earlier, under the "noblest English"
heading; he has turned, mentally if not physically, from one sector of the
army to another. The imputation that one group of soldiers can be
expected to fight better than another because of its birth is offensive and
self-defeating. It is, simply, bad psychology. Of course, these syntactic
implications will not come out plainly on stage. The right actor could
make Falstaff's tavern bills sound exciting. But the rhetorical hollowness
remains. There is something "off" about the Harfleur speech, an element
that correlates with its effective failure.

Between Harfleur and Agincourt, Henry continues to learn, and his
crucial encounter comes with the English soldiery on the eve of the great
battle. They test his rank and identity. Who *is* Henry? Pistol puts it
well, in his exaggerated fashion: "Art thou officer? Or art thou base,
common, and popular?" (4.1.37). Henry opts for "a gentleman of a
company." This, says the latest editor, meant "a volunteer who received
no pay, provided his own clothing and equipment, chose the captain or
general under whom he served, and was beyond the reach of normal
military discipline."[6] It is in this shape that Henry has to withstand
Michael Williams' interrogation. There is a certain instinctual bristling
between the two. The King does not care to be checked by a private
soldier, and Michael Williams senses that the nameless gentleman is
passing down some fraudulent line of the Higher Command's. He has also
a well-founded suspicion that if things go badly, the men of rank can
always arrange a ransom. It is to allay this suspicion that Henry comes
out with what in three plays is his only silliness: "If I live to see it, I will
never trust his word after" (4.1.194). Michael Williams guffaws at that, as
well he might: "You'll never trust his word after! Come, 'tis a foolish
saying." And the King, for all his anger, has to take it. It is the lot of a
"gentleman of a company."

Identity remains. In Shakespeare's insidious way, the idea is prepared
well in advance, with the word "brother." Henry opens Act 4 by addressing Bedford and Gloucester as "brother," but then, they *are* his brothers.
A little later he admits Fluellen as his "kinsman," under questioning from
Pistol. Then he overhears Alexander Court's solitary line: "Brother John
Bates, is not that the morning which breaks yonder?" These sayings, and
the sense of the crisis at hand, prepare Henry for his great oration. It is
cued in by the (necessarily rhetorical) offer of pre-battle leave, and

We would not die in that man's company
That fears his *fellowship* to die with us.
This day is call'd the feast of Crispian.
He that outlives this day, and comes safe home,
Will stand a tip-toe when this day is nam'd,
And rouse him at the name of Crispian.
He that shall live this day, and see old age,
Will yearly on the vigil feast his neighbours,
And say "To-morrow is Saint Crispian."
Then will he strip his sleeve and show his scars,
And say "These wounds I had on Crispin's day."
Old men forget; yet all shall be forgot,
But he'll remember, with advantages,
What feats he did that day. Then shall our names,
Familiar in his mouth as household words—
Harry the King, Bedford and Exeter,
Warwick and Talbot, Salisbury and Gloucester—
Be in their flowing cups freshly rememb'red.
This story shall the good man teach his son;
And Crispin Crispian shall ne'er go by,
From this day to the ending of the world,
But we in it shall be remembered—
We few, we happy few, we band of brothers;
For he to-day that sheds his blood with me
Shall be my brother; be he ne'er so vile,
This day shall gentle his condition;
And gentlemen in England now a-bed
Shall think themselves accurs'd they were not here,
And hold their manhoods cheap whiles any speaks
That fought with us upon Saint Crispin's day.

                                                    (4.3.40–67)

History is assimilated into myth—not myth as falsehood, but myth as
illustrious truth. And the essence of myth is a new beginning. Those who
fight at Agincourt will be reborn: "this day shall gentle his condition."
King and subject will share the fellowship of Agincourt, and its aftermath.
The psychic objective of the battle, as Henry presents it, is not to defeat

the French. They have no place whatsoever in the oration. The objective
is to be part of the annual, seasonal celebration of a great episode in the
nation's history. It is that imaginative vision, with all its homely reality,
that enables Agincourt to be won. Beyond the day's fighting lies a future
in which all classes are transmuted into equality of fellowship with the
Warrior-King. The soldiers fight in order to attend the Agincourt reunion.

Before that vision, irony retreats. And the sober accounting for the
day's work leaves intact the vision, as it does the social structures:

> Where is the number of our English dead?
> Edward the Duke of York, the Earl of Suffolk,
> Sir Richard Keighley, Davy Gam Esquire:
> None else of name, and of all other men
> But five and twenty.
>
> (5.7.100–4)

A duke, an earl, a knight, a (Welsh) gentleman, twenty-five others. That
is parity of sacrifice. There is nothing in the casualty lists to contradict the
vision in Henry's Agincourt speech.

CHAPTER FIVE

The Major Tragedies

HAMLET

*T*he *Tragedy of Hamlet, Prince of Denmark*—every word tells, but only one concerns us here. *Tragedy* is the mystery of the entire event. *Hamlet*, the name of father and son, links identity to ancestry. *Denmark* is the nation, the soil from which everything grows. *Prince* is the rank at the center of the play. How does *prince* structure the play, and all events and relationships within it?

Prince is not *King*, and most of the play is Hamlet's coming to terms with that fact. He becomes King in the last few minutes of his life, as the courtiers fail to intervene in his killing of Claudius and listen silently to his directions for the new reign. He has, after all, put right a failure. Denmark, as it emerges slowly throughout the play, is an elective monarchy, and Hamlet's failure to become King is the unexplored hinterland of everything that ensues. Whether he was in Denmark at the time of King Hamlet's death, or abroad, the play does not make clear. The situation is ambivalent: son of the late King, passed over (or outmaneuvered) for the succession, faced with a problem of revenge that is inherently all but insoluble. In these exceptionally difficult circumstances, to be "Prince" begs all the questions.

It is nonetheless the given of the play, and the best lead-in. To be a Prince, one must behave in a princely manner. And Hamlet does so. Consider his affable relations with all social classes. Horatio and company find him in intense depression, but his recovery is swift. He remembers Marcellus's name, and while Bernardo's is beyond him he covers up well with "Good even, sir." The Players, addressed as "Good friends," are obviously just that. The Pirates, "these good fellows," are soon set to running his errands. The Gravedigger—who would put out a less accommodating Prince—is persuaded to talk. So is the reticent Norwegian Captain, who under Hamlet's assiduous pumping comes up with a spurt of bitter military intelligence concerning the objectives of Fortinbras's Polish campaign (for which he receives "I humbly thank you, sir"). This is a Prince with the common touch. When Claudius says "he's loved of the distracted multitude," this is nothing other than the truth.

Affability is all very well, but princeliness suggests something more. The stage has been receptive to acting which promotes a social model of grand style. Alec Clunes's Hamlet, for example (1945), was on the Castiglione model, all sprezzatura. As Kenneth Tynan saw it, "Clunes' Castiglionean Hamlet was more than Italian: it was European in the wider sense."[1] To see Hamlet as *Il Cortegiano* works best, I think, in the final scene, when Hamlet is very consciously presenting himself to the Danish Court as a finished product within a certain cultural frame. Still, the apotheosis of Hamlet is only acceptable if it states formally what has been implied in his earlier conduct. Of recent years, the stage has been less interested in transmitting this image of Hamlet. But Derek Jacobi has maintained the Gielgud tradition of the Renaissance Prince, and it remains an available model for actors.

Congruent with this ideal of the Prince is that of the gentleman. Hamlet does not in fact claim it for himself. But Rosencrantz and Guildenstern, reporting back to Claudius and Gertrude, are happy to reassure the Queen that he received them "most like a gentleman" (3.1.11). And the entire relationship between Hamlet and Laertes is based on Hamlet's recognition that Laertes is "a very noble youth," a genuine social model. Wittenberg has to keep up with Paris.

The contours of the gentlemanly ideal are as described by Polonius, in his advice to Laertes (1.3.59–80). E. A. J. Honigmann remarks that the ideal "has to be firmly stated because it asserts itself, in one disguise or another, in so many scenes." The ideal becomes critical to the action when Claudius remembers Lamord ("Here was a gentleman of Normandy") (4.7.82). The factor common to Lamord, Laertes, and Hamlet is the gentlemanly exercise of fencing. Thus Claudius is able, by associating the three, to set up the fencing match. "Claudius," says Honigmann, "more or less equates Lamord and Laertes, one perfect gentleman vouched for by another, claims that Hamlet wished to match himself against Laertes, and thus implicitly measures Hamlet against Lamord, the 'gem of all the nation.'"[2] The ideology explains the action.

The ideal is naturally subject to distortion and indeed caricature. Polonius's view of it is subtly self-erasing, through its own hard shallow worldliness. Michael Long is right, I think, to detect the "Philistinism" of the Polonius household.[3] Everything that Polonius says to Laertes by way of precept is just, and much of it has passed into the language. It is proverbial, and proverbs do not lie. And yet proverbs distort the truth through their simple generalizations, just as Polonius can find nothing better to denote Hamlet's mental state than "mad." In his briefing of Reynaldo it emerges that Polonius regards swearing, quarreling, drabbing as acceptable pursuits in a young man-about-town. Drabbing, yes, incontinency, no. One draws the line. The quintessential Polonius comes out in what he knows about clothes.

> For the apparel oft proclaims the man;
> And they in France of the best rank and station
> Are of a most select and generous chief in that.
>
> (1.3.72–4)

What he says about French fashion is perfectly true, but it is the sort of information one could pick up from an in-flight magazine.

Polonius knows what everybody else knows, and nothing else. If he endangers the gentlemanly ideal, Osric lampoons it. Laertes, the rising star of the provincial Danish Court, is singled out for gushing praise:

Believe me, an absolute gentleman, full of most excellent differences, of very soft society and great showing. Indeed, to speak feelingly of him, he is the card or calendar of gentry, for you shall find in him the continent of what part a gentleman would see. (5.2.106–11)

Nothing could be better calculated to irritate Hamlet, and to make him rise to the bait. One reflects afterwards, though not at the time, that Osric is more intelligent than he looks. That sort of buffoon often is. The outcome is a challenge, not only overt. Laertes, as Hamlet well realizes—and he uses the word thrice to Osric—is a *gentleman*. To fence with him is an act of public theater, before the eyes of the court, that will confirm whatever claims Hamlet can make in that direction. It might be a distortion to say this is the metropolis versus the provinces again: it is Paris/Elsinore versus Wittenberg/Elsinore, at all events. But it must above all be an exercise in social polish, and the Queen, who yearns for these things, gets a message through to her son: "The Queen desires you to use some *gentle* entertainment to Laertes before you fall to play" (5.2.197). "She well instructs me," replies Hamlet, and his apologia before the court is the apotheosis of the Renaissance Prince as gentleman:

> Give me your pardon, sir. I have done you wrong;
> But pardon't, as you are a gentleman.
>
> (5.2.218–19)

That is one line of approach, through Hamlet as a model of princely courtesy and accomplishment.

> The courtier's, soldier's, scholar's, eye, tongue, sword,
> Th' expectancy and rose of the fair state,
> The glass of fashion and the mould of form
>
> (3.1.151–53).

Ophelia is the gauge of Hamlet's best self. But this is only a part of Hamlet. Much of the play shows him behaving badly. Hamlet's conduct is a continuation of Shakespeare's interest in the shuttling between behavior proper to rank and behavior that betrays it, on view in *Love's Labor's Lost* and *A Midsummer Night's Dream*. "A gentleman," ran the saying, "is one who is never offensive unintentionally." Hamlet can be extraordinarily and ingeniously offensive, and unless one accepts the pleas of diminished responsibility entered on his behalf (and by him), always with intent.

Hamlet's relations with Claudius are superb variations on superior/ subordinate insolence, and are so from the first council scence. Claudius, well knowing that he has a problem on his hands, broaches it with a form of address as ingratiating as he can make it: "But now, my cousin Hamlet, and our son" (1.2.64). Hamlet's "a little more than kin, and less than kind" fills out the ill-defined space occupied by aside, muttered comment— semi-audible insolence, as it were—and, in the extreme case, interruption audible to the King. It depends on performance. ("Aside" scarcely exists as a Folio stage direction. It is almost invariably an editor's inference.) Hamlet is being awkward, obviously. He is also testing the ground. When Claudius continues with the pacific, wounded line, "How is it that the clouds still hang on you?" Hamlet ventures on a direct rebuttal of the King: "Not so, my lord, I am too much in the sun." Kings are not habitually contradicted by subjects. We have in four lines a paradigm of a relationship: Claudius handles the problem with caution, refusing to take offense; Hamlet, seeing his advantage, goes as far as he dares. The immediate point of the exercise is to prohibit Hamlet's plan of escaping to Wittenberg *and to make him accept it on record.* He won't do it for Claudius, but the Queen's tactful intervention enables the face-saving but still acerbic formula of "I shall in all my best obey *you*, madam" (1.2.120). A sticky situation has been got over, and Claudius is unfeignedly glad— "Why, 'tis a loving and fair reply"—as he takes an immediate exit calling for a drink, the first of the day no doubt.

It's a fair bet that Hamlet's "Those that are married already, all but one, shall live" (3.1.148) is a conscious hit at Claudius, lurking behind the arras. His main affronts are in open court, though. The play scene finds a highly strung, excited Hamlet approaching "madness," which covers his strange jests on "chameleons" in the King's presence. The actor in Hamlet finds the production intensely stimulating, and his behavior to Ophelia, with its stream of brutal sexual innuendo, is outrageous. It even seems designed to make the Queen jealous: "No, good mother, here's metal more attractive," and for a moment he seems to be playing the younger woman off against the elder. This flood of semi-hysteria bears him up in his challenge to Claudius. When the King is unwise enough to ask "Have you heard the argument? Is there no offense in't?" Hamlet gets in "No, no, they do but jest—poison in jest" and "Your Majesty, and we that have free souls, it touches us not" (3.2.227–36). All these are finely calibrated affronts: Hamlet is using his own high spirits, saying, you can't touch me here, I am obviously in a manically elated mood and can get away with murder. At the core of the play scene is a spoiled stepson and a stepfather who would love to throttle the wretch but cannot. Not with the boy's mother looking on, anyway.

The relations between Claudius and Hamlet are paradoxical. Claudius has everything but cannot assert his will; Hamlet is a defeated subject but knows how to exploit his privileged position. Each man knows that the other knows. The contest is, therefore, one of provocation and self-control. The dialogue in 4.3 is brilliantly tense and dangerous. Hamlet, in "Your worm is your only emperor for diet" (4.3.21) uses a locution still current. "Your worm" is the language of the barroom expert, holding forth to his unenlightened crony about the way things work. Claudius, who prudently declines the bait, is well advised to counter with "Alas, alas" [poor fellow; only a madman would address his sovereign in this way]. It leads to the level exchange:

> *Hamlet*: For England?
> *King*: Ay, Hamlet.
> *Hamlet*: Good.
> *King*: So is it, if thou knew'st our purposes.
> *Hamlet*: I see a cherub that sees them.

Messages are received. "Thou" is one of them; it is the only occasion when Claudius so addresses Hamlet, and its intimacy is also a threat.

Hamlet exits on a rather contrived word game—"Farewell, good mother"—an easy trick to score off Claudius, and a way of keeping the contest alive. Hamlet's talent for offense reemerges in the exaggerated deference of his letter to Claudius: "High and mighty . . . Tomorrow I shall beg leave to see your kingly eyes . . ." It is all the "card or catalogue," as Osric would say, of insolence. And it culminates in Hamlet's last words to Claudius, "Here, thou incestuous, murd'rous, damned Dane,/ Drink off this potion" (5.2.317–18). The brutal physicality of the line contains everything that Hamlet has longed to do. For it to make sense, he has to be holding Claudius by the back of the head while he forces the wine down his throat. With it goes the contemptuous "thou." Hamlet not only kills Claudius, he insults him.

Hamlet, in fact, exploits his princely position in ways that are ingeniously varied while expressing an ungovernable soul. His behavior to Ophelia is adequatedly described as sadistic. He cuts up Polonius figuratively ("you are a fishmonger") and literally. With Laertes, he loses his temper badly (and is ashamed of it). He spends an entire scene lecturing his mother on the sexual propriety of sleeping with her husband, immediately after he has killed an innocent man. And yet the audience forgives him. With us as with Claudius, Hamlet gets away with it. Nevertheless, actors in recent years have been more ready to emphasize, or admit to, the negative side of Hamlet. Anton Lesser's Hamlet in Jonathan Miller's production (1982) actually cheated in the fencing match. Laertes was shocked. (So was I.) Hamlet is something other than the pattern of chivalry, and today's actors know it.

And yet one comes back to the word *prince*, as one must, for the text never relinquishes it. Hamlet does not in fact claim the word and the rank for himself. Others do it for him. Polonius, recounting to Claudius and Gertrude his warning to Ophelia, quotes himself (not altogether accurately) as saying "'Lord Hamlet is a prince out of thy star. This must not be'" (2.2.140–41). That is an absolute statement of class discrepancy: a union is impossible. And the prohibition could be viewed as an imperative of state, though Gertrude thinks otherwise: "I hop'd thou shouldst have been my Hamlet's wife" (5.1.238). It is an available view of Ophelia and Hamlet. *Prince* in this sense is one sharply limited by his rank, who may only marry within the degree. Yet nothing of this applies to Horatio's final tribute, "Goodnight, sweet prince." *Prince* is now an assemblage of comely virtues. It combines nobility of temperament with rank, Horatio's assertion that the composite image of the Renaissance Prince is what should stand as Hamlet's memory. As for Hamlet himself, he speaks the word but

once, and of another man. It is in his final soliloquy, as he watches the
Norwegian army pass through the Danish corridor on its way to Poland:
"Witness this army, of such mass and charge, /Led by a delicate and
tender Prince" (4.4.47–48). In this play of analogues, the example of
Fortinbras is what hardens Hamlet into action. "When honor's at the
stake" (4.4.56) is, at the same time, Hamlet's admission that *honor* must
govern his conduct. It is a superb compliment paid by one prince to
another, and Fortinbras repays it. He does not, at the play's end, laud
Hamlet for being princely. He recognizes a fellow soldier.

> Let four captains
> Bear Hamlet like a soldier to the stage;
> For he was likely, had he been put on,
> To have prov'd most royal; and for his passage
> The soldier's music and the rite of war
> Speak loudly for him.
>
> (5.2.387–92)

The carbon dating of rank is war.

KING LEAR

If *prince* is the entry to *Hamlet*, then *king* seems the way into *King Lear*.
But *king* needs to be qualified. *King Lear* is only marginally concerned with
kingship, royalty, and high politics; this is not an English history play
transferred to the Dark Ages, a *Richard II* in furs. *King* in *King Lear* is the
apex of the social hierarchy, and in this play symbolizes all forms of
authority. *Authority* is the word used by Kent and Goneril of Lear and by
Lear himself:

Thou hast seen a farmer's dog bark at a beggar? . . . And the creature run from the
cur? There thou mightst behold the great image of authority: a dog's obeyed in
office.

(4.6.154–59)

What the mad King sees is a world in which all rank, all office caricatures
itself. Hence the play's business is to dwell on the decomposition of title
and rank, before resting on the exhausted reordering of the state in the
final lines. *King Lear* is fascinated with the inversions, paradoxes, and
betrayals of social rank.

One has first to get right the play's period signals. Its Dark Age primitivism ought not to be overstated. There's no question of the misty, pre-Conquest aura of *King Lear*, but there are threads of sophisticated, courtly activity worked into the texture. The opening scene has the atmosphere of a great and well-ordered court ceremonial—the greater, because violated. Peter Brook is right in characterizing the opening speech of Goneril:

The words are those of a lady of style and breeding accustomed to expressing herself in public, someone with ease and social aplomb. As for clues to her character, only the façade is presented and this, we see, is elegant and attractive.[4]

On a later occasion, Lear says something to Regan that could no doubt apply as well to Goneril:

> Thou art a lady;
> If only to go warm were gorgeous,
> Why, nature needs not what thou gorgeous wear'st,
> Which scarcely keeps thee warm.
>
> (2.4.266–69)

Light, fashionable court dress—with a suggestion of exposed skin—is not the raiment of primitives. The combat in Act 5 is in the vein of chivalry, and thus technically medieval (an anachronism here, of course). The customary class structures are often spoken of. *King Lear* is not like *Macbeth*, rooted in savagery. The whole point of the play is that the descent into barbarism is from *something*, a plateau of established and functioning social order. The horrors are proposed as the failure of civilization, as much as the regular condition of barbarism.

The opening scene registers economically a challenge to the social order—bastardy. It is a masterly vignette of implied motivation. Three men enter, two of them middle-aged courtiers talking court politics. One of them says, "Is not this your son, my lord?" (1.1.7) and we realize that the young man on the fringe has not even been introduced. And it is his father who has not introduced him. Gloucester now explains, with a combination of embarrassment and lip-smacking appreciation of the sexual exploit involved, that the young man is his bastard. Presumably the dialogue between Gloucester and Kent is a little apart from Edmund, but it can hardly be entirely out of earshot. (Kent has just asked, "Is not *this* your son?" not "*that*.") Gloucester calls his son over. "Do you know this noble gentleman, Edmund?" (This is polite, and disingenuous. Edmund does *not* know this noble gentleman, nor would he, if it were left to his father.) With what iron self-control does Edmund reply, "No, my lord"! The introductions are made; the young man is personable and cultivated. But when he says, "Sir, I shall study deserving," it is clear that it will do him little good. His father immediately intervenes; no point in giving the lad false ideas about his chances at court: "He hath been out nine years, and away he shall again" (1.1.31–32). *Nine years* away, brought up in obscurity away from the court, which is the only place to make a career in. And after a glimpse of courtly delights, to be banished again. Edmund is a bastard, and his father is ashamed of him.

I labor the social points here because in the play that follows Gloucester is the victim of an appalling crime, and the object of the audience's most intense pity. But here, in some thirty-odd lines, is sketched a type of callousness and insensitivity—the aristocrat who will neither acknowledge properly nor cut off his bastard, and thereby breeds a malcontent. When Edgar in his moralizing way says, "The gods are just, and of our pleasant vices/Make instruments to plague us" (5.3.170–71), the play supports him, but not in the sense he intends. *King Lear* is not a tract on the evils of sexual promiscuity. It depicts, with unillusioned clarity, the consequences of a failure to assimilate a well-born outsider into the social order.

The point is heavily stressed later. Edmund's soliloquy (1.2) spells out the implications of the opening. The full-blooded embrace of a Darwinian nature, "Thou, Nature, art my goddess," is also a grapple with society's words: "Why brand they us/With base? with baseness? bastardy? base, base?" There's also the stereotype illustrated in *King John*, that legitimacy is effete and bastardy has vitality:

> Who, in the lusty stealth of Nature, take
> More composition and fierce quality
> Than doth, within a dull, stale, tired bed,
> Go to th'creating a whole tribe of fops
> Got 'twixt asleep and wake?
>
> (1.2.11–15)

The makings of a doctrine are here, the notion that bastards have a natural right to overthrow custom—that, indeed, social forms are destined to be overthrown.

Edmund makes the case for himself, and it is oddly close to Lear's case, "I am a man more sinn'd against than sinning," with its shift of personal responsibility elsewhere. But the case goes beyond Edmund's subjectivity. In accusing Edgar, Edmund quotes his brother as saying:

> Thou unpossessing bastard! dost thou think,
> If I would stand against thee, would the reposure
> Of any trust, virtue, or worth in thee
> Make the words faith'd?

(2.1.67–70)

It is a lie, but a plausible one. It is meant to deceive and does. Edmund projects upon his brother a commonplace of social experience. Then later, even the mild Albany bears down hard upon him in the aftermath of the victory and will accept no divergence of view: "Sir, by your patience,/I hold you but a subject of this war,/Not as a brother" (5.3.60–62). When Edmund asserts himself during the Regan-Goneril imbroglio, Albany's response is brutal: "*Half-blooded fellow, yes*" (5.3.81). The evidence is unequivocal: whatever personal qualities of blood and breeding Edmund may have, the stigma of bastardy never lapses. It is always in waiting, ready to be hurled at the victim. This is no predestined criminal; Edmund is a personable and talented young man who takes the only road open to him and follows it to the end. In the origins and circumstances of bastardy lies a force for evil.

Legitimacy, as presented in the court scene, is mainly an affair of property and inheritance. It is a will implemented before death, a property settlement entered into so as to defeat claims on the estate. Lear's object is to settle matters while he can; and his solution is a continuation of his life-time policies. Post-Lear Britain is to be a tripartite division among Regan/Cornwall, Goneril/Albany, and Cordelia/husband (probably, because of strategic convenience, France). In other words, Britain is to be divided into the North of England and Scotland (which is what "Albany" denotes), the West plus its share of the heartland (Cornwall), and the Southeast (Cordelia, to whom Kent is feudatory). This division is not really arbitrary. Since the great Dukes are already in possession of their regional territories, Lear's settlement merely formalizes the present state of affairs with the addition of heartland areas. It also maintains the present jealousies and rivalries of the inheritors, which are neatly contained within a triadic system. The map of Britain that Lear unfolds is a working diagram of a settlement that corresponds reasonably well to the current situation. The future will have to depend on the fertility of the three daughters, anyway—or their husbands.

The settlement fails because of an emotional outburst that has family and personal origins, hence is beyond my scope here. What matters is the nature of the arrangement Lear has in mind. It is a weighty and complicated version of the bourgeois contract in *The Taming of the Shrew*. Since Cordelia is not yet betrothed, her portion is linked with her marriage settlement, and is, as Lear makes clear, her *dower*. In sum, the court scene is designed, with lavish ceremonial, to embrace several operations. It is an abdication; the announcement of a division of property that is in effect a will; and the final settlement of dowries upon three daughters. The way is open for the final bids of Cordelia's two suitors. It is a complex and serious business involving the fate of the realm, and must have been deeply pondered. In presentation, these decisions call for a solemn and public protestation of fealty and devotion by the beneficiaries. But when one of them cannot swallow the form of words and says so, Lear loses his temper—like his daughter. He blunders, but he has some cause.

The court scene fractures these arrangements of state. A great ceremonial occasion demands that its forms be accepted. The choreography is laid down. Incompetence is allowed for, of course—peers trip, crowns slip, mitres cant at an angle, elderly notables go to sleep—but open repudiation is a blasphemy. That is what Cordelia commits and what Lear reacts to. And Kent makes things far worse. A modern audience may miss some of the disgusted contempt in "be Kent unmannerly,/When Lear is mad. What wouldst thou do, old man?" (1.1.144–45) with its unpardonable "thou." That is an assault upon authority itself, and authority chooses to make its stand there. The rest of *King Lear* is not a cause-and-effect demonstration of social dissolution stemming from one (or three) headstrong actions, but it shows a fractured society. After the violated ceremonial of Act 1, scene 1, *King Lear* enters a savage parody of social order.

A domestic dimension comes into view in Goneril's household: this is a daughter finding her aged father a burden, determined to ally herself with her sister to curb him. She has a case. "His knights grow riotous," all hundred of them. Lear is a problem guest, demanding his dinner as soon as he comes home from hunting, making trouble with his unruly followers. He has lost none of his gift for vituperation: "clotpoll," "mongrel," "whoreson dog." Things cannot go on like this, and ceremonial, unsurprisingly, yields to the lack of "ceremonious affection" with which Lear is entertained. No one puts it better than the Fool:

Lear: Dost thou call me fool, boy?

> *Fool*: All thy other titles thou hast given away; that thou wast
> born with.
>
> (1.4.147–49)

And for all the "authority" that the disguised Kent discerns in Lear's
countenance, it is now stripped from him. Rank is identity: identity shorn
of title becomes madness.

  King Lear. That is what the center of the drama is, "every inch a king."
An ex-king is conceptually impossible; like Richard II, Lear loses his vital
essence with his throne. Since the essence is authority, its loss is imaged
through social subjection. When called upon by Regan to go back to
Goneril, Lear flashes

> Return with her?
> Why, the hot-blooded France, that dowerless took
> Our youngest born—I could as well be brought
> To knee his throne, and, squire-like, pension beg
> To keep base life afoot. Return with her?
> Persuade me rather to be slave and sumpter
> To this detested groom.
>
> (2.4.210–16)

None of these terms has independent worth in Lear's eyes, not even
"squire." They are merely types of subjection. "Base" (as Edmund has
seen) is a concealed metaphor, in which moral values are transferred to
social position. "Noble" is good, and "base" is bad. For Lear, the
ultimate threat to identity comes from loss of authority, hence the existential horror of the lowest social ranks.

  It is this threat that the heath scenes make actual. The social purgatory
of the hovel, the dirty straw and the degraded company, is the pit of the
King's experience. It is registered partly through shocked observers.
Gloucester reacts through his class consciousness: "What, hath your
Grace no better company?" (3.4.138). Cordelia, when she hears of it,
thinks of the physical conditions as well as the company:

> And wast thou fain, poor father,
> To hovel thee with swine and rogues forlorn,
> In short and musty straw?
>
> (4.7.38–40)

The point repeatedly made is that human degradation is also social degradation.

The heath scenes are deeply imbued with social class. Shakespeare insists on the reality of the heath as something measurable in terms of the ordinary stratified world. The Fool, who like all his brethren is himself classless, or at least hard to place within the social hierarchy, puts a riddle to Lear:

> *Fool*: Prithee, nuncle, tell me whether a madman be a gentleman or a yeoman?
> *Lear*: A king, a king!
> *Fool*: No; he's a yeoman that has a gentleman to his son; for he's a mad yeoman that sees his son a gentleman before him.
>
> (3.6.9–14)

Even the common social aspirations are a form of madness. The fallen Edgar presents himself as an ex-servingman—"three suits to his back, six shorts to his body"—who is now a mad rogue, "whipp'd from tithing to tithing, and stock-punish'd, and imprison'd." Behind these types of pride and abasement stand the forms of earthly justice. And the mock trial that Lear presides over—"I'll see their trial first. Bring in their evidence"(3.6.35)— is a mad charade of justice.

So, in a different key, is the interrogation and blinding of Gloucester. Cornwall detaches the event from ordinary justice:

> Though well we may not pass upon his life
> *Without the form of justice*, yet our power
> Shall do a court'sy to our wrath, which men
> May blame but not control.
>
> (3.6.23–26)

Justice is the appetite of the strong. In the same vein is Cornwall's promise to Edmund, "True or false, it hath made thee Earl of Gloucester" (3.5.15–16), which coolly asserts the ducal right to fill a title by killing off the present holder. Against these wrongs, the single act of natural justice is the intervention of the nameless Servant.

> *1 Serv.*   Hold your hand, my lord.

I have serv'd you ever since I was a child;
But better service have I never done you
Than now to bid you hold.

(3.7.71–74)

Upon him is vented the rage of both mistress ("How now, you dog") and master ("My villain!"). It is the old formula, the aristocrat's rejection of all challenge. "A peasant stand up thus!" is Regan, and "throw this slave/Upon the dunghill" is Cornwall's. What a text is Cornwall's incredulous "My villain"! The word assimilates the sense of *villein* (serf, bondslave) into *villain* (one of base, low qualities). Yet again, the social hierarchy translates into moral values. Against this is the fact of the drama. The blinding of Gloucester is a great noble's crime, followed by a peasant's rebellion.

Out of all this emerges, indistinctly yet detectably, a kind of proto-socialism, the need of which each of the major sufferers sees. Lear on the heath shares the anguish of the homeless, "You houseless poverty":

Poor naked wretches, wheresoe'er you are,
That bide the pelting of this pitiless storm,
How shall your houseless heads and unfed sides,
Your loop'd and window'd raggedness, defend you
From seasons such as these? O, I have ta'en
Too little care of this! Take physic, pomp;
Expose thyself to feel what wretches feel,
That thou mayst shake the superflux to them,
And show the heavens more just.

(3.4.28–36)

Justice, a later generation would comment, is also social justice. And Gloucester's sense of things parallels Lear's. The blind Earl meets on the heath an Old Man: "O my good lord, I have been your tenant, and your father's tenant, these fourscore years" (4.1.13–14). The Old Man is told to leave Gloucester with "the naked fellow," Edgar, and when he demurs is told sharply to obey: "Do as I bid thee, or rather do thy pleasure." It is infinitely pathetic, this reflex flash of the old hauteur that fades into the realization of powerlessness. It prompts Gloucester to say:

Let the superfluous and lust-dieted man
That slaves your ordinance, that will not see
Because he does not feel, feel your power quickly;

> So distribution should undo excess,
> And each man have enough.
>
> (4.1.68–72)

Lear's "pomp" is Gloucester's "superfluous and lust-dieted man," broadly, "the wealthy." Each sees the need for the wealthy to yield something to the poor, and the curiously modern ring of Gloucester's last two lines comes close to "redistribution of income." *King Lear* is not reducible to a political thesis, but the intensity of the heath experience creates a vision of human need.

The play continues to pit against each other aspects of a fragmented world. For instance, the audience receives the slaying of Cornwall as an absolute moral necessity, and its revulsion has to be acted out on stage. Yet the Messenger who bears the news to Albany recounts it neutrally, as a kind of convulsion of Nature:

> A servant that he bred, thrill'd with remorse,
> Oppos'd against the act, bending his sword
> To his great master; who, thereat enrag'd,
> Flew on him, and amongst them fell'd him dead;
> But not without that harmful stroke which since
> Hath pluck'd him after.
>
> (4.2.73–78)

"Bred" suggests a certain paternal responsibility, which the Duke of Cornwall had for his servant and which the Servant himself had acknowledged. That bond has been violated, so the Servant, too, must pay for his assault on degree. The moral coloration comes from Albany:

> This shows you are above,
> You justicers, that these our nether crimes
> So speedily can venge!
>
> (4.2.78–80)

It is justice of a kind, which must eke out earthly justice, to whose inadequacies the mad King returns:

A man may see how this world goes with no eyes. Look with thine ears. See how yond justice rails upon yond simple thief. Hark, in thine ear: change places and, handy-dandy, which is the justice, which is the thief?

(4.6.150–53)

This is close in spirit to the mock trial of Act 3, but Lear has now stepped down from the bench. Authority—"thou rascal beadle," "the usurer"—is now the primal sham, and "that whore," "the cozener" are its victims. Another kind of inversion appears in the encounter of Oswald and Edgar. In a caricature of social relations, Oswald takes on the contemptuous airs of his betters, using such forms of address as "bold peasant," "slave," "out, dunghill!" Edgar, speaking an exaggerated form of Mummerset, does his yokel act: "Good gentleman, go your gait, and let poor volk pass" (4.6.239–40). The ensuing fight is won by the peasant, who is also a disguised nobleman and heir to an Earldom. Thus, Act 4 takes us to what is virtually a collapse of all order, a deliquescence if not reversal of all classes and all roles.

From this abyss, Act 5 conducts the audience away, and it does so through yet another paradox, a forgotten resource of social rank. The combat that determines the outcome of the play is in that most archaic of modes, chivalry:

> *Albany*: Come hither, herald. Let the trumpet sound,
>   And read out this.
> *Herald*: If any man of quality or degree within the lists
>   of the army will maintain upon Edmund, supposed
>   Earl of Gloucester, that he is a manifold traitor,
>   let him appear by the third sound of the trumpet.
>   He is bold in his defence.
>
>   (5.3.108–14)

"The age of chivalry is dead," said Burke, pointing out what seems inherent in the nature of chivalry. Chivalry is always an anachronism, an Arthurian bequest that looks back to Camelot as a golden age. It can have no place in the brutal and fallen world of *King Lear*. And yet it does. Edgar responds to the trumpet in terms that could have been taken from the Coventry tournament in *Richard II*:

> Behold, it is the privilege of mine honors,
> My oath, and my profession. I protest—
> Maugre thy strength, youth, place, and eminence.
> Despite thy victor sword and fire-new fortune,
> Thy valor and thy heart, thou art a traitor.
>
>   (5.3.129–33)

Edmund assents to the presumption of social equality in his challenger:

> In wisdom I should ask thy name;
> But, since thy outside looks so fair and warlike,
> And that thy tongue some say of breeding breathes,
> What safe and nicely I might well delay
> By rule of knighthood, I disdain and spurn.
>
> (5.3.141–45)

And the play, after all, is determined by knightly combat between noble brothers. The elder wins.

The contest between right and wrong is fought out within a class and is so emphasized. "If th'art noble,/I do forgive thee," says the dying Edmund. "Let's exchange charity./I am no less in blood than thou art, Edmund" is Edgar's response (5.3.165–67). And Albany is quick to confirm this aspect: "Methought thy very gait did prophesy/A royal nobleness" (5.3.175–76). The resonances of "noble" are behind Albany's offer to hand over the government to Edgar and Kent. But the old structures of fealty are still there. Kent, says Edgar, "in disguise/Follow'd his enemy king, and did him service/Improper for a slave." And it is the role of liegeman that weighs finally with Kent: "I have a journey, sir, shortly to go./My master calls me, I must not say no."

King Lear is the picture of a feudal society, organized on strong vertical lines. The leaders have great power and call for loyalty and obedience. Those in subordinate positions can expect protection and occasional reward, but must never challenge their masters. The play traces the exercise of power, as seen with Lear, Gloucester, and Cornwall. It shows the reaction against what is felt as the abuse of power, notably by Cordelia and Kent, Edmund, and the nameless Servant. *King Lear* does not, I think, simply ally itself with the rebels, nor could it. Each member of the resistance has faults, if only hotheadedness. What the play offers is a society in which individuals have a stark choice, submission or revolt. Kent's identity is that of liegeman to Lear, and his challenge and return are equally grounded in the urge to do service to his master. Cornwall's servant grounds his challenge on fealty. This limitation of choice to yielding or taking the consequences is the disabling weakness of the social order that Shakespeare diagnoses. Moreover, the mental pressure on subordinates is the greater for this, that terms of subordination are terms of abuse: "slave," "peasant," "groom." The honorable position of vassal, which Kent holds, is in fact the first flout Lear gives him: "O vassal!

Miscreant!" (1.1.160). Since, in Shakespeare, social characteristics are related always to the temperament of the ruler, the structures of *King Lear* refer ultimately to the sclerotic, passionate, and unyielding nature of the King. Authority hardens into the authoritarian, and falls.

OTHELLO

Class as motivation is the principle of *Othello*. The formula covers the title part easily enough. Othello is a study of racial insecurity in an alien society: his failure to understand Desdemona is also an alien's incomprehension of Venetian society. The main psychological issue is the extent to which Othello is truly "jealous" (a trait he disclaims) or not. The contours are clear to the point of banality, and it is no accident that of all Shakespeare's plays *Othello* adapts most easily to opera. But around Othello and Desdemona is a subtle and varied social context. *Othello* is a military play as well as a tragedy rooted in the circumstances of Venetian society. In the relations between military rank and social class lie the causes of the tragedy.

Class comes first here, since it precedes and informs the restrictions of military life. Venice is a great city-state, dependent on its maritime trade and capacity to protect its trade: hence a successful general, as Othello is, can name his social price. There are indications that Venice is far from color-blind, but the Duke has no intention of using his weight to support Brabantio in the council scene. Desdemona has chosen Othello, and that is that. Othello can take his aristocratic bride to Cyprus with the Establishment's blessing. He thus disappoints Roderigo, *a gull'd Gentleman* (there is Folio authority for the dramatis personae here), who follows the pair abroad. In Cyprus, Othello becomes what we recognize as Governor-General and sets up a small military-social group that is a microcosm of Venetian society. In it the tensions, resentments, and pairings of society are magnified. The four main acts of *Othello* are the inner story of the Governor-General's residence.

A word on military rank is in order. As always in Shakespearean drama, the need is to register gradation in ways that are serviceably flexible. An army is like a court in this respect. You cannot stand by scrupulous distinctions between Third Gold Stick-in-Waiting, the Lord Chamberlain's assistant, an equerry, a major-domo, and Garter King of Arms who happens to be around that day. Somebody (as it might be Philostrate in *A Midsummer Night's Dream*) will have to do it all, with a couple of spare courtiers to help out, if casting permits. With a company of fifteen to sixteen actors, which has been established as the playing strength of the King's Men, doubling was always necessary and so was flexibility of organizational role. Applied to an army, this means that one cannot expect the ranks to be precisely confirmed. Othello is a general, but at times, as in the opening of 2.3, for example, he seems more like the Colonel of the Regiment, discussing guard duties with his adjutant. (And also dropping a kindly hint that the Adjutant's known weakness with the bottle will have to be watched.) Cassio, in turn, is about to check up on the Orderly Sergeant, Iago. These are regimental matters; and yet Cassio ends as Acting Governor of Cyprus, with large diplomatic, administrative, and military responsibilities. What the playwright offers is a sketch, not a diagram. *Lieutenant* and *Ancient*, especially, are not so much hard-and-fast categories, as suggestive containers.

Of these containers, the most important is Iago's. "If I take it on," said Olivier, "I don't want a witty, Machiavellian Iago. I want a solid, honest-to-God N.C.O."[5] The first Othello of our times, measuring the options of stage tradition, chose an Iago based on his military rank. Anthony Quayle, when he played Iago, offered according to Speaight "a *rusé* sergeant-major, or adjutant risen from the ranks."[6] Evidently those with military experience (which includes Olivier and Quayle) see Iago in terms of rank. And this corresponds well to the text. *Ancient*, Iago's rank, means "ensign." There is no direct modern equivalent, but "Colour-sergeant" is a reasonable approximation, or perhaps "Warrant-Officer." Iago is ambitious for promotion, which goes, however, to Cassio, *an Honorable Lieutenant*. Rank goes with class, and Iago is bitter: "mere prattle without practice/Is all his soldiership" (1.1.26–27). It is an old story. Iago has the combat experience; Cassio has some sort of staff college background ("bookish theoric") and pull. The staff candidate gets the appointment.

Objectively, this is a correct decision. Othello's second-in-command has to function at a number of levels. But one can scarcely expect the passed-over to acquiesce gracefully. "Accelerated promotion," as Paul Jorgensen remarks, "in an army of any period, is bound to produce jealousy."[7] The relations between Cassio and Iago are continuously tense: they are based on class corresponding to rank, with the Lieutenant knowing perfectly well that his subordinate has in some respects a better claim to the post. It is that tricky situation when the successful applicant has to work with a subordinate passed over for promotion. Cassio is naturally wary and also compensatory. There is in his address a scarcely

veiled policy of putting Iago down. And since he can hardly do this
through strictly military and professional means, he chooses the social
route.

It comes out right away, on the Cyprus quayside. Cassio kisses (or
embraces) Emilia, remarking,

> Let it not gall your patience, good Iago,
> That I extend my manners; 'tis my breeding
> That gives me this bold show of courtesy.

(2.1.97–99)

This is decidedly cool. "Between•that condescending 'good Iago' and the
word "Sir" with which the ancient replies, an Elizabethan audience must
have recognized a familiar class barrier," as E. A. J. Honigmann puts it.[8]
Later in the conversation, Cassio takes Desdemona aside, saying, "He
speaks home, madam. You may relish him more in the soldier than the
scholar." "A blunt fellow, not polished, but amusing enough." And in the
drinking scene,

> *Cassio*: For mine own part—no offence to the General, *nor any
> man of quality*—I hope to be saved.
> *Iago*:   And so do I too, Lieutenant.
> *Cassio*: Ay, but by your leave, not before me; the Lieutenant is
> to be saved before the Ancient.

(2.3.98–102)

Those who believe that alcohol merely licenses its consumers to behave as
they wish to behave anyway, can point to this passage. It appears less a
slip than something Cassio has been saying all the time to Iago.

Cassio himself is clearly defined. Personable, socially accomplished,
agreeable to both sexes, he is everything that Iago is not, and Shakespeare
uses him to get at Iago. "Unless I am mistaken," said A. C. Bradley, "he
[Iago] was not of gentle birth or breeding . . . for all his great powers, he is
vulgar."[9] This seems true, but Bradley goes on, surprisingly, to add "and
his probable want of military science may well be significant." What can
"military science" have to do with the play? And yet, I think Bradley is
right. By "military science" he means not simply an extended Renaissance training in the theory and practice of war, but a larger comprehen-
sion of issues and contexts, of causes and implications. A good

platoon officer may be altogether deficient in the understanding of war. There is something extraordinarily limited in the self-defeat of Iago.

The principal cause, however, is the class resentment that permeates Iago, and is nourished by many subtle touches. William Empson has written illuminatingly, for example, of *honest*, a word constantly applied to Iago. It seems such a straightforward term. And yet, says Empson, Shakespeare "never once allows the word a simple, hearty use between equals."[10] It can have a patronizing ring (as in "honest Thompson, my gardener"). "Honest" places Iago in a position of limitation and subordination: that is the way he is perceived. In this respect, the landing scene is revealing. Following the passage quoted above, "you may relish him more in the soldier than the scholar," comes

He takes her by the palm. Ay, well said, whisper. With as little a web as this will I ensnare as great a fly as Cassio. Ay, smile upon her, do; I will gyve thee in thine own courtship. You say true; 'tis so, indeed. If such tricks as these strip you out of your lieutenancy, it had been better you had not kiss'd your three fingers so oft, which now again you are most apt to play the sir in. Very good; well kissed! and excellent courtesy! 'Tis so, indeed. Yet again your fingers to your lips? Would they were clyster-pipes for your sake!

(2.1.166–77)

Since nothing of this can conceivably be spoken in the company's hearing, the speech must be an aside. It is so long, however, that "aside" cannot denote, as it usually does, a momentary turning away from the stage company so that the actor can address the audience directly. Iago is therefore set apart from the other actors on stage. There is nothing in the dialogue to suggest that Iago has turned away from the others. The others have turned away from him. Cassio has taken Desdemona by the palm, as Iago says, and has led her to one side. The ancient is excluded. Hence the concentrated viciousness of Iago's commentary, directed especially at Cassio's facility for kissing "which now again you are most apt to play the sir in." Behavior appropriate to rank often looks like bad acting to those of lesser station, placed as audience. And Iago's frustrations culminate in simple obscenity. ("Clyster-pipe" is a syringe for a vaginal douche.) The class feeling, so sharply detailed here, is a motive at least as strong as the sexual fantasies of the soliloquies.

Furthermore, unlike the sexual fantasies, the class factor is in place from first to last. The opening dialogue between Roderigo and Iago is a sustained rage against being left "his worship's ancient." Roderigo, to his face, is "thou silly gentleman" (2.3.307). The class antagonisms between

Cassio and Iago fill out the second act. Iago in power is the story of Acts 3 and 4. During this phase, the public expression of self through blank verse, the province of the gentleman, comes to Iago easily. He seems keen to mix on good terms with Montano and the others in the drinking scene. Of the passages in 5.1, Honigmann perceptively notes that Iago "continues to caress the Venetians with the word 'gentlemen,'" and that he is eager "to be accepted as an equal to gentlemen." Not till that scene does Shakespeare place the final missing piece: "If Cassio do remain,/He hath a daily beauty in his life/That makes me ugly" (5.1.18–20). It is a haunting admission of what, after all, Iago finds in Cassio to envy.

Othello has the precision and inner balance of a beautifully regulated piece of machinery. It does not have the tolerances and wide ambiguities of the other major tragedies. It is designed to work in the way it does, and in no other way. Hence in the theater it is not considered a director's vehicle, but an actor's vehicle. The main parts are designed to lock on to other parts, which are themselves closely specified. The cast is numerically small, and parts that matter the New Arden editor reckons as no more than seven.[11] Ultimately, the drama is confined to those in and near the Governor-General's residence, and this tight grouping contains all the personal and social forces that bring about the catastrophe.

What appears, therefore, as a duet between Othello and Iago in the temptation scene is a relationship activated by others offstage. The relationship between Iago and Cassio is crucial. But so is the relationship between Othello and Cassio. Othello has rightly appointed Cassio for the very qualities he lacks—the social skills, excellent connections with the Venetian Establishment, a general worldly savoir faire. These qualities emerge in Cassio's man-of-the-world's liaison with Bianca, which he is careful to conceal from his superior. And he is on good terms with Desdemona, as the second-in-command should be. It is the ease of his relations with Desdemona, two well-born Venetians striking up a natural rapport, that contributes so powerfully to the disaster. Desdemona herself is exactly placed. "Our general's wife is now the general," says Iago (2.3.305), voicing a commonplace of military life. To her is attached Emilia, "the gentlewoman that attends the general's wife," as Cassio calls her (3.1.24). Emilia would seem to share the approximate standing of her husband, and her command of blank verse (in the willow scene, especially) confirms this. Emilia and Desdemona also display the camaraderie of the married quarters. Each is in part an extension of her husband's rank and each values and needs the companionship of the other. The communications and the reticences between wives and husbands are the unseen mechanisms of the plot. Again and always, this play is enclosed within a narrow and coercing frame.

There is then no escape for Othello, and his mind is poisoned by a single malign agent. The dispassionate reason of Venice, speaking through Lodovico, comes too late to save him. At the end, the inner logic of the situation, which is also a social logic, asserts itself. Cassio gains yet another promotion. Iago fails yet again. More than any other villain in Shakespeare, Iago demonstrates the banality of evil.

MACBETH

It is all in the "bleeding Sergeant's" report of the battle, and Duncan's response. Macbeth, says the Sergeant,

> carv'd out his passage
> Till he fac'd the slave;
> Which ne'er shook hands, nor bade farewell to him,
> Till he unseam'd him from the nave to th'chaps,
> And fix'd his head upon the battlements.

(1.2.19–23)

Macbeth, fighting his way to his chief adversary, Macdonwald, has ripped him open from belly to throat. At word of this feat, Duncan exclaims, "O valiant cousin! *Worthy gentleman!*"

Words shift according to context. A gentleman in this play is one who is spectacularly good at unseaming opponents. That is cardinal, while the implications of culture, education, and breeding are irrelevant. Macbeth's exploit evokes "valiant cousin!" from the King, an admiring admission and claim of kinship. Kinship itself depends on unseaming here: blood is allied to the warrior's prowess, which holds together the community. The primitive Scotland of *Macbeth* looks upon social rank in ways far removed from, say, Windsor, Padua, or even Elsinore.

Although stage history has instances of modern-dress productions—Sir Barry Jackson's and Komisarjevsky's—*Macbeth* is essentially a play of the Dark Ages and should be placed there. The Beowulf-type loyalties of the tribe are the morality that Macbeth violates. What we see are the *origins* of class, rather than the later developments of class. The society of *Macbeth* is regulated by warrior-leaders and followers, whose loyalty is the only guarantor of the tribe's existence.

Loyalty is the prime virtue of such an era, and it needs an imaginative effort to reclaim it from the past. *Loyalty* today refers to something different; it is almost a concealed metaphor. It may be the code word of a political leader, calling upon supporters not to transfer their backing to another contender. This is far removed from a time when the tribal leader really did defend his people against a foreign invasion (which is what the Norwegians mount here), and keep some kind of order in a primitive land. "The service and the loyalty I owe," Macbeth's submission to Duncan (1.4.22), is more than a form of words. It is the principle upon which the community depends.

The society pictured in *Macbeth* is easily described as pre-feudal, with relations based on personal obligation. It seems however to be in transition to a later, feudal type of social organization, in which blood ties, though important, are not the only determinants of position. The crux is the scene in Duncan's palace at Forres, when he makes the announcement concerning the succession:

> Sons, kinsmen, thanes,
> And you whose places are the nearest, know
> We will establish our estate upon
> Our eldest, Malcolm, whom we name hereafter
> The Prince of Cumberland; which honor must
> Not unaccompanied invest him only,
> But signs of nobleness, like stars, shall shine
> On all deservers.
>
>   (1.4.35–42)

The announcement puts a sharp question to Macbeth: either he deals with the Cumberland problem shortly, or it will defeat him. And it can also be taken as a personal affront to Macbeth, this sudden declaration of the succession. The interest lies in the social arrangements Duncan plans for the realm and in their underlying sanctions. At least two major points can be inferred. First, Malcolm has undergone some kind of rite of passage previous to the announcement, which can only have been his participation in the battle. Although he has not done particularly well in it—the Sergeant apparently saved him from being taken prisoner ("fought/ Gainst my captivity") still, he was there and passed the test: the future king must be battle-worthy. Second, the elevation of Malcolm brings with it corresponding rewards for supporters, "On all deservers." To avoid jealousies and perhaps future rebellions, titles will be granted with discrimination as sweeteners. Rank in this analysis is simply a means of buying off future disaffection, cash down.

A social paradox emerges, here and throughout the crucial scenes in *Macbeth*. Disloyalty is the primal sin, and Macbeth admits as much in his soliloquy: "He's here in double trust:/First, as I am his kinsman and his subject—/Strong both against the deed; then, as his host . . ." (1.7.12–14). On the other hand, there is a great deal of disloyalty around. The late Thane of Cawdor, suborned no doubt by dollar-rich Norwegians (1.2.64), stands for that: "He was a gentleman on whom I built/An absolute trust" (1.4.13–14). It seems that loyalty and disloyalty are the reactivating impulses of this society, and Duncan's public pronouncement implicitly admits this. He cannot take loyalty for granted.

What then makes a rebel and murderer of Macbeth? "Ambition" is not really sufficient as a labeling trait, and Lady Macbeth sees it as not dominant in him: "Art not without ambition" (1.5.16). "Perception of opportunity" is perhaps nearer. The general savagery of life has already made him a killer, if not a murderer: that is a predisposing factor. Beyond that is another social value, of even deeper origin, but obviously related to the social order of this play: masculinity. "I dare do all that may become a *man*;/Who dares do more, is none," says Macbeth, in the decisive scene with Lady Macbeth. And she quells him with her reply:

> What beast was't then
> That made you break this enterprise to me?
> When you durst do it, then you were a *man*;
> And to be more than what you were, you would
> Be so much more the *man*.
>
> (1.7.46–51)

Underneath *gentleman*, the class of warrior-leader, is *man*, the warrior himself.

It is this sense of "man" that Lady Macbeth fortifies. She seems the archetype of the socially ambitious wife who drives her husband beyond his limits. But that may be too simple a reading. He consults her, and she finds the winning arguments: in the symbiosis of marriage, who comes first? "The Macbeths need to be married," as Sybil Thorndike used to say, meaning that the actors need to impart a sense of relationship. Relationship is motivation, in *Macbeth* especially. Lady Macbeth's presence, as well as the subtext of her arguments, lends a sexual coloration to the decisive encounter. The concealed argument is that a *man* must be so to other men, and to his wife. The one sense affirms the other.

Again and again, "manhood" surfaces for inspection as the principle of conduct by which the dramatis personae demand to be judged. Macbeth projects the value even upon the Murderers he hires: "Now, if you have a station in the file,/Not i'th'worst rank of manhood, say't" (3.1.101–2). "Dispute it like a man," says Malcolm to Macduff when the news of his family's slaughter breaks. "This tune goes manly," is his commendation of Macduff. "But like a man he died," is the epitaph on Young Siward whose father, in Roman fashion, accepts the tribute to a valiant brief life. To show cowardice is the worst of all, and Macbeth dies in that belief.

The public aspect of social rank is given a single extended view in the scenes of Macbeth's reign, the banquet scene. As so often in the tragedies there is a domestic, even a bourgeois dimension to an event of public magnitude. Lady Macbeth's disastrous dinner party must evoke echoes of many less spectacular fiascos. It starts as a place dinner, "You know your own degrees, sit down," where the host, however, decides to move around. "Ourself will mingle with society/And play the humble host" (3.4.3–4) is a rather odd confusion of conventions, making it for Macbeth something of a buffet occasion. The host is distracted by news and neglects his guests. Worse, he dismays the company with a passionate fit, causing the hostess to cover up for him:

> Sit, worthy friends. My lord is often thus,
> And hath been from his youth. Pray you, keep seat.
> The fit is momentary; upon a thought
> He will be well again.
>
> (3.4.53–56)

The host pulls himself together and tries to restore the evening with a toast, "I drink to th'general joy o'th'whole table" (3.4.89), but lapses again into his fit. Lady Macbeth tries once more:

> Think of this, good peers,
> But as a thing of custom. 'Tis no other;
> Only it spoils the pleasure of the time.
>
> (3.4.96–98)

But it is now over, and the tone of her next remarks acknowledges the defeat: "You have displac'd the mirth, broke the good meeting,/With most admir'd disorder." Even her nerve has now snapped, and the guests are bidden to get out, fast: "At once, good night./Stand not upon the order of your going,/But go at once." Exclude the apparition of Banquo, visible only to Macbeth, and what is left is a failed dinner party not a league away from the worst experiences of the audience. It is really the play's climax for Macbeth, "*unmanned* in folly," and for his wife, cheated of her social triumph in what should be the moment of grandeur.

The last moments of *Macbeth* are the individual against the social order. Macbeth dies alone, his self-image the bear tied to the stake. All that is left is a final spurt of fighting rage against Macduff. For Malcolm, the inheritor of the new order, the arrangements are an improved version of those proposed by his father at Forres:

> We shall not spend a large expense of time
> Before we reckon with your several loves,
> And make us even with you. My Thanes and kinsmen,
> Henceforth be Earls, the first that ever Scotland
> In such an honor nam'd.
>
> (5.8.60–64)

"Reckon with" means "reward you for". There is to be no delay. Not only will titles be bestowed, a new title will be created: Earl. Men of high rank will henceforth trace their descent from those who supported Malcolm in his victory over the tyrant Macbeth. And all is to be consecrated at Scone. "It is very interesting," remarks Peter Hall, "that the politically adroit, more modern man, Malcolm, does not engage in hand-to-hand fighting; that is left to Macduff."[12] Malcolm has left his warrior days behind. So there is a social progress in the outcome of the tragedy. The anarchy of individual will has been defeated, and the victors solidify their triumph with titles.

CHAPTER SIX

The Problem Plays

ALL'S WELL THAT ENDS WELL

> A poor physician's daughter my wife! Disdain
> Rather corrupt me ever!
>
> (2.3.113–14)

There is no getting away from the crux of *All's Well That Ends Well*. Everything comes down to this explosive rejection. Bertram, Count of Roussillon, will have none of Helena, a gentlewoman and daughter to Gerard de Narbon. *All's Well* is focused on class as is no other play in the canon save *Coriolanus*. And yet it is not clear what the crux means.

To get at Bertram's rejection of Helena one has to cast it. Of the variations possible in staging, consider the following two scenarios:

Scenario 1. Helena is played by the most radiantly attractive young actress available to the company. She approaches the role as though it were Rosalind, to which part she has ambitions. That makes Bertram an Orlando who has the bad taste to decline his fate. Bertram is played by an actor of average looks who is unable to generate much sympathy for his plight. The result is foreordained. At the King's command, the audience will ask: What is the young fool waiting for? Why doesn't he accept the fortune lavished on him by the gods? Away with outmoded distinctions!

Scenario 2. Helena is played by an actress of less lustrous parts, who is able to mask her ambitions for Rosalind or Portia. She is not the natural focus of audience devotion, which the great Shakespearean parts are. Bertram is taken by a handsome and appealing young actor, somewhat more distinguished in bearing than the King's choice of consort, who knows how to tone down the most offensive lines and play up those which support his position. He deploys his charm, of which Evelyn Waugh tells us to beware, but which is a low professional necessity for actors. The audience will now judge matters differently. Why shouldn't the young man make his own choice? It is what the audience demands for itself.

Setting aside the professional charm of the actor playing Bertram, there's a case for him developed in the lines and context of the rejection. Here is a young man brought up at home in the provinces, glimpsing court life for the first time, with all its exciting vistas of military service in Italy where he can find out if what they say about Italian girls is really true (2.1.19). To be ordered home to breed, not even with the girl next door, but with a ward brought up under the same roof—that's hard. Then consider the peer group aspect (in both senses). Helena is paraded in the court scenes before four young lords, "This youthful parcel/Of noble bachelors" (2.3.50–51). The young courtiers stand in line, ready to do their duty, but rather hoping that they will not need to be of, well, service. Their words are polished enough, but Lafeu's comments are unequivocal: "Do they all deny her? . . . These boys are boys of ice; they'll none of her" (2.3.84–89). Lafeu, like the audience, generously wishes right to be done. Those in the front line of social progress hope that someone else will supply the heroics. There are four social analogues to Bertram, and none of them instinctively wants to make the choice that is wished upon them. In this they may well be reflecting a prejudice common to the nobility. Lawrence Stone tells us that "as late as the middle of the seventeenth century a gentleman was refusing the offer of marriage with the daughter of a rich doctor since 'the very thought of the clyster-pipes did nauseate his stomach.' " [1]

Then, take the words. In the crises of human decision, Shakespeare always plots the moves with great care. When Hamlet declines to kill Claudius at prayer, the reasons he gives are already pre-empted by "Now might I do it pat" ["but I won't"], which is the instinct at work, not reason. So here, Bertram's first reaction to the royal command is:

> My wife, my liege! I shall beseech your Highness,
> In such a business give me leave to use
> The help of mine own eyes.
>
> (2.3.104–6)

This is not unreasonable, surely. In Tyrone Guthrie's production, says Tynan, "the young man's initial reaction is to treat the whole matter as a joke; he cannot believe that the daughter of a medical practitioner could seriously contemplate marrying into the aristocracy." [2] The next exchange is even:

> *King*:   Know'st thou not, Bertram,
>   What she has done for me?

> *Bertram*:   Yes, my good lord,
> But never hope to know why I should marry her.
>
>   (2.3.106–08)

This is good honest selfishness, on a raw human level: why should *I* pay *your* debts?

> *King*:   Thou know'st she has rais'd me from my sickly bed.
> *Bertram*: But follows it, my lord, to bring me down
>   Must answer for your raising? I know her well:
>   She had her breeding at my father's charge.
>   A poor physician's daughter my wife! Disdain
>   Rather corrupt me ever!
>
>   (2.3.109–114)

The King's "rais'd" triggers off the Count's "bring me down": one impulse activates the counterimpulse. The reasons now follow, charged with social contempt but also with exasperation at the royal command that has mobilized the cadres of reasons.

Social contempt, as Shakespeare shows throughout his work, is linked with an angry reaction to challenge. That is what the terms are used for. "A poor physician's daughter" is not the same thing as a generalized disdain for medical families in straitened circumstances. It is a specific reaction to a woman publicly forced upon the speaker, a problem that, Bertram might well feel, should never happen to anyone. But what are the feelings that precede his reasons?

We come to sex. There is no question of Bertram's physical attraction for Helena, as she herself makes plain:

>   'Twas pretty, though a plague,
> To see him every hour; to sit and draw
> His arched brows, his hawking eye, his curls,
> In our heart's table—
>
>   (1.1.86–89)

This is the language of overwhelming physical desire, *Vénus toute entière à sa proie attachée*. But Venus, as Shakespeare well knew, had her problems with Adonis. Desire cannot guarantee its reciprocal, and there is no trace whatsoever of attraction on Bertram's side. During the opening scene, his single address to Helena has a cold hauteur: "Be comfortable to my mother, your mistress, and make much of her." The reminder in "your mistress," a phrase with parallels elsewhere in *All's Well*, implies, among other things, "know your place." Some vestigial instinct is stirring here. If one substitutes "adopted daughter" for "ward," which is Helena's official category, one can see that adoptions are not always popular with the rest of the family. There is between Bertram and Helena nothing of that easy-going raillery that Parolles and Helena fall into, in the same scene. The subtextual suggestion is that this raillery comes from a perceived social parity: two outsiders together in the great house. But Bertram is decidedly aloof. One can find motives, but the main line is easy and surely incontestable: Bertram simply doesn't like Helena.

The real problem now emerges: the relation of class to sex. How does one cut the crystal here? The given, I think, is Bertram's distaste for Helena. But that is the manifestation, and the roots are obscure. Has class disabled the sexual component of the relationship? In other words, does Bertram find Helena impossible *because* she is "a poor physician's daughter"? Or is sex the essential difficulty, manifesting itself through class?

The problem widens. Helena can be read as a Shavian New Woman, an implacable Life Force stalking her man until he succumbs out of sheer exhaustion. Or she can be seen as needing to expiate her own sense of social guilt, "That I should love a bright particular star/And think to wed it, he is so above me" (1.1.84–85). Certainly, anyone who chooses the Grizelda role can expect hard times. Bertram is granted, as it were, a kind of license in which to discharge his brutalities. My point is that Helena and Bertram fit each other rather well, their formation offering more long-term prospects than an observer might conclude. Helena's report on their night together is a rare sexual document in the canon:

> But, O strange men!
> That can such sweet use make of what they hate,
> When saucy trusting of the cozen'd thoughts
> Defiles the pitchy night. So lust doth play
> With what it loathes, for that which is away.
>
> (4.4.21–25)

The makings of a deal are here. The resonances of "strange" and "play" suggest a dimension of the first night that will have to be re-created. Bertram's chosen partners are Diana and Maudlin (Lafeu's daughter); what he gets is Helena. She will always be a mental substitute for "that which is away." The future has its possibilities, but no one would offer a confident prognosis, certainly not the King, in "All yet seems well."

The frictions between Bertram and Helena do not in the end threaten the play's account of social order. Whatever else *All's Well* is, it is not a rejection of the claims of aristocracy. Time and again it proposes models of conduct that events do not subvert. The French court, the guarantor of tradition, is guided by a civilized and percipient monarch with a shrewd sense of the adjustments every system must make to survive. His praise of the dead Count of Roussillon, Bertram's father, is definitive:

> Who were below him
> He us'd as creatures of another place;
> And bow'd his eminent top to their low ranks,
> Making them proud of his humility
> In their poor praise he humbled.
>
> (1.2.41–45)

Equally, the Countess is presented as a living model. "She illustrates," says Robert Speaight, "the relaxed protocol and quiet courtesies of a life lived deep in the country; an aristocrat with a quick eye for the *arriviste*."[3] She is also vastly more liberal than her son, and well inclined to look kindly upon Helena but without making false promises. The Countess and Lafeu are the old school at its best. Consider, for example, their beautifully struck duet on that delicate problem of stopping over for the night:

> *Countess*: I have letters that my son will be here tonight.
> I shall beseech your lordship to remain with me
> till they meet together.
> *Lafeu*: Madam, I was thinking with what manners I might
> safely be admitted.
> *Countess*: You need but plead your honorable privilege.
> *Lafeu*: Lady, of that I have made a bold charter; but,
> I thank my God, it holds yet.
>
> (4.5.77–84)

The air of gallantry here, as of two who remember an unspoken and perhaps unacted past, is enchanting.

It is in this context that Helena's submissiveness should be read. The order to which she aspires, and to which she cannot admit her aspirations, is shown as polished, benign, deeply respectful of life as expressed through its forms. The paradox of Helena's story is that only through knowing her place can she rise. Her own account of matters is

> The Count Roussillon cannot be my brother:
> I am from humble, he from honored name;
> No note upon my parents, his all noble.
> My master, my dear lord he is; and I
> His servant live, and will his vassal die.
>
> (1.3.146–50)

And that sense of relationship is clearly transferred, more or less intact, to her marriage with Bertram. The formal standing of the matter is plain. The King has the right to create in Helena title, "honor and wealth from me." Bertram, crushed, admits it:

> I find that she which late
> Was in my nobler thoughts most base is now
> The praised of the King; who, so ennobled,
> Is as 'twere born so.
>
> (2.3.168–71)

Virtue and honor are thus united by the King. What remains seems to me best categorized as a sexual rather than a social problem.

So far so good, if somewhat homiletic. Life, however, is more than the approved assimilation of the talented middle classes into the upper echelons. We need an outsider, and a disgrace. Parolles is the man. He is, says Jonathan Miller, "the kind of young man the Countess wishes her son would not bring back to the house." Guthrie made him the archetypal bounder, described by Kenneth Tynan as "a breezy, overdressed road-house cad, fore-doomed to failure in his social climbing by the possession of an accent that is ever so slightly 'off.'"[4] I am not sure this is quite right. Parolles must be able to take in even Lafeu for a while, as Lafeu admits. He is a plausible fellow, hence Lafeu's indignation—which is partly with himself: "You are more saucy with lords and honorable personages than the commission of your birth and virtue gives you heraldry" (2.3.254–56). Parolles's essential crime is that unlike Helena, he does not know his station. This is compounded by his disgraceful conduct with the International Brigade in Italy, but that is the occasion of his public unmasking, not the basic offense itself.

Parolles, in fact, contains an engaging analysis of how the system works.

Rebecca West's phrase for Michael Arlen, "every other inch a gentleman," hits him off nicely. Parolles gets there by sheer plausibility and push, attaching himself to a younger man of great rank. He overplays his hand with a shrewd old aristocrat, and is put down badly. (And is, if I mistake not, the first victim in English literature of that venerable insult, Lafeu's "Pray you, sir, who's his tailor?" 2.5.15.) The pattern holds in Italy, where his fellow officers conspire to trap and unmask him. There follows his great existential manifesto:

> Captain I'll be no more;
> But I will eat and drink and sleep as soft
> As captain shall. Simply the thing I am
> Shall make me live.
>
> (4.3.308–11)

This is unaccommodated man, forcibly divested by rank—"Captain I'll be no more"—and discovering that there is life beyond rank. And so there is. Lafeu, finding a Parolles shorn of pretensions (and therefore purged of contempt) is prepared to take him up again: "Sirrah, inquire further after me. I had talk of you last night. Though you are a fool and a knave, you shall eat" (5.2.49–50). Parolles's edgily ambidextrous performance during the King's investigation secures his rehabilitation, and Lafeu confirms him as one with whom to collapse into prose:

> Mine eyes smell onions; I shall weep anon.
> Good Tom Drum, lend me a handkercher.
> So, I thank thee. Wait on me me home, I'll make sport
> with thee; let thy curtsies alone, they are scurvy ones.
>
> (5.3.314–17)

Parolles finishes up as a private jester to Lafeu, holding much the same position as Lavache does with the Countess. It is a wry final comment on social order. The system can assimilate a penitent Pretender, too. The French court of *All's Well That Ends Well*, apparently ruled by form, is penetrable to a variety of social talents.

TROILUS AND CRESSIDA

Buried a millimeter under the surface of *Troilus and Cressida* is its major class issue, the discrepancy in rank between Troilus and Cressida. It is never discussed and always there. Linked with class is another issue that is never discussed: marriage. The lovers skirt around these unmentionables and in the end are defined by them.

It is obvious that the play calls on two stereotypes of folklore, Faithful Troilus and Faithless Cressida, and allows these stereotypes to go forward on the evidence. You can believe in them if you want to. Troilus does, and so for that matter does Cressida. Equally, the play subverts the stereotypes by suggesting a subtly supportive case for Cressida and a subtly hostile account of Troilus. The cases can be sketched with a few blunt questions. What is Cressida supposed to do for herself, the only woman in a military camp, without a protector? Why does Troilus let her go? What is the nature of his commitment toward her, and what right does he have to complain when she turns? The stereotypes clearly have some answering to do for themselves.

Another approach is through the forms of the plot. As everyone sees, *Troilus and Cressida* suggests a replay of *Romeo and Juliet*, with the Nurse's role taken over by Pandarus. But in *Romeo and Juliet* the question of marriage is raised early on, by Juliet. Romeo assents instantly. He loves her, his intentions are honorable, the Montagues and Capulets inhabit the same social plane. There is no mental barrier to marriage, whatever the physical obstacles. Nothing like that happens in *Troilus and Cressida*. What Pandarus is called on to set up, what Troilus wishes and Cressida assents to, is quite different. It is never named, but its status is assumed all round. It is an affair.

The boulevard-comedy tone of Trojan life implies an affair as a natural feature of the landscape. Nothing else fits the vital tonal scene of Act 3, scene 1 (the only scene in which Helen appears), with its remorseless café chatter and endless talk of love. "This *love* will undo us all," Helen sighs. Of Cressida's sexual past nothing is known (in part, because she insists with Pandarus on her own privacy), but her soliloquy at the end of Act 1, scene 2 has the knowingness of experience. Troilus is young ("he never saw three and twenty"), and presumably is not a sexual ingénu. "I am giddy, expectation whirls me round" is the speech of a connoisseur of the flesh, concerned lest he "shall lose distinction in my joys" (3.2.26). Pandarus has no doubt of his mission, which is to bring them to bed. He does so in a scene that offers a parody of marriage as the broker-priest joins the hands of the lovers. "Amen," they all cry to his sense of the union. This odd ceremony makes it more than a mere bedding, if something less than a marriage. What is it, then?

The shape of the event is dimly visible through Cressida's form of address: "Prince Troilus, I have lov'd you night and day/For many weary months" (3.2.111–12). Troilus is a prince, son of King Priam, by birth a member of the highest Council of Troy. Cressida is daughter to the renegade Calchas, a priest. She is certainly well connected. Pandarus, who when visiting (3.1) is "Lord Pandarus," is her uncle, and refers to her as "cousin" (the usual term of aristocratic kinship). But Pandarus, when concerned to put a servant right about these matters, fixes the standings definitively: "It should seem, fellow, that thou hast not seen the Lady Cressida. I come to speak with Paris from the Prince Troilus" (3.1.36–37). That is it, for practical purposes. A prince of the blood royal has an affair with a lady who is well connected but not of exalted rank. Cressida's deportment toward Troilus (her calling him "my lord") indicates not only shyness but also the respect due to one of his rank.

The affair is consummated. Neither then nor later is there any talk of marriage. In itself this calls for no special comment. If all affairs were predicated on a discussion of marriage, the operations of this world would be much circumscribed. Still, Troilus does raise it, oddly enough as a hypothetical possibility during the Trojan council scene, "I take today a wife," adding "and my election/Is led on in the conduct of my will" (2.2.61–62). The will is absent here, evidently. One can of course take Jan Kott's line that this is a wartime liaison in which the question of marriage never arises: "These war-time lovers have been given just one night. And even that night has been spoilt."[5] Much as I respect Kott's commentaries on Shakespeare, this seems a misreading. "War" is not a block category, nor has it spoiled the night. The war is a long-term feature of the scene rather than a real threat to personal relations. The Troy of *Troilus and Cressida* resembles nothing so much as the Paris of 1914–18, a great and opulent capital city near the fighting but also safe from it. Life goes on much as before for the wealthy (to the stupefaction of those on leave from the front). The purely military aspects of *Troilus and Cressida* suggest a tournament, where deeds of knightly prowess can conveniently be enacted on a day-to-day basis and from which people habitually return unscathed (the happy consequence of wearing armor). Paris, for one, has a relaxed attitude toward this fighting business: "I would fain have arm'd today, but my Nell would not have it so" (3.1.129–30). The Trojan War in intimate close-up! This is the supreme epic of antiquity, fought over immortal Helen—and its main beneficiary cannot even get out of bed to fight for her. His Nell has rung.

The idea of war has to be qualified here. Until the death of Hector, it does not seem genuinely to threaten the participants. When the lovers part, Cressida in no way touches on the dangers which her warrior-lover might be supposed to incur. Troilus has no doubt that he can handle the sentries. It is a quiet sector of the line. The war has become an institution, bringing administrative and personal inconvenience rather than anguish and loss.

Act 4, scene 2: Troy, the courtyard of Pandarus's house. Troilus and Cressida enter together, with Troilus urging his lover to go back to bed: "Dear, trouble not yourself; the morn is cold." It is an early getaway. Cressida helpfully offers to call Pandarus down to open the gates, a suggestion Troilus finds distasteful: "Trouble him not." It is early for Pandarus-type jokes. Twice more Troilus tries to get Cressida to leave him: "To bed, to bed . . . I prithee now, to bed." A touch overanxious, this, eliciting a pouting "Are you aweary of me?" But what an idea!

> O Cressida! but that the busy day,
> Wak'd by the lark, hath rous'd the ribald crows,
> And dreaming night will hide our joys no longer,
> I would not from thee.
>
> (4.2.8–11)

The crows would have been even more ribald had they stayed around to watch Troilus's departure. "You will catch cold, and curse me." A moment later it is all up, for Pandarus is awake and the resigned Troilus can only say, "It is your uncle." The first phase of the getaway is over, and it is a failure.

This heartless sketch of the morning after, the young man stealing away at first light without, so far as one can tell, breakfast, must give pause to anyone placing the idyll among the great romances in history. Troilus is obviously embarrassed, and anxious not to be found at Pandarus's house. That anxiety is shared by Cressida, for when the knocking is heard, "I would not for half Troy have you seen here." The discovery or imputation of the liaison would, both feel, harm *his* reputation—not hers.

The crux follows immediately. Aeneas has to break down some loyal resistance from Pandarus, but gets through to Troilus with the bad news of the exchange of Antenor for Cressida. And Troilus's response, on which the play turns, is "Is it so concluded?" (4.2.66). No protest, no anger, no attempt to see Priam to get the agreement reversed! And this is the man who in the council scene argued passionately for a war policy. Troilus can contend for grand strategy, but not for a personal favor from his own relations. The reason is contained within the deadly line Shakespeare gives him: "and, my lord Aeneas, /We met by chance; you did not find me here" (4.2.70–71). This is admirable self-possession, but it is not necessary to read the line as pure calculation; it is the pattern of conduct that counts. Troilus, as Act 4, scene 2 develops, is eager to get away from Cressida, ready to acquiesce in the arrangements that will take her away, and anxious to preserve his reputation. The liaison, as he places it, is neither for marriage nor acknowledgement. A sexual accord can be presumed. The available interpretation is therefore that the disparity in rank is crucial. It is a case of social embarrassment.

How does Troilus manage the feat of self-deception contained in their parting? The repository of his beliefs is a chivalric ideology, much on display with the combatants of both sides. It is a value system whose key words are "troth," "pledge," "knight," and other properties of a knightly code belonging to the world of Froissart and Malory. Chivalry is always an anachronism, as Achilles demonstrates with mathematical if not physical elegance. Nevertheless, it is accepted by Greeks and Trojans. Hector, in his challenge to the Greeks ("He hath a lady wiser, fairer, truer, /Than even Greek did couple in his arms" [1.3.275–76]), invokes the language and values of the Middle Ages, even if "the splinter of a lance" does not occur. Ajax accepts the challenge and its assumptions and is ready enough to pause after a few blows so that the real business of the truce—an inter-army drinking session—can begin. Within this mode of military/aristocratic chivalry, Shakespeare does not pursue social distinctions. It is enough that all subscribe to it, though they follow it with differing degrees of devotion.

When, therefore, Troilus views Cressida with Diomedes in the discovery scene (5.2), he is the victim of this ideology. He has imagined that talk of "faith," "pledge," and "troth" has bound Cressida to him for as long as he requires, even though he has given no commitment bar a glove and is powerless to do anything that will protect Cressida. His system fractures, with "This is, and is not, Cressida," but in truth it was no system, merely a set of postures. It is fitting that Troilus should lose Cressida to Diomedes, one of the play's few realists. His epitome of the war, the "hell of pain and world of charge" (4.1.59), is cut with diamond on glass. The end is a refutation of two dreams of honor, Troilus's and Hector's. The one reinforces the other. "Pale Ebenezer thought it wrong to fight;/But Roaring Bill, who killed him, thought it right." Belloc on pacifism is much like Shakespeare on chivalry. To confuse chivalry with warfare is to accept a troubadour's version of relations between the sexes.

MEASURE FOR MEASURE

There are at least two kinds of problem child: first the genuinely abnormal child, whom no efforts will ever bring back to normality; and second, the child who is interesting and complex rather than abnormal: apt indeed to be a problem for parents and teachers but destined to fulfilment in the larger scope of adult life. Now *All's Well* and *Measure for Measure* are like the first problem child: there is something radically schizophrenic about them. *Hamlet* and *Troilus and Cressida* are like the second problem child, full of interest and complexity but divided within themselves only in the eyes of those who have misjudged them.

> E. M. W. Tillyard, *Shakespeare's*
> *Problem Plays*[6]

Measure for Measure is the problem child par excellence. It seems to change direction halfway through in Act 3, scene 1, where a comedy of intrigue starts to emerge from a tragic chrysalis. The problems of judgment laid upon the audience are acute. And the conclusion can leave the audience aghast at the pairings. What is Isabella to say to the Duke's proposal? She says nothing, and speculation has been rampant of recent years. "I think," says William Empson, "that this is a complete and successful work of the master, but the way is a very odd one, because it amounts to pretending to write a romantic comedy and is in fact keeping the audience's teeth slightly but increasingly on edge."[7] "Teeth on edge" is exactly right for the impression this play creates. It starts early and leaves off late. Setting aside the obscurities of the opening scene, *Measure for Measure* starts to emit its malign social signals in scene two, with the gentlemen.

The pox was the great Elizabethan joke, and I suppose there could scarcely be a comedy of this era without some honest mirth over venereal disease. But there is something gratingly unfunny in the keen, competitive way in which Lucio and his friends discuss the side effects of their sexual athleticism. "Behold, behold, where Madam Mitigation comes! I have purchased as many diseases under her roof as come to" is Lucio's claim, before being interrupted by his friend's estimate, "three thousand dolours a year" with a pun on "dollars." Sex may be an expensive and painful business, but no sacrifice is too heavy for its devotees. Among the young gentlemen here, the brothel is the accepted medium for their class recreation.

Lucio, as this dialogue makes clear, is no solitary enthusiast but a member in good standing of the young men's sporting club. He is representative of his class, if an extremist—"*a Fantasticke*" as the Folio listing puts it in its dramatis personae. What is one to make of him then? Shaw, in his incisive way, coupled him with Benedick to the latter's disadvantage:

Lucio is much more of a gentleman than Benedick, because he keeps his coarse sallies for coarse people. Meeting one woman, he says humbly "Gentle and fair: your brother kindly greets you. Not to be weary with you, he's in prison." Meeting another, he hails her sparklingly with "How now? which of your hips has the more profound sciatica?" The one woman is a lay sister, the other a prostitute. Benedick or Mercutio would have cracked their jokes on the lay sister, and been held up as gentlemen of rare wit and excellent discourse for it.[8]

Shaw is technically in error here—it is the First Gentleman, not Lucio, who asks Mistress Overdone the "sciatica" question. No doubt the line was reassigned in the performance that Shaw reviewed. Substantially, though, he is right. Lucio is a different person with Isabella, and the rest of the world. Linguistically, he has two modes; the decent, rather unctuous, "best behavior" verse for public occasions, and the bawdy, witty prose that is his preferred speech. This seems an acceptable division. And yet there's a strange moment when Lucio, at the nunnery, encounters the novitiate nun—he does not yet know her to be Isabella—with

> Hail, virgin, if you be, as those cheek-roses
> Proclaim you are no less.
>
> (1.4.16–17)

In effect, he says "You look healthy, so you must be a virgin." As a man-of-the-world's address to a stranger, this leaves something to be desired. So, no doubt, does the society in which that joke can begin to make sense. Is he nervous? A moment later, learning of Isabella's identity, he overcompensates with "I hold you as a thing enskied and sainted/By your renouncement," which places the virtuous woman on a pedestal. The signals continue to jar and reassure. Lucio is obviously being a good friend to Claudio, doing what he can to pull strings for commutation of sentence. But when Pompey appeals, there is nothing doing:

> *Pompey*: I hope, sir, your good worship will be my bail?
> *Lucio*:   No, indeed will I not, Pompey; it is not the wear.
>
> (3.2.67–69)

Heartless beast, Pompey might well reflect. "Not the wear" makes it a matter of fashion, morally neutral. It is a hard little cameo of class relations: Lucio is on perfectly good terms with Pompey, but at the sight of trouble makes a prudent distinction between servant and service industry, which can look after itself. The despairing Pompey makes one more appeal as he is led off, "You will not bail me then, sir?" and gets an unambiguous answer from the unfeeling Lucio, "Then, Pompey, nor now" (3.2.75–76). There can be no public acknowledgement of the services that Pompey has rendered the *ton* of Vienna. The services are in any case illegal.

It makes no sense to examine class relations in this play in an abstract or general way, since *Measure for Measure* is unremittingly focused on sex, and its language, people, and plot are all saturated with sexuality. In *Othello*, the sexuality is on the surface (except for a couple of Iago's soliloquies). Here it is everywhere, but prohibited, punished, repressed. The café chatter of the gentlemen in 1.2 is one side of things: the proclamation "All houses in the suburbs of Vienna must be pluck'd down" is the other. It is one of those periodic crackdowns on vice that authority is accustomed to administer, when archaic laws are put to use. The plot of *Measure for Measure* is sometimes thought of as outrageously improbable, but almost all states retain laws that have not been prosecuted for many years. (Massachusetts and other New England states have, for example, had on their statute books until very recently punishments for adultery and other sexual offenses.) There is nothing inherently improbable in the plot of *Measure for Measure*, merely a dramatic intensification of a commonplace of legal and social history. The movement against vice brings with it an exposure of the ways in which Viennese society orders its sexual affairs, and itself.

Two social institutions are on view here, prostitution and marriage. They are the foreground and background of the composition. Prostitution, according to the Duke, has been thriving, yet Mistress Overdone reports a recession in the trade: "Thus, what with the sweat, what with the gallows, and what with poverty, I am custom-shrunk" (1.2.78–80). Layoffs will be necessary, and Pompey is reduced to temporary employment as a barman (tapster), a resource not unknown to later societies. Nevertheless, those close to the trade feel that it will come through its current difficulties. "The vice is of a great kindred; it is well allied," observes Lucio (3.2.94), nicely suggesting the trade's powerful friends. As for marriage, two case histories are supplied here. Angelo, once contracted to Marina, has broken off the spousals on hearing of the loss of her dowry. He alleges that "her reputation was disvalued/In levity" (5.1.219–20). Claudio and Julietta, having exchanged vows, have consummated their union but not gone through a church ceremony: the clandestine arrangement is designed to protect the "dower/Remaining in the coffer of her friends" (1.2.143–44) to which Julietta is entitled. The factor common to both unions is a substantial dowry. Without heavy underlining, Shakespeare indicates the connections between money and sex, licit and illicit, in Vienna.

Vienna suggests a two-story, upstairs-downstairs image of matters sexual. Downstairs is the brothel, the vicious underworld that contains the sexual activities of the Viennese. To it is annexed, as it were, the garden house within the vineyard, part of "the garden circummur'd with brick" (4.1.26), the discreet trysting place where Angelo makes his clandestine appointment. Secrecy is the characteristic of these people. Upstairs is marriage, of which the play offers no visible example. It is an ideal, which has been debauched by Claudio and Julietta.

These two are interesting, not because of any particular individuality they possess, but because they subscribe wholeheartedly to the code that condemns them. Claudio and Julietta are conventional people, which is useful when one wants to learn about conventions. Claudio's entrance line tells a great deal: "Fellow, why dost thou show me thus to th'world?" (1.2.110). This is a shame culture. Claudio's agony at being paraded through the streets reflects Angelo's "special charge" in the matter: the one punishes, the other admits the pain. And Claudio finds great difficulty in even naming the problem to Lucio, much less discussing it. (Note that Lucio, a good friend of Claudio's, has no inkling of the relationship with Julietta.) Shame has all but silenced Claudio, and he needs euphemisms ("liberty," "a thirsty evil") even to approach the subject. There is no rebellion here, merely an appeal to his sister via Lucio to try a personal intervention. In the same way, Julietta confesses and repents (2.3) under the Friar's (Duke's) urgings. She submits to what is a short sermon on sin and shame, making without demur the required affirmation of penitence:

> I do repent me as it is an evil,
> And take the shame with joy.
>
> (2.3.35–36)

What links Julietta and Claudio is shame, the conviction that they have infringed the complex and contradictory laws on marriage. They acquiesce in the code that imputes guilt to them, if not in the severity of the sentence.

Euphemism is the key to Claudio's attitudes. The unnameable is the
thing itself. That is a condition of the gentry, but the same trait appears in
the low-life quarters—an itch for respectability. The other side of Pompey's ilk is a craving for gentility and propriety, with an instinct for
euphemism close to Claudio's. The whole social mode is caricatured in the
examination of Pompey and Froth (2.1), in which the vile offense allegedly
committed by Pompey cannot be named and is not charged. "Stewed
prunes," a notorious bordello specialty, are named with an apology "and
longing, saving your worship's presence, for stewed prunes." An impene-
trable secrecy masks the other actors in Pompey's narrative:

> *Pompey*: Very well; you being then, if you be remember'd,
>   cracking the stones of the foresaid prunes—
> *Froth*:   Ay, so I did indeed.
> *Pompey*: Why, very well; I telling you then, if you be
>   remember'd, that such a one and such a one were
>   past cure of the thing you wot of, unless they
>   kept a very good diet, as I told you—
>
> (2.1.101–9)

"And so he goes off on a branch line," remarks Brian Vickers, "showing
ludicrous gentility as he disguises the name of a certain person suffering
from a certain disease (but in his profession any fool knows what the
disease is)."[9] Pompey and Claudio have more in common than might
appear.

Abhorson adds his footnote to the mode of respectability. The public
executioner is discovered in a dilemma of some poignancy: "his office
lacks a helper" (4.2.8), but the authorities propose to appoint Pompey as
part of the Governor's rehabilitation scheme: "if you will take it on you to
assist him, it shall redeem you from your gyves" (4.2.8–10). Against the
gain to status that an assistant provides must be set his deplorable record.
Abhorson's reputation might be disvalued in levity. "A bawd, sir? Fie
upon him, he will discredit our mystery," Abhorson protests. Hanging,
after all, is a skilled trade, and the interview between Abhorson and the
trainee hangman turns on that status-claiming word, "mystery." Pompey
gets the job, but has to do all the dirty work—"Sirrah, bring Barnardine
hither . . . Go in to him and fetch him out"—while Abhorson reserves to
himself the fun of actually hanging the man. In its decorum, its bureaucratic forms, its consciousness of status, Abhorson's occupation is a
vestigial parody of the society it serves. Pompey sees it as a step up the
ladder.

There are really only two classes in *Measure for Measure*, the respectable class and the rest. This play is less interested in depicting social gradations within the over-Viennese, than in making plain the chain of authority: Duke, Angelo, Escalus, Provost, Abhorson, Pompey. All are "instruments of some more mightier power/That sets them on" (5.1.235–36), as Angelo puts it. At the end of the line come Barnardine, Ragozine, and Claudio. They are there not to be poor, but to be punished. And the essential crime of this play is sexual. Not killing, not theft, not forgery— none of these crimes is enlarged in *Measure for Measure*. The clear statement of the system is, as usual, put into Pompey's mouth. So far as he is concerned, the prison population is the brothel's clientele: "I am as well acquainted here as I was in our house of profession" (4.3.1–2), followed by a catalogue of business acquaintances, "all great doers in our trade." The brothel is the net for a range of social malefactors. So is prison.

In charge of the prison population is that archetype of the reformist Governor, the "gentle Provost." He regards Barnardine as a long-term challenge. When the Duke suggests "He wants advice"—an opening here for the Friar?—the Provost has to extinguish his hopes. "He will hear none. He hath evermore had the liberty of the prison: give him leave to escape hence, he would not" (4.2.139–41). All possible privileges, including a run of the prison, unlimited liquor, unstinted legal advice ("his friends still wrought reprieves for him"), and moral suasion in the ducal mode, all have been lavished to no avail on the hardened wretch. The liberal Governor, who needs no prodding from the ducal Home Office, has done his best but it is wasted on the old lag. *Measure for Measure* is perhaps more conservative than the penal reformers in it.

Better results may come from less ambitious forms of social direction. A key episode is the judicial hearing of 2.1. The fun of Elbow's deposition is also a neat demonstration of social control. Escalus comes out of it very well. Endlessly patient, he sticks to his examination while the irritable Angelo moves off. He does what he can to sift some sense out of the knavery and inarticulacy before him. He permits himself only a few mild jokes at the solecisms of the uneducated. He lets Pompey off, but with a warning that if he appears before him again, there will *really* be trouble. He is at pains to arrange for Elbow's replacement, without hurting the man's feelings. "How long have you been in this place of constable? . . . Alas, it hath been great pains to you: they do you wrong to put you so oft upon't" (2.1.245–53). The local householders, it seems, have paid Elbow to look after things. It is time for a change. "Look you bring me in the names of some six or seven, the most sufficient of your parish." Without fanfares or parade of authority, Escalus quietly attends to the improve-

ment of local policing in Vienna. It is Justice of the Peace's work and
society's work. Social control is an affair of making the right appoint-
ments.

The dynamics of rank are on display in the final scene, the apotheosis of
ducal power. Pairings, rewards, punishments—all are assigned as from
"power divine." The Provost is to be promoted, and Barnardine released.
The task of bringing about Barnardine's spiritual regeneration is prudently delegated by the Duke: "Friar, advise him; /I leave him to your
hand" (5.1.483–84). Some challenges are best left to one's subordinates.
The institution of marriage is to be honored by Claudio, Angelo, and
Lucio, in that order. That leaves Isabella. The pairing of the Duke and
Isabella is a demand of the form, the expectation of a romantic ending.
Yet there are certain concealed difficulties, which include their vast
disparity in rank and the possibility that a novitiate nun might have
doubts about marriage with anyone, including her moral supervisor. The
Duke has in no way broached the matter before the final scene. He does so
now in terms that again justify Empson's phrase, "setting the teeth on
edge." The Duke first hints at his intention:

> As I was then,
> Advertising and holy to your business,
> Not changing heart with habit, I am still
> Attorney'd at your service.
>
> (5.1.380–83)

Isabella, who as with Angelo is good at not understanding what men
mean, plays it back carefully: "O give me pardon, /That I, *your vassal*, have
employ'd and pain'd/Your unknown sovereignty." A moment later it is
"dear maid," "O most kind maid." After Isabella's plea for Angelo's life
(which are her last words in the play), and the revelation that Claudio
lives, the Duke gives unmistakable signs of his intentions:

> If he be like your brother, for his sake
> Is he pardon'd; and for your lovely sake
> Give me your hand and say you will be mine.

At this point the drama becomes intolerable. The gap between the needs
of fiction and the objections of reality opens wider. Why this sudden and
public proposal? Is it gaucherie, insensitivity, impulsiveness, a reliance on
rank to do the work of persuasion? At any rate, the Duke, for whatever

reason, then *drops the subject*: "But fitter time for that." A proposal is customarily the staple of conversation for a while. The Duke returns to it only in the last few lines of the play.

> Dear Isabel,
> I have a motion much imports your good;
> Which if you'll a willing ear incline,
> What's mine is yours and what is yours is mine.
>
> (5.1.532–35)

That is not a proposal, but notice to renew a proposal. It seems final. Rhymed couplet, end of scene, end of play. Only it is not the end. Whatever inflection of response is contained in Isabella's silence must be registered in the "so" that follows, the beginning of what is really the last couplet:

> So, bring us to our palace, where we'll show
> What's yet behind that's meet you all should know.

Of the possible meanings of "So," two it suggests are (a) *There* (satisfied, he takes her hand), or (b) *Very well, we'll talk about this later* (because Isabella is still unresponsive). It is always very difficult to deny a Renaissance Prince, especially when he makes an honorable offer in public. But it is conceivable that Isabella is now playing the Angelo game, one rank up.

"A great part of the grace (I confess) lay in action," as Webster remarked of *The Devil's Law-Case*. Not only the grace, but the meaning of *Measure for Measure* can only reside in performance. Shakespeare's cunning and provocative refusal to mark his score decisively means that the relations between Isabella and the Duke will be determined by the actress and actor. I cannot prejudge the outcome, of which stage history has offered widely differing versions. But the essential plotting of the conclusion seems marked. What has been veiled, suppressed, repressed in Vienna comes into the open for inspection above all in the Duke's overtures to Isabella. Marriage must be held to be about sex, and the Duke's early disclaimer ("Believe not that the dribbing dart of love/Can pierce a complete bosom" [1.3.2–3]) yields to a public admission of interest. The Duke's change of heart signals his kinship with his subjects, the other Viennese.

CHAPTER SEVEN

The Roman Plays and Timon of Athens

TITUS ANDRONICUS

Peter Brook, who in 1955 directed the play's most celebrated revival, described *Titus Andronicus* thus: "Everything in *Titus* is linked to a dark flowing current out of which surge the horrors, rhythmically and logically related—if one searches in this way one can find the expression of a powerful and eventually beautiful barbaric ritual."[1]

His judgment makes *Titus Andronicus* a ritual drama, which later practice has largely confirmed as the best way of staging the play. The horrors are central, and the director's first duty is to determine the mode of presenting them. Little seems to propose a social context for the horrors, or suggests other than a remote and barbarous past. And yet there is an early sketch for a context.

Titus Andronicus opens with an embryonic explanation for itself in Saturninus's address to the Roman Senators and Tribunes:

> Noble patricians, patrons of my right,
> Defend the justice of my cause with arms;
> And, countrymen, my loving followers,
> Plead my successive title with your swords.
> I am his first-born son that was the last
> That ware the imperial diadem of Rome;
> Then let my father's honors live in me,
> Nor wrong mine age with this indignity.
>
> (1.1.1–8)

This unadorned appeal to primogeniture is schematic in its clarity. From the authority of fathers, rooted in *patricians, patrons*, descends the *title* of the first-born son, which is imposed on *followers*. It is a clear vertical system. Set against it is Bassianus's appeal:

Romans, friends, followers, favorers of my right,
If ever Bassianus, Caesar's son,
Were gracious in the eyes of royal Rome,
Keep then this passage to the Capitol;
And suffer not dishonor to approach
The imperial seat, to virtue consecrate,
To justice, continence, and nobility;
But let desert in pure election shine;
And, Romans, fight for freedom in your choice.

                                                        (1.1.9–17)

Bassianus's plea, "let desert in pure election shine," opposes merit to primogeniture. It is the way of the future. It is also well justified, in its own terms. Saturninus is corrupt and wayward, while Bassianus is a man of honor and integrity. Still, the people would prefer Titus Andronicus to either. But Titus, granted a kingmaker's privilege, chooses "our Emperor's eldest son, /Lord Saturnine . . . Then, if you will elect by my advice, / Crown him, and say 'Long live our Emperor!'" (1.1.224–29). Patriarchy has endorsed primogeniture.

And that, really, is it. Ideas about the social origins of the tragedy go no further in this play than exposing the failings of patriarchy and primogeniture. There is a hint in the bickering between the unappetizing Chiron and Demetrius over the possession of Lavinia: "'Tis not the difference of a year or two/Makes me less gracious or thee more fortunate:/I am as able and as fit as thou" (2.1.31–33). That is Chiron, to whom his elder brother, Demetrius, makes this lofty response: "Youngling, learn thou to make some meaner choice:/Lavinia is thy elder brother's hope" (2.1.73–74). This is the precedence of louse over flea; and if one had to go on *Titus Andronicus* alone, one would say that Shakespeare regards primogeniture as an absurd system. Titus, who backs it, is a crazed patriarch. He disposes of his sons as though they were any other kind of chattel, and he kills his daughter, Lavinia, because of the shame done to her. In short, he symbolizes a system that is rigid and oppressive, but Roman society sanctions his acts, and there are no internal criticisms of Titus's conduct. In *Titus Andronicus* the patrician order needs and gets renewal from outside. Its salvation comes from a son of Titus and an army of Goths.

JULIUS CAESAR

Titus Andronicus has total power over his children. In *Julius Caesar*, that power is exercised, as it were, from beyond the grave. The later play shows a fascinating shift of angle to address the same phenomenon, patriarchy. Sons are everywhere in *Titus Andronicus*—Titus's, Tamora's, and Aaron's. In *Julius Caesar*, nobody has children. Dramatically they are excluded from the cast, and the opening procession draws attention to Calphurnia's infertility. To compensate for their lack of children, the Romans have an abundance of ancestors, all of them male. And these ancestors are living presences. "I am the son of Marcus Cato, ho!" cries young Cato, twice (5.4.4,6). "Think you I am no stronger than my sex, /Being so father'd and so husbanded?" asks Portia (2.1.296–97). "But woe the while, our fathers' minds are dead," says Cassius (1.3.82). A father in *Julius Caesar* does not have to mean an immediate progenitor, a person one actually knows. The idea of father is absorbed into *patres*, city fathers, elders; he is an ancestor, a standard of conduct, an ideal. "I, as Aeneas, our great ancestor" says Cassius (1.2.112). Even over several generations, the patriarchal grip is fastened upon the minds of the Romans. "The dead are more powerful than the living," said Fontenelle.

Honor, therefore, is a patrician's acknowledgement of the claims of ancestry. Children make no competing claims, for they do not exist. Pride of ancestry has a clear field here, and determines conduct. It is the key to Brutus from first to last. His name is the reminder of the Brutus who led the opposition to Tarquin, driving him from the throne. Not to take up the challenge, not to lead the conspiracy against Caesar, would be a betrayal of his ancestors, his name, his identity. "Shall Rome, etc," the anonymous message left for him, is an enigmatic Rorschach on which Brutus at once prints his values. Brutus is fixed in the patrician cast of mind, imbued with a sense of family duty toward his country. That is easily seen. More interesting are the ways in which he interprets his license to do his duty, and the extent to which others cede to him their own rights. The central figure of *Julius Caesar* is a study in patrician dominance, in whose personal and class traits is rooted the failure of the conspiracy.

Peter Ustinov once defined "inflexible integrity" as "a quality which has led to as many errors of judgement as any other." That locates the problem nicely. Brutus has unswerving integrity and commits many errors. But why does he make them, and why do the others let him?

The point about Brutus is not that he is wrong part of the time, or even most of the time. He is wrong *all* of the time. Most of us can claim a few correct decisions here and there. It takes a Brutus to avoid the statistical chances of occasional success that mankind is prone to. From the initial decision to join the conspiracy, to his conduct at Philippi, the play is a catalogue of Brutus's errors. And yet he never questions his own judgment, not even at the end. He feels no regret. This cast of mind is surely class-based, revealing itself through an extraordinary personal arrogance. But Brutus is not "arrogant" as the world understands it, haughty in manner. His behavior toward his slave Lucius is exemplary. But in arrogating to himself powers and rights unjustified by performance, in making undue claims for himself, Brutus is the epitome of patrician self-confidence.

His actions are inner-directed and seem unaffected by others—unless one counts proposals from others, which elicit from Brutus a veto. His key soliloquy *begins* with a decision—"it must be by his death"—and thereafter consists of a laborious shunting around of available reasons until they are acceptably in position. To call this the record of an agonized dilemma seems to me a total misreading. The choice is already made; the mental process is a search for comfortable furniture. There follows the meeting with the conspirators, during which Brutus in rapid succession overrules proposals first, to bind them by oath; second, to bring in Cicero; and third, to kill Mark Antony with Caesar. No one has thought of bringing in Caius Ligarius, till Metellus Cimber mentions him, and Brutus is happy to vouch for the man, no further discussion being needed. All this is accomplished without significant opposition from the others, who capitulate in the face of Brutus's wishes. The decision to let Mark Antony speak at Caesar's funeral, and to speak second, is Brutus's alone. Throughout, the unspoken principle is that *Brutus knows best*. Nothing can shake that conviction, not even his 100 percent record of disaster. Brutus is every inch a leader—or, more exactly, one who accepts the role of leader.

His leadership extends to his method of paying his troops, an issue explored in the quarrel scene. The encounter between what the old commentaries used to call the "realist," Cassius, and the "idealist," Brutus, is about coins, which emblematically possess two faces.

> *Brutus*:   I did send to you
>   For certain sums of gold, which you denied me;
>   For *I* can raise no money by vile means.
>
>   (4.3.69–71)

MacCallum is good on Brutus's self-righteousness here: "What does all this come to? That the superfine Brutus will not be guilty of extortion, but that Cassius may: and that Brutus will demand to share in the proceeds."[2] One can see in this an exercise of the chain of command vital to Brutus's moral well-being. It is for subordinates to nourish the leader's sense of self. Or one can see here the archetypal liberal, a man who knows the value of everything and the price of nothing. Whichever way, it is an aristocrat's insistence that the world conform to his sense of things.

In all this, class plays a decisive role. Why do the others let Brutus get away with it? They too are "noble Romans," and this is the record of their dispute within the patrician order. The only answer I can see is that Brutus is of a higher rank within that order. In *Julius Caesar* one cannot expect straightforward analogues to the class system elsewhere. Dukes, earls, and counts cannot be rendered in Roman terms. But there is family distinction, a title of nobility, which gives the patronymic "Brutus" immense standing among the conspirators and among Romans generally. "Let him be Caesar!" is the crowd's naive tribute to Brutus. The conspirators feel that they need his name, much as a company might like a letterhead peer on the board. Unlike that company, they also feel the need to defer to him. It is the conspirators who confirm Brutus's identity: he leads, they acquiesce in his leadership. Effectively, the family record is a special claim upon Romans. No one questions it, not even in the quarrel scene. Brutus's dominance over his fellows is based on family name.

Brutus's standing with the conspirators and with other Romans corresponds to the later reputation with audiences and scholars of Brutus the stage figure. There is a general, not a universal, readiness to take Brutus at close to his own valuation, with a few reservations. In my stage-going experience, only John Wood (RSC, 1972) has put forward a radical questioning of the claims Brutus makes for himself. And yet the play exposes those claims. "Honorable men" contains, in Antony's Forum speech, a widening base of irony. With "honorable" is linked "noble." Here as elsewhere the word unites two senses: the formal claim to belong to the order of the nobility and the qualities associated with magnanimity, or greatness of mind. And Brutus is noble. Cassius says it at the beginning, "Well, Brutus, thou art noble" (1.2.307), and Antony says it at the end, "This was the noblest Roman of them all," which puts the question back, with unwinking candor, to the audience. Brutus unquestionably has greatness of mind, if that faculty is held to be undisturbed by self-righteousness, self-confidence in the face of all evidence and experience, and a determination to lead the state his way whatever the consequences.

In all the circumstances, "noble" might seem to have had a battering in *Julius Caesar*. And yet it is the play's trick to leave audiences disinclined to contest Antony's eulogy. In part, of course, that is the nature of eulogies. One goes along with them. But in the main, it is because the criticisms of

Brutus are unformulated in the dialogue. Brutus, an active politician, is supported or opposed but is never queried. The audience has to do it for themselves. "*Julius Caesar*," wrote Mary McCarthy, "is about the tragic consequences that befall idealism when it attempts to enter the sphere of action."[3] Either Miss McCarthy is mistaken in linking idealism with Brutus, or she is drawing attention to conduct that used to give idealism a good name.

ANTONY AND CLEOPATRA

Antony, the survivor of *Julius Caesar*, is the victim of *Antony and Cleopatra*. This play can scarcely be said to raise any class issues, unless one regards it as a phase of Roman decadence in which the patrician order turns to exogamy. *Antony and Cleopatra* is founded on the polarity of Egypt and Rome. And Antony can been seen as a proconsul succumbing to the lure of the East, as Beerbohm Tree did in his 1906 production. In following the text ("a tawny front," 1.1.6), Tree chose to play up this Roman-Egyptian cultural clash. But this view is not current. Suggestions of a cultural or ethnic divide are played down on the contemporary stage. The RSC's most recent productions, in 1978 and 1982, have concentrated on a "chamber" Shakespeare approach, avoiding the scenic splendors of Alexandria and Rome together with their cultural implications. The differences between Antony and Cleopatra belong to a different order of psychology.

The play's subject is a single relationship, Antony and Cleopatra's, which bypasses the categories of social class. The Queen and the Consul are of approximating eminence, and the question of the drama is their commitment toward each other. Throughout, there are hints of a domestic dimension far removed from the grandeurs of the imperial theme. In this, Antony and Cleopatra are simply people living together, endlessly bickering about the mistress's status as non-wife. It is an ordinary, even a commonplace story of a woman unable to marry her lover, in the end claiming him for her own. The culmination of the drama, in this reading, is "Husband, I come./Now to that name my courage prove my title!" (5.2.285–86). Between the splendors and duplicities of a single relationship this play oscillates. The great exploration of social class in Rome is left to *Coriolanus*.

CORIOLANUS

Namier, I have been told, was once asked the difference between Left and Right. "It is very simple. The Left invented the class war, and the Right implements it." *Coriolanus* depicts both sides in open and enthusiastic pursuit of the class war. On the one hand are the patricians, so termed throughout. On the other are the plebeians, referred to on one occasion as *plebeii*, with the sense of estate of the realm. The plebeians are led by tribunes, officers elected by the people. The story of *Coriolanus* personalizes a phase in the contest between the classes, set formally in the early history of Rome. The analogies between the politics of Shakespeare's Rome and those of any modern state are so obvious as to need no underlining, but neither do they bear much softening or reservation. The whole is presented with a hard clarity, as though incised upon marble. In *Coriolanus* there is no question, as with *Twelfth Night*, of undetermined social counters. The roles are fixed. The open question is what Shakespeare makes of these class transactions.

The opening, which looks like an insurrection, turns into a debate. The stage directions, reckoned to be Shakespeare's own and wonderfully expressive, give an immediate fix: *Enter a company of mutinous Citizens, with staves, clubs, and other weapons.* Surely this is a mob, such as we have seen before in *Julius Caesar*? No, and *mob* is not the word. The lynching mob that destroys Cinna the Poet is a refuge for the individual conscience, a collective able to do things the individual dare not. Here the members of the "company" (not a pejorative term) retain their identity, and fall to discussion which they prefer to serious stave-work. This is a Victorian Working Men's Institute, whose representative figures are 1st Citizen, patently of the militant tendency, and 2nd Citizen, the archetypal Working Class Tory. For the 1st Citizen, Coriolanus symbolizes the oppressive policies of "authority" (the ruling class) that are starving people: let him be put to death, and the price of corn will come down. The 2nd Citizen points out Coriolanus's distinguished military service. The matter is unresolved, and 1st Citizen is urging the company toward the Capitol, when Menenius enters. He defuses matters through a blend of calculated bonhomie and political sermonizing. First comes the straight party line: "I tell you, friends, most charitable care/Have the patricians of you" (1.1.63–64). The famine is the work of the Gods, not the patricians. Then comes the prolonged Fable of the Belly, a discourse that provokes the crowd to listlessness. Economic theory usually does, and a later generation, which knows the same fable as the trickle-down theory, behaves in much the same way. At any rate, Menenius is allowed with minimal heckling to expound his view that the belly supplies the rest of the body. "'Though all at once cannot see what I do deliver out to each'" (1.1.140–41), all parts of the body benefit from the belly's work. Argument by metaphor is always a tricky business, and the 1st Citizen, of whom one could have expected something crisper, has only the lame "It was an answer" (1.1.145). The fable means that "The Senators of Rome are this good belly, /And you the mutinous members" (1.1.146–47). The discussion is halted by the entrance of Coriolanus, but the debate is eternal. Essentially, two theories of society are being offered.

The 1st Citizen sees a direct confrontation in class terms, patricians versus plebeians, the few against the many. Even without the intervening concept of the bourgeoisie (which has no standing in *Coriolanus*), the 1st Citizen is easily seen as a spokesman for proto-Marxism. Against him, the doubts and reservations of the 2nd Citizen—who simply does not care for attacking aristocrats with an outstanding war record—are expanded by Menenius into a theory of social interaction, in which the nobility and wealthy are vital to the well-being of the community. The unresolved debate between these two theorists of society, interrupted by the specific problem of Coriolanus, is the intellectual frame to the action.

The role of Menenius is central. He is a kind of party manager, the acceptable face of patrician rule. His manner, at once genial and patronizing, covers an astute blend of tactics. Note his early address to the Citizens: "Why masters, my good friends, mine honest neighbors" (1.1.60). "Honest neighbor" was also Leonato's address to Dogberry— and Dogberry's to the Watch. But the essential idea is in his opening line, "What work's, my countrymen, in hand?" with its subliminal suggestion that they ought to be *working* and the open appeal of "my countrymen," to patriotism as the binding social agent. Of Menenius as a person it is possible to hold diverse views. His qualities are a gift to the character actor. His functions are unambiguous. He is there to make liaison between the classes, to keep an eye on what the opposition is up to, and to present the actions and motives of his class in the best light. And Menenius would agree to that description of his functions, holding that they are essential to the decent ordering of society.

Against Menenius are set the two tribunes, Sicinius Velutus and Junius Brutus. Shakespeare's handling of his characters is not quite so modern here; party managers often get on rather well with their opposite numbers, who are ideally placed to sympathize with them in the burdens they carry. But in this early stage of social progress, Menenius has unmitigated loathing for the tribunes, which, if they reciprocate, they control far better. About the tribunes there is no question of function. Their duties are plain. There is, nevertheless, a question of judgment. They have usually had a bad press, being identified with agitators and troublemakers generally. On stage, they are usually played so as to resemble a contemporary trade union figure. And yet it is hard to see how they could discharge their duties otherwise, given the impending election of Coriolanus, who can only be taken at his own word as a tyrant to the plebeians. John Palmer's assessment of the tribunes' conduct is admirably judicious:

Their tactics in handling this very difficult situation are masterly. To denounce them as mean and contemptible is to forget that *Coriolanus* is a political play and to display a remarkable ignorance of the conduct of public affairs during a popular election. They do not *oppose* the nomination of Martius as a consul, but suggest, not unreasonably, that, if he desires to be the first magistrate of Rome, he should show less contempt for her citizens.[4]

Sicinius and Brutus strike me as thoroughgoing professionals. They are realists and experts, categories that are beyond the question of likeableness, and they keep their temper in the face of extreme provocation from Menenius (2.1). "Here they are," as Granville-Barker says, "playing the game by its rules, yielding smoothly to their mastery, condoning no smallest breach of them.[5] In them can be seen the general attachment of the Left to protocol, rules, forms, precedents. Sicinius and Brutus are not revolutionaries but constitutionalists, which may be why Menenius finds them so detestable.

The election of Act 2 is the political center of the play. In some respects the practices it depicts are not far removed from those of Elizabethan elections. J. E. Neale, whose *The Elizabethan House of Commons* is the authority, stresses that an election to the Elizabethans did not mean a choice between candidates; it was the confirmation of a candidate whom the governing circles had put forward.[6] No direct analogue to Coriolanus seems recognizable among the records of Elizabethan elections, but similar situations can be traced in memoirs of the twentieth century— Harold Nicolson's, for example.[7] Coriolanus wishes to be elected, but the humiliation of campaigning is beyond him. The need for, shall we say, door-to-door canvassing brings out the worst in him, a contempt for the plebeians with which is coupled nausea at their insanitary habits: "Bid them wash their faces/And keep their teeth clean" (2.3.59–60). He also proposes to remind the electorate of its military shortcomings against the Volscians. No wonder Menenius is aghast: "O me, the gods! /You must not speak of that." Only a devoted party worker would take on the job of campaign manager to Coriolanus.

The 1st Citizen has it. He may not be the same "1st Citizen" as in Act 1, but he has the same sense of the point, and when Coriolanus puts it to him, "Well then, I pray, your price o'th'consulship?" he answers grimly, "The price is, to ask it kindly" (2.3.72–73). I don't think a later generation can improve on that. The ritual humbling of the electoral process is the arch through which all leaders must pass, bowed. And the rules for war heroes remain the same as for everyone else. It is not surprising that Coriolanus should resist the rules; what is truly curious is the grounds of his revulsion against "most sweet voices":

> Why in this wolvish toge should I stand here,
> To beg of Hob and Dick that do appear
> Their needless vouches? *Custom calls me to't.*
> What custom wills, in all things should we do't,
> The dust on antique time would lie unswept
> And mountainous error be too highly heap'd
> For truth to o'erpeer.
>
> (2.3.112–18)

This, as Palmer mildly remarks, "is a strange observation to fall from the lips of a conservative nobleman."[8] Coriolanus's attachment to hereditary privilege is unconnected with any general or principled devotion to tradition. Palmer again: "He dislikes having to seek the suffrage of the commons. Let the suffrage be abolished. His election is opposed later on. Let the tribunes be removed."[9] At the heart of this play's politics is an odd paradox: the radicals are strict constitutionalists, the aristocrat is contemptuous of tradition. In accusing Coriolanus of being "a traitorous *innovator*" (3.1.174), Sicinius phrases the charge with consistency and precision.

In the electoral process, a certain humbug can be taken for granted. More nakedly revealing is the patrician reaction to the news of the Volscian approach in Act 4. Cominius and Menenius rend the plebeians, beginning with Cominius's "O, you have made good work!" (Again, the subliminal charge: "Now look what you've done: you should have stuck to your *work*.") Cominius expands it, cheerlessly cataloguing the disasters about to befall the ingrates of Rome:

> You have holp to ravish your own daughters, and
> To melt the city leads upon your pates,
> To see your wives dishonor'd to your noses—

Menenius, who would like some hard news, tries to interrupt this torrent, but Cominius continues. He has a point to make:

> Your temples burned in their cement, and
> *Your franchises, whereon you stood, confin'd*
> *Into an auger's bore.*
>
> (4.6.80–88)

This, he says, is what comes of you people having the vote! Menenius takes up the cry:

> You have made *good work*,
> You, and your apron-men; you that stood so much
> Upon the voice of occupation and
> The breath of garlic-eaters!
>
> (4.6.96–99)

"Voice of occupation" means workmen's vote. That is what the patricians deride, even more than the tradespeoples' badges of work. "Stood upon" ("set store by") is the phrase both Cominius and Menenius use, to refer to the vote, and the message is emphatic: next time you vote, listen to the words of authority. The passage is really a single tirade, delivered in relays by Cominius and Menenius. Their objective is to enforce among the guilt-stricken plebeians a sense of their sin in banishing the noble Coriolanus. It succeeds, too. Against Menenius's jeer, "You and your crafts!" and Cominius's warning of the danger to Rome, the tribunes have only the limp, "Say not we brought it." There is naturally no admission from Cominius and Menenius that the patricians' selection committee has blundered in nominating an unelectable candidate, thus putting in jeopardy a safe seat.

Cominius and Menenius put forward the undiluted party line. The essence itself is Volumnia. This monster, whom Shakespeare draws with a fascinated blend of wonder and loathing, is fully stated in her opening scene. There is about her nothing further to reveal, only to recount. Volumnia tells her daughter-in-law, Virgilia, how she "was pleas'd to let

him [Coriolanus] seek danger where he was like to find fame." And to
Virgilia's "But had he died in the business, madam, how then?" Volumnia responds, "Then his good report should have been my son; I therein
would have found issue" (1.3.12–21). She means it. When the news
arrives of her son's triumphal return, her reaction is "Oh, he is wounded,
I thank the gods for't" (2.1.114), at which point Menenius remarks
compassionately, "So do I too, if not too much." The point of Volumnia's
delight soon emerges: "There will be large cicatrices to show the people
when he shall stand for his place" (2.1.139–40). She and Menenius
engage happily in a wound-counting competition, leading to a positive
incantation on her lips as the trumpets sound for the triumphal entry of
Martius. As Vickers remarks, "It is one of the songs that the mother
serving the fatherland sings when she sends her son off to the trenches."[10]
And indeed, Volumnia is extraordinarily reminiscent of certain posters of
World War I.

Her teachings on the ordering of society are recalled by her son:

> I muse my mother
> Does not approve me further, who was wont
> To call them woollen vassals, things created
> To buy and sell with groats; to show bare heads
> In congregations, to yawn, be still, and wonder
> When one but of my ordinance stood up
> To speak of peace and war.
>
>   (3.2.7–13)

Nowhere in the canon is there a plainer statement of aristocratic contempt
for the people. Their role in life is to listen, hats off, when a patrician
speaks. But Coriolanus has misunderstood the drift of this doctrine. It
must not come between a patrician and his assumption of power. Power is
the point: "I would have had you put your power well on/Before you had
worn it out" is his mother's advice. A formal submission to the people is
perfectly in order, explains Volumnia, and she elaborates her position in
this telling passage:

> *Volumnia*:   If it be honor in your wars to seem
>   The same you are not, which for your best ends
>   You adopt your policy, how is it less or worse
>   That it shall hold companionship in peace

> With honor as in war; since that to both
> It stands in like request?

Coriolanus: Why force you this?

Volumnia: Because that now it lies you on to speak
> To th'people, not by your own instruction,
> Nor by th'matter which your heart prompts you,
> But with such words that are but roted in
> Your tongue, though but bastards and syllables
> Of no allowance to your bosom's truth.
> Now, this no more dishonors you at all
> Than to take a town with gentle words,
> Which else would put you to your fortune and
> The hazard of much blood.
> I would dissemble with my nature where
> My fortunes and my friends at stake requir'd
> I should do so in honor.

(3.2.46–64)

Honor has always to be redefined in whatever context it appears. Volumnia's exposition of aristocratic honor is especially fascinating for drawing on the imagery of war. In other words, "the class war" is with her not an overheated hyperbole, but a mental reality. Hence, the stratagems of war are admissible in dealing with the plebeians, since they constitute a threat to the patrician order. Coriolanus is to "spend a fawn upon 'em," rather than, through frowning, alienate "our general louts."

Coriolanus now stands explained. He is a creature formed by his class and his mother, who is herself the mouthpiece of her class. Coriolanus is not, in himself, vastly interesting. His few soliloquies have little individuality and no originality. His wife, Virgilia ("my gracious silence"), hints at unassuaged areas of his mind, emotions not fulfilled by the public career of a Roman hero, but these are necessarily undefined. The real interest of Coriolanus lies in this, that through his impossible pride and legendary shortness of temper he says the things no one else would admit under torture. Coriolanus tells the truth. It is a rare quality, and one which Shakespeare exploits to great advantage in the explosive scene of Act 3, scene 1, when Coriolanus reacts to the challenge of the tribunes. What follows is an exposition of patrician doctrine.

"It is a purpos'd thing, and grows by plot/To curb the will of the nobility" (3.1.38–39) is Coriolanus's reflex: the patricians' suspicions are ever on the alert for encroachment upon privilege by "foes to nobleness."

The issue of corn, raised by Brutus, is inflammatory. Corn stands not only
for food and the means of life, but also power—authority has it—and
wealth, for it is controlled by business interests and "usury." Hence the
word sets Coriolanus off, "Tell me of corn!" and he develops it into a
metaphor for the dangers of plebeian encroachment:

> In soothing them, we nourish 'gainst our Senate
> The cockle of rebellion, insolence, sedition,
> Which we ourselves have plough'd for, sow'd, and scatter'd,
> By mingling them with us, the honor'd number
> Who lack not virtue, no, nor power, but that
> Which they have given to beggars.
>
> (3.1.68–73)

The good corn of the nobles must not be mingled with the plebeian weed.
The next, and fatal trigger word is "shall." Coriolanus has the faculty of
instantly reacting to innocuous-seeming words, whose implications he
understands. Sicinius has said, "It is a mind/That shall remain a poison
where it is" (3.1.86–87). The assertion of "shall" is the point, and
Coriolanus launches into a condemnation of divided authority:

> You are plebeians,
> If they be senators . . . and my soul aches
> To know, when two authorities are up,
> Neither supreme, how soon confusion
> May enter 'twixt the gap of both, and take
> The one by th'other.
>
> (3.1.101–12)

The damage is done now. Cominius and Menenius cannot restrain their
man. Coriolanus goes on to the standard position of the ultras through the
ages: If we concede anything, all goes. Concession to "the greater poll"
(3.1.134), the weight of numbers, leads to a general anarchy, "where
gentry, title, wisdom, /Cannot conclude but by the yea and no/Of general
ignorance"(3.1.144–46).

Holding these views, Coriolanus has no chance of accommodating the
Roman citizens, and the rest of the play traces his banishment, return,
and final departure to an exile's death. The only possible alliance is with a
foreign aristocrat, Aufidius, and this too founders on Coriolanus's pride.

The decisive insult that provokes Coriolanus to his final paroxysm of rage, being called "boy," is partly a class term: "boy" implies not merely youth, but subordination. Hence he transfers it upon Aufidius with the very meaning that Aufidius had intended, "'Boy'! O slave!" (5.6.104). Pride is indispensable as a partial explanation for Coriolanus's fall. The individual trait, however, is seen as a class trait, of which it is a magnification. The tragedy of Coriolanus is that he cannot *think*, except in class terms: he is defined by his class and his mother; there is nothing left over.

Coriolanus is patently a play of class. Less obviously it is a play of groups, and the stage directions show that Shakespeare had the identity of groups much in mind. The comprehensive term for the Roman leaders is "patricians," and this is widely used. The stage directions also refer to "Senators," and Nicanor refers to "the Senators, patricians, and nobles" (4.3.14). Not everyone within the class grouping could be a senator; and the effective distinction between the other terms is that "patrician" is an objective noun of rank, whereas "noble" retains the rich ambiguity of adjective and noun, rank, and quality. There is a curious stage direction at the beginning of Act 4: *Enter Coriolanus, Volumnia, Virgilia, Menenius, Cominius, with the young Nobility of Rome.* Have the elders deserted him, asks Granville-Barker? Or is there a faction of young aristocrats, the ultras of their day, ready to back Coriolanus should he decide to fight?[11] It looks like an idea Shakespeare wanted to register in the text, but could not develop beyond the stage directions. I incline to couple this stage direction with that in the last scene (5.6.8): *Enter three or four Conspirators of Aufidius' faction.* The principle is that groups are identified as having distinctive characteristics.

This applies even more strongly to the popular side, for their characteristics change. The initial *company of mutinous Citizens* becomes *a rabble of Plebeians with the Aediles* at 3.1.179. ("Aediles" are assistant officers to the tribunes.) There is a tumultuous moment, however, at which Menenius cries "On both sides more respect." At other times, the stage directions specify simply *Citizens* or *Plebeians*, and at 4.6.129, *Enter a troop of Citizens.* These collective nouns have varying inflections, and such simple plurals as *Enter Citizens* make a guarded point by contrast, declining the identity of a collective noun. But beyond that are the generic terms themselves. *Plebeian* here is a precise statement of class and political affiliation. *Citizen* is not a perfect synonym for *plebeian*, nor is it so neutral as it seems. It makes a claim, for in *Coriolanus*, *city* is a word of power (which it is not in *Julius Caesar*), mentioned many times, and ultimately with a value in sight. The city is the sum of its people. A citizen is a member of this community.

It is not a mere linguistic curiosity that in the development of the English-speaking peoples *citizen* has driven out *plebeian* from general usage. "What is the city but the people?" asks Sicinius, and his hearers chorus back "True, /The people are the city" (3.1.199–200). A fair claim, one might think. But Shakespeare does not exactly grant it. The chorus of "The people are the city" is given the speech-heading *All [Ple.]*, not *Cits.* The city is not coextensive with the plebeians. The patricians belong too.

Coriolanus is acidly objective in its account of the class struggle in Rome. Its subject is a military athlete, perfectly unfitted for political office, who is advanced as a front for the class interests he represents. These interests are given a fair run, however, and Coriolanus is allowed to expound at length his sincerely held views, which are those of the classic ultra. He embodies an issue that is crucial to all societies: the aristocrat-warrior is essential for the defense of the state, but may become too fond of practicing what he is good at, war. Coriolanus, his other defects aside, is ominously pleased with the news that the Volsces are in arms, "I am glad on't" (1.1.223). The plebeians, having no class attachment to warfare, appear less keen on it than Coriolanus. One small scene (1.5) shows Roman soldiers bearing off spoils. This seems a sensible precaution against the rigors of civilian life, given the bread discipline that their leaders like to enforce. At other times, the plebeians are shown as arguing intelligently (1.1) and exercising their ballot power with decency and good sense (2.3). Whatever else *Coriolanus* is, it is not a condemnation of the plebeians. It does show, however, a society in which the accommodation between the classes is still far off.

And what society is that? Roman, of course, as always in the Roman plays: Shakespeare was a stickler for historical accuracy there, knowing that Ben Jonson and others would not allow him the license of Navarre, Illyria, and Bohemia, where he could operate much as he pleased. And yet the analogies emerge. No play with such a plot can fail to suggest its parallels. The delicate flavor of English institutions is imparted, here and there: both the Volsces and the Romans have a *commons*, and Coriolanus's final entry is to Antium, *the Commoners being with him*. As pronounced by Sicinius, the word "commons" has weight and dignity:

> Assemble presently the people hither;
> And when they hear me say "It shall be so
> I'th'right and strength o'th'commons."

(3.3.12–14)

Commons suggests something more than a loose collective of the common people. It signifies an estate of the realm, and the term vibrates in the same way as "the House of Commons" does. *Gentry* is cunningly worked into the texture. Brutus believes that Coriolanus wants the consulship only "by the suit of the gentry to him/And the desire of the nobles" (2.1.228–29). Coriolanus, in one of his rages, speaks of the ruling class as "gentry, title, wisdom" (3.1.144). And they are mentioned in the major stage direction which opens Act 3: *Cornets. Enter Coriolanus, Menenius, all the Gentry, Cominius, Titus Lartius, and other Senators.* It is an unmistakable thread, by which Shakespeare keeps hold of the English connection, and is realized most strikingly in Coriolanus himself. Exiled, disgraced, and nameless, when he is asked by a serving man at Aufidius's house to identify himself, he replies: "A gentleman" (4.5.27).

The English connection, tenuous though it is, keeps open this play's line of escape from Rome and into the future. *Coriolanus* was for centuries thought of as a right-wing play. It is now viewed benignly by the Left, and with some perplexity by stage directors. Tynan thought it best served when either everything in it was slanted, or nothing. To slant nothing, however, begs all the questions; and there is something oppressive in the play's stony detachment from its issues and its protagonist. Coriolanus himself is unarguably a disaster. But those who expect history to provide a final refutation of the 1st Citizen or Menenius are still waiting.

TIMON OF ATHENS

If *city* is the word that matters in *Coriolanus*, *City* is the compass bearing of *Timon of Athens*. Lower case *city* is the community, the polity of Rome. Capitalize it, and *City* means much what we mean by it, the financial center of London. This sense is what Timon invokes, as he bids his guests to be seated:

Make not a City feast of it, to let the meat cool ere we can agree upon the first place. Sit, sit.

(3.6.66–67)

That is meant to suggest a banquet as given in the City of London. And the Folio, our only source for *Timon*, does in fact supply the capital, "Citie Feast." The Act 3 banquet is, like Macbeth's banquet, the symbolic center of the play. The secret equation is: Athens = London.

Timon goes on to strengthen the equation. The blasphemous grace before the feast begins:

The gods require our thanks. You great benefactors, sprinkle our society with thankfulness. For your own gifts make yourselves prais'd; but reserve still to give, lest your deities be despised. Lend to each man enough, that one need not lend to another; for were your godheads to borrow of men, men would forsake the gods.

(3.6.69–75)

The ironic "You great benefactors" covers the Gods, to whom the thanks are nominally addressed, and the City magnates at table, who are the targets of the satire. The men of money, "Most smiling, smooth, detested parasites" (3.6.90), are the leaders and emblems of what Athens has become, the type of a corrupt and decadent society. That is why *Timon of Athens* translates so well on stage into contemporary idiom. Jonathan Miller's 1984 television production, which retained Elizabethan costuming, nevertheless brought out, for example, the Pseuds Corner flavor of the Poet and Painter ("A thing slipp'd idly from me" 1.1.22), and the assorted hangers-on attending Timon's levée. The dialogue between Timon and the Cartier salesman (1.1.167–75) is pure Bond Street. What jewelers say to their clients does not vary much through the ages. The vignettes of the late friends avoiding contact with the servants of the distressed Timon are etchings of metropolitan hollowness and venality. Overall, the implied linkages between Athens and London are the essence of *Timon*, just as *Volpone*, its close contemporary, cannot be confined to Venice. And these linkages work just as well for productions held in Paris, or Rio de Janeiro, or New York. Shakespeare knew only one metropolis intimately, and the type is code-named "Athens."

In Athens, and later out of it, dwells Timon. At the heart of this play is a large question, and perhaps an emptiness. Who is Timon? The title, with that opaque clarity that is so Shakespearean, tells us merely that he is "of Athens," perhaps implying "formed by Athens." G. R. Hibbard views Timon as a figure easily recognizable in Shakespeare's day, one who

goes in for the "conspicuous consumption" which became such a pronounced feature of upper-class life in England during the last twenty years or so of Elizabeth's reign and continued under her successor. There was a passion for building new and elaborate houses; men appeared at court with "whole manors on their backs" in the form of rich clothes; they put on lavish and spectacular shows for their sovereign; and as a result "the great frequently found themselves short of ready money, and proceeded to borrow it."[12]

In this view, Lord Timon is simply a nobleman who carries to excess the extravagances of the day. And there was undoubtedly an Elizabethan sense that a nobleman should behave magnificently. But that in itself does not explain Timon's compulsive spending. Tyrone Guthrie, with his shrewd sense of the social landscape, chose to stress "the upstart element in Timon's genial distribution of largesse," as Tynan put it.[13] That is an attractive coloration, but there is nothing in the text to support it; and "to Lacedaemon did my land extend" (2.2.155) is surely the mark of the landed gentry. There is no explanation of the origins of Timon's wealth, nor is other vital information forthcoming. We have no idea how old he is; while Timon is generally taken as around the middle years, Peter Brook cast him as a young man (M. François Marthouret), a member of the *jeunesse dorée*. Timon's sexual inclinations are enigmatic, though as a good host he entertains his guests with "Amazons." All that is shown is a man insulated by wealth from the world, giving his matinée performance of generosity each day. Timon buys his satisfactions with borrowed money; one can see in this the pattern of a parvenu, or one born to such wealth that he never understands it. The play steers clear of the question: *Why* does Timon want, and choose, to be so insanely generous?

The audience is left with a presented fact, which overshadows the explanations. The play's dominant feature is the great tirades of Part Two. Those are what everyone remembers of the play: Timon denounces a corrupt and decadent society. Part One exists to bring Part Two into being, a platform on which the tirades can be mounted. But in performance it does not work like that at all. Part Two is a villainous and largely intractable problem for the director and the title actor, who have to cope with monotonously high-pitched denunciations, lack of interesting incident, and a static storyline. Unless done with great expertise, Part Two is poor theater, astonishingly so for its author. Part One, on the other hand, is first-rate. The acrid Jonsonian comedy of Athenian high life is tellingly done. One thinks of the marking on Walton's score, *con malizia*. It has a glittering vivacity altogether lacking in the post-interval *Timon*. Hence there is, I think, a certain disjunction between form and content, between the dramatic effect of *Timon of Athens* and its message.

That message seems unmistakable: gold is the emblem of Athenian corruption, and usury its characteristic device. It is what Alcibiades denounces: "Banish me?/Banish your dotage, banish usury, /That makes the Senate ugly" (3.5.98–100), following up with a reference to the "usuring Senate." All the same, the play's targets are not nearly so well defined as might appear. The "usuring Senate," faced with a monstrous bad debt, has a case. The senator is allowed to make it:

> My uses cry to me; I must serve my turn
> Out of mine own; his dates and times are past,
> And my reliances on his fracted dates
> Have smit my credit. I love and honor him,
> But must not break my back to heal his finger.
>
> (2.1.20–24)

Fairly put: creditors have their rights too, as Shakespeare would know, having taken a man to court over the repayment of £1.15.10. There are always two sides to debts, that of lenders and that of borrowers. Still, the time to denounce usury is before a debt crisis, not after. The task of recycling Timon's debts might well daunt a consortium of creditors, the more so as he shows no understanding of the situation's gravity. Moreover, the many references to money are confusing. Since the sums spiral upward, they can be taken as signs of inflation, an objectively depreciating currency, or Timon's diminishing hold on reality. (He asks at one point for a thousand talents, an enormous sum.) The playgoer might well second Tynan's plea:

May I add how helpful it would be if the programme were to give some hint of the current exchange-rate in crowns, ducats, and talents? It is much easier to form an opinion of a man who owns five talents when you know whether he needs, to restore his credit, a thousand pounds or eight and sixpence. Few bank-managers in the audience . . . would be likely to trust a man who owed only eight and sixpence.[14]

All in all, the usury aspect of the play's arraignment is not unequivocal, nor could it be.

The same point holds good for gold. Marx greatly admired the passage on "Gold? Yellow, glittering, precious gold?" (4.3.26–43), which he quotes in *The Power of Money in Bourgeois Society*, praising Shakespeare for anticipating his insights. Money, says Marx, is "the alienated *ability of mankind*. That which I am unable to do as a *man*, and of which therefore all my essential individual powers are incapable, I am able to do by means of *money*."[15] And a good thing too, many will feel. It simplifies life. But what matters here are Marx's fallacies of drama, not money. The cardinal sin of a commentator is to quote a speech, and to say: "This is what Shakespeare thinks." What Shakespeare does is to enter imaginatively into the minds of his characters. The Timon of Part Two is an embittered self-exile, unbalanced if not deranged, unable to form a relationship with any other human being. What he says about gold might passingly coincide with the opinions of a larger audience in a black mood. In itself, it represents nothing but Timon.

For Timon, as for Lear, all rank and position is provisional, a matter of luck and perspective. This is Timon's account of social gradation:

> Raise me this beggar, and deny't that lord,
> The senators shall bear contempt hereditary,
> The beggar native honor.
> It is the pasture lards the brother's sides,
> The want that makes him lean.
>
> (4.3.9–12)

I paraphrase: "If beggars were raised in wealth and privilege, they would hold the esteem now granted to the nobility. The chance of being first-born makes one man fatter and wealthier than his brother." This is another gird at primogeniture to add to those in *Titus Andronicus* and *As You Like It*. Basically, Timon's attack denatures society. If chance and a lucky upbringing create social station, what is left of essence? Timon's diatribe is a nihilist rejection of all social order.

The play "protects" itself by not allying itself with Timon's outpourings. As Apemantus says, "the middle of humanity thou never knewest, but the extremity of both ends" (4.3.301–2). The discriminations Timon cannot make are made by the action. Any sort of a moral code is left to two groups, servants and soldiers.

The servants are exemplary. Alone in a corrupt Athens, they cling to their master, doing their duty to the last ("Yet do our hearts wear Timon's livery" [4.2.17]). The affecting emblem scene of Act 4, scene 2, written in a noble and passionate blank verse, shows the Steward sharing the last of his money with his fellow workers, over their silent protest; "Nay, put out all your hands." His diagnosis of Timon is "undone by goodness." The same Steward seeks out Timon in the woods, to serve him still. Even Timon admits him "one honest man." So the relationship of master and man, which might seem to be founded on money, escapes the play's nihilism.

But that is a kind of static frame to the action. It changes nothing. Only a military coup can overthrow the Athens régime, which appears to be undefended against assault. Alcibiades, "noble and young," is the revolution incarnate. He comes over as no kind of saint, but a hard, just man, loyal to his friends, the necessary man in all circumstances. Alcibiades has only to march his followers to the walls of Athens, "Sound to this coward and lascivious town, /Our terrible approach" (5.4.1–2), and wait for the Senators to outbid each other's concessions. And there is in Alcibiades' triumph a sense of revolutionary energy backed with moral force:

> Now the time is flush
> When crouching marrow, in the bearer strong,
> Cries, of itself, "No more." Now breathless wrong
> Shall sit and pant in your great chairs of ease.
>
> (5.4.8–11)

He has the right to order the culling operation the Athenian leaders admit to be necessary—the decimation of the corrupt. And when the Resistance takes its toll in the aftermath of victory, its inspiration will be Timon. "Dead/Is noble Timon, of whose memory/Hereafter more" (5.4.79–81). In the end, blood-letting is the only cure for Athens, as Alcibiades' image promises.

> Bring me into your city,
> And I will use the olive, with my sword;
> Make war breed peace, make peace stint war, make each
> Prescribe to other, as each other's leech.
> Let our drums strike.
>
> (5.4.81–85)

"Leech" means physician and bloodsucker. English has both meanings, French must choose; and Peter Brook, in his 1974 production at the Bouffes-du-Nord, chose to end on "*que l'une soit prescrite à l'autre comme sang-sue et vice versa. Tambours, frappez.*" As with *Titus Andronicus*, salvation must come from outside. It takes an invading army to cure the sickness within the City.

CHAPTER EIGHT

The Romances

PERICLES

Pericles is a fable of Mediterranean antiquity, and much of it bypasses questions of social class. The main personages are of royal blood, and their mingled disasters and fortunes are the story of the play. In a romance, the triumph of the virtuous and royal is generically determined. And yet there has to be in Shakespeare some token resistance to their victory. Pericles has to assert his princely qualities after being shipwrecked. The brothel scenes are a kind of anti-masque, in which disturbing and uncouth figures make threatening gestures. More, the brothel scenes and the fishermen's dialogue (2.1) transport the audience to England, and thus to structures from which the rest of the play is an escape. This Mediterranean fable is not without its Northern overtones.

As usual in Shakespeare's low-life scenes, the names are English. Pilch and Patchbreech ply their trade nearer home than Pentapolis. Their dialogue is of the same order. The 3rd Fisherman puts up an inviting chance to his fellows, "Master, I marvel how the fishes live in the sea," which the 1st Fisherman seizes. Fish in plays are always symbolic. No one ever seems just to eat them.

Why, as men do a-land—the great ones eat up the little ones. I can compare our rich misers to nothing so fitly as to a whale: 'a plays and tumbles, driving the poor fry before him, and at last devours them all at a mouthful. Such whales have I heard on o'th'land, who never leave gaping till they've swallow'd the whole parish, church, steeple, bells, and all.

(2.1.28–34)

A pretty moral, as Pericles remarks. The 3rd Fisherman, liking the radical tone of this, goes on to propose some social reforms of his own: "But if the good King Simonides were of my mind . . . We would purge the land of these drones, that rob the bee of her honey" (2.1.43–47). No doubt this is a hint that something should be done about enclosures, but the matter is not one to pursue. State action on drones will have to wait for a more

165

favorable opportunity. Making his presence known on this equivocal cue, Pericles stirs up some social frictions of his own: "Peace be at your labor, honest fishermen!" (2.1.52). The 2nd Fisherman reacts sharply to this piece of class patronage: "Honest! good fellow, what's that? If it be a day fits you, scratch't out of the calendar, and nobody look after it" (2.1.53–55). *Honest*, the word so thoroughly explored in *Othello*, gets people's backs up. Pericles compounds this mistake in the passage that follows. Sticking to blank verse, while the others speak prose, he presents himself as one "that never us'd to beg," who nevertheless needs—"pity." The conversation turns to begging, which according to the 1st Fisherman is the major Greek welfare program: "Here's them in our country of Greece, gets more with begging than we can do with working" (2.1.64–65). How that complaint echoes across the centuries! The benefits of unemployment have always been keenly scrutinized by those in work. Still, 1st Fisherman lends Pericles a gown and promises him a meal. Second Fisherman, a rancorous sort, is reluctant to let his advantage go: "Hark you, my friend; you said you could not beg," to which Pericles has only the lame "I did but crave." When 2nd Fisherman exits, Pericles does well to confine to an aside "How well this honest mirth becomes their labor!" (2.1.94). The scene perfectly illustrates a gentleman down on his luck, needing the help of his social inferiors and finding it rather trying.

The same class factors emerge for inspection in the later part of the scene, like the dripping armor on which the dialogue is focused. Pericles, left alone with 1st Fisherman, has dropped into prose, a decent acknowledgement of human kinship. Once the other two Fishermen return, *drawing up a net*, Pericles at once reverts to blank verse. The armor is his class, is himself: "And though it was mine own, part of mine heritage, / Which my dead father did bequeath to me" (2.1.121–22). It is identity, lost and rediscovered. He begs the armor of the Fishermen that he may take it to the court of Simonides "Where with it I may appear a gentleman." (*Gentleman* is freely used in this play.) First Fisherman grants the plea, but 2nd Fisherman, in his coarse way, reminds Pericles that a salvage reward is customary: "Ay, but hark you, my friend; 'twas we that made up this garment through the rough seams of the waters; there are certain condolements, certain vails" (2.1.146–49). It is curious how, over the centuries, "my friend" retains its sense of hostility.

The court scenes of Act 2 show Pericles renewing his identity. At the presentation before the tournament, Pericles' appearance is scoffed at by the Lords: "For by his rusty armor he appears/To have practis'd more the whipstock than the lance" (2.2.50–51). (That is, Pericles has worked as a carter.) Others take the same view, and the stage direction reads *Great shouts, and all cry "the mean knight!"* But Pericles does well in the lists, not shown on stage, and is admitted to the banquet that follows. "Knights," the first word of King Simonides' address to his princely guests, is the tuning-fork of the banquet scene. Pericles' deportment is knightly, though Simonides affects to cry him down, "He's but a country gentleman" (2.3.33). Wanting to know "of whence he is, his name and parentage," the King sends his daughter Thaisa to make inquiry. She repeats to the word her father's formula, and Pericles answers it: "A gentleman of Tyre; my name, Pericles; /My education been in arts and arms" (2.3.82–83). That is satisfactory, and Pericles is invited to take part in "a soldier's dance," a sword dance, in which with his fellow knights he acquits himself well: "So this was well ask'd, 'twas so well perform'd." For the next test, Simonides invites Pericles to dance with his daughter, "Come, sir, here's a lady wants breathing too," and amidst the company *Pericles and Thaisa dance*. It is the climactic test of knightly prowess, passed with flying colors: "Thanks, gentlemen, to all; all have done well, /But you the best" (2.3.108–9). And off the knights go to their lodgings, the best being reserved for Pericles. The matter is essentially decided. Thaisa is of Simonides' mind, and Pericles is the chosen man. Next day Pericles is summoned to the King's presence for the vital conference. He stands up well to pressure from the prospective father-in-law, proclaiming:

> My actions are as noble as my thoughts,
> That never relish'd of a base descent.
>
> (2.5.58–59)

A moment later Thaisa enters, and Simonides announces in his bluff way that she is to marry the stranger knight—who, he reflects, "May be (nor can I think the contrary)/As great in blood as I myself" (2.5.78–79).

The entire sequence of Act 2, scenes 2 through 5, is a kind of dramatized wish-fulfillment dream. The pageant of the knights is Pericles' peer group: though belonging to them by birth and breeding, he has to reassert his qualities in the tests that follow, until the King grants him the hand of the Princess. Nobility has to be restated in performance. The "rusty armor," that ambivalent symbol, is still Pericles' passport from degradation to triumph. Act 2 is the main evidence that the *Prince of Tyre* is a late Shakespearean analogue to the *Prince of Denmark*.

The brothel scenes are "rancid with Hogarthian realism," says Speaight,[1] and they pair off with *Measure for Measure* for low-life accuracy.

Mytilene, we gather, has a shortage of recruits to the trade, possibly an extension of the begging problem explored in the Fishermen's dialogue. People are unwilling to work, and the risk factor among the clientele is alarming: "The poor Transylvanian is dead, that lay with the little baggage" (4.2.21). Pandar seems to have lost his zest and talks of retiring once he has made his pile. "Besides, the sore terms we stand upon with the gods will be strong with us for giving o'er." Shocked at this defeatism, the Bawd remarks, "Come, other sorts [classes of people] offend as well as we." "As well as we? ay, and better too; we offend worse. Neither is our profession any trade; it's no calling" (4.2.32–38). Pandar, one feels, has been talking with Abhorson. He has lost his sense of professional pride.

Into this gloom Marina comes as a shaft of sunlight. Here is a genuine prospect, one that Pandar unhesitatingly accepts at the asking price of one thousand marks. She is cried throughout the market, with all the thrilling additions at which Boult is adept: "There was a Spaniard's mouth so water'd that he went to bed to her very description" (4.2.100–2). All things are ready, if her mind be so. But instead, Marina elects to convert the ungodly. The two Gentlemen who emerge from the brothel forswearing bawdy houses for ever (4.5) resemble Victorian drunks strayed into a temperance meeting. Worse follows. Chief amongst the regular clientele is Lord Lysimachus, a disgrace to the peerage no doubt but a consistent and discerning patron of the trade. He is "an honorable man," as the Bawd is at pains to impress upon Marina, "the governor of this country, and a man whom I am bound to." So will she, please, "use him kindly?" (4.6.49–57). What Marina does is to engage in a kind of Isabella-Angelo fencing with Lord Lysimachus, which completely defeats the governor. He puts the best face on it, "Had I brought hither a corrupted mind, /Thy speech had alter'd it" (103–4), a line that has found the sympathetic support of a number of editors, including the New Arden, who believes that it "was surely not Shakespeare's intention in the play" to have Lysimachus "visit the brothel with wicked intent."[2] I really cannot see what other intent Lysimachus could have had, unless he were going in for Gladstone-type reform of the brothels himself. His opening pleasantry to the Bawd, "How a dozen of virginities?" does not, to my ear, have the ring of the social worker, and those employed in the trade have no doubt that the defection of Lord Lysimachus is a serious economic blow. As Gareth Lloyd Evans remarks, "And what infinite heart-ache lies behind this affronted cry: 'worse and worse, mistress; she has here spoken holy words to the Lord Lysimachus.'"[3]

The trade does its best in the face of these buffetings. Boult, concerned like Pandar for the image of prostitution, sees that its reputation must suffer: "She makes our profession to stink as it were afore the face of the gods" (4.6.134–35). More, her conduct is an affront to good social relations between the classes. "The nobleman would have dealt with her like a nobleman, and she sent him away as cold as a snowball; saying his prayers too" (4.6.137–39). It is a time for firmness, and Boult is instructed to ravish the recalcitrant Marina. There is a perceptible squaring of shoulders as Boult accepts his hard duty: he does not expect to enjoy it, but he will do it. "An she were a thornier piece of ground than she is, she shall be plough'd" (4.6.143–44). This resolution fades before the tirade Marina unleashes at him. Marina, it turns out, wants to be a teacher—and now one thinks of it, there was always a touch of the academic there—and co-opts Boult for the publicity:

> Proclaim that I can sing, weave, sew, and dance,
> With other virtues which I'll keep from boast;
> And I will undertake all these to teach.
> I doubt not but this populous city will
> Yield many scholars.
>
> (4.6.181–85)

The scene ends with Virtue Triumphant, and Boult, like Lord Lysimachus, abjectly defeated. It is that sort of play.

Pericles concludes with the confirmation of identities, with Marina joining Thaisa and Pericles in the rediscovery of family and station. Identity here is social as well as personal. Again and again the dialogue turns to Marina's "parentage," to confirm that "thou cam'st/From good descending" (5.1.126–27). Lysimachus, who has been unaware of Marina's parentage, volunteers:

> She's such a one that, were I well assur'd
> Came of gentle kind and noble stock,
> I'd wish no better choice, and think me rarely wed.
>
> (5.1.66–68)

Royal blood, virtue, beauty unite: the fable transmutes the structures it invokes. *Pericles* escapes from England, yet shows traces of its provenance. After all the testings of mischance, the Prince's family reunites as the nucleus of good order and the model of identity.

CYMBELINE

"Unresisting imbecility" was Dr. Johnson's view of *Cymbeline*. A later generation amended this blunt verdict to "experimental drama," which puts a better face on the same difficulties. Experiments have always been assessed less rigorously in the arts than in the sciences. Even so, *Cymbeline* is notoriously hard to come to terms with. Its bases of reality shift vertiginously, and the action is placed in four countries of the mind: the Ancient Britain of Cymbeline's court, Wild Wales, Renaissance Italy, and Ancient Rome as evoked by its soldiers. The reader and playgoer might think they need extreme mental agility to traverse these settings, but I doubt it. By the fifth act, trying to keep a clear head is good only for headaches. One is better off submitting passively to the episodic and dreamlike nature of the romance, which shuttles between fantasy and varying kinds of reality. Everything in *Cymbeline* is going to remind one, fairly soon, of something else. Shaw's criticism of an inferior production touches a nerve. "Mr. Gordon Craig and Mr. Webster are desperate failures as the two noble savages. They are as spirited and picturesque as possible; but every pose, every flirt of their elfin locks proclaims the wild freedom of Bedford Park."[4] At this distance it is not for me to defend Craig and Webster. But Bedford Park, or something like it, is surely the issue.

Shaw wanted a "Mohican" effect, and the actors gave him something nearer home. Not unreasonably: Guiderius and Arvigarus have been gently brought up by Belisarius, within the limits of the Welsh caves, and must be able to take their places in Cymbeline's court at the end. A cavedweller is not, so to speak, a troglodyte. These two minor parts suggest a general problem of presentation, which is to convey an intermittent sense of social reality via the furs, caves, Roman uniforms, and other paraphernalia. And yet the dramatis personae often fall into the attitudes and manners of Shakespeare's day. In particular, social class is a recurring issue. It opens the play and returns often, ultimately being absorbed into the theme of Britain's imperial future. The play's discussion of class forms around the two contenders for Imogen, Posthumus and Cloten.

Posthumus, a gentleman at Cymbeline's court, has married the king's daughter, Imogen, and is banished for it. The two courtiers who discuss the affair at once establish Posthumus's background—which goes back one generation only. "What's his name and birth?" "I cannot delve him to the root" (1.1.27–28). All that is known is that Posthumus's father received his titles for military service against the Romans, and that his mother died in giving birth to Posthumus, who was brought up as a ward in Cymbeline's court. He is admitted to be a gentleman of outstanding qualities, yet the King is enraged at his daughter's misalliance: "Thou took'st a beggar, wouldst have made my throne/A seat for baseness" (1.1.141–42). Anger, throughout the canon, distorts the sense of social distinction.

Posthumus's breeding is on display in the wager scene, conducted, as Vickers remarks, in Shakespeare's best aristocratic vein.[5] The setting is Renaissance Rome, where a cosmopolitan gathering (including Italians, a Frenchman, a Dutchman, and a Spaniard) shows to advantage. Philario, the host, strikes the note of international courtesy: "Here comes the Briton. Let him be so entertained amongst you as suits with gentlemen of your knowing to a stranger of his quality. I beseech you all be better known to this gentleman, whom I commend to you as a noble friend of mine" (1.4.25–29). Posthumus and the Frenchman have met before, the latter's good offices being called upon to avert a duel. "Can we with manners ask what was the difference?" inquires Iachimo. "Safely, I think: 'twas a contention in public, which may, without contradiction, suffer the report" (1.4.48–52). The exquisitely tuned social antennae of the speakers establish the high plane of sophistication on which the meeting is conducted. Granville-Barker, who analyzes the scene with great tact, says that "Iachimo's tactics are to lead his man on to challenge *him* to make good his boast . . . Patently, that will be the better position to be in; and we mark him feeling for the steps to it, every faculty alert. In this finesse lies the interest of the scene."[6] Since the wager is integral to the plot, it can scarcely be criticized on moral grounds. Shakespeare wishes to embed it in a passage worthy of the center of Renaissance civilization, Rome. The setting tests Posthumus's social credentials. Here, the play proposes, is a model of how gentlemen resolve their differences. What a gentleman is not is illustrated by Cloten.

It hardly seems worth while to denounce Cloten. "Oaf," "tailored brute," "degenerate debauchee," "barbarian" are some of the milder terms used to describe him in the commentaries. We can safely hiss at Cloten. He is less a character than a tissue of class attitudes, a target for girds at uncouth lordlings. Class is what Cloten insists on talking about, and class is what kills him in the end, when a country dweller resents being called "rustic mountaineer." But there is dramatic energy and observation in the part, and Shakespeare is more engaged with Cloten than Posthumus.

His swearing, for example, is the mark of the fashionable young buck. It has given offense to some proto-Puritan of the palace: "and then a whoreson jackanapes must take me up for swearing, as if I borrowed mine oaths of him, and might not spend them at my pleasure" (2.1.3–5). Much good it did him, says a companion Lord: Cloten broke his head for it. The principle as laid down by Cloten is: "When a gentleman is dispos'd to swear, it is not for any standers-by to curtail his oaths. Ha?" (2.1.9–11). I like the "Ha?" with its expected assent to a great moral truth. Cloten is not offering a private opinion, but appealing to doctrine received by all right-minded people. The asides of the 2nd Lord instruct the audience in its reactions; so Cloten's "Would he had been one of my rank!" is covered by the Lord's "To have smelt like a fool" (2.1.14–16). The problem with being noble, as Cloten sees it, is that no one dare fight with him, which is a great pity, seeing that "it is fit I should commit offense to my inferiors" (2.1.28). Etiquette imposes constraints upon the great that others know nothing of. This Italian newcomer to the court, for instance: "Is it fit I went to look upon him? Is there no derogation in't?" (2.1.41–42). And on being assured "You cannot derogate, my lord," he goes.

This is good fun, but a more serious vein of class pride is tapped in Cloten's scene with Imogen. He reproaches her for her connection with Posthumus:

> You sin against
> Obedience, which you owe your father. For
> The contract you pretend with that base wretch,
> One bred of alms and foster'd with cold dishes,
> With scraps o'th' court—it is no contract, none,
> And though it be allowed in meaner parties—
> Yet who than he more mean?—to knit their souls—
> On whom there is no more dependency
> But brats and beggary—in self-figur'd knot,
> Yet you are curb'd from that enlargement by
> The consequence o'th'crown, and must not foil
> The precious note of it with a base slave,
> A hilding for a livery, a squire's cloth,
> A pantler—not so eminent!
>
>   (2.3.111–24)

This icy assessment of misalliance has the ring of social reality. It is not the speech of a fool. But Imogen responds in terms of a reciprocal class analysis, finding "base" and "groom" the words for Cloten.

> Thou wert dignified enough,
> Even to the point of envy, if 'twere made
> Comparative for your virtues to be styl'd
> The under-hangman of his kingdom.

$$\text{(2.3.127–30)}$$

"Under-hangman" was Pompey's job. Again one sees Nietzsche's perception illustrated, that moral values are equated with social position—by those in a position to assign them.

Cloten is really a clothes horse, which is what the imagery declares him to be. In pursuit of Posthumus and revenge, he travels to Wales, takes over Posthumus's clothes, and is then confronted by Guiderius:

> *Cloten*:   Thou villain base,
>   Know'st me not by my clothes?
> *Guiderius* :   No, nor thy tailor, rascal,
>   Who is thy grandfather; he made those clothes,
>   Which, as it seems, make thee.

$$\text{(4.2.81–84)}$$

A palpable hit. Cloten is quick to defend himself against the imputation of ill-fitting attire. "Thou precious varlet!/*My* tailor made them not" (4.2.84–85). People who wear others' clothes are sensitive to slights. The quarrel that Cloten forces upon Guiderius leads to the majestic disclosure of rank: "I am son to th'Queen" (4.2.94), which does not impress Guiderius. He has to defend himself, and moreover "Yield, rustic mountaineer" (4.2.102) is provocative. G. L. Brook explains that "we think of a *mountaineer* as a hardy, admirable man, but to Guiderius it is a fighting word."[7] (Compare the American *hill-billy*, which suggests a conviction like the Elizabethans' that civilization begins with valleys and plains.) It is the last of Cloten's social insults.

His death is the nemesis of inordinate class pride. But it is treated gently, with Belisarius's insistence that Cloten be buried after his degree:

> Our foe was princely,
> And though you took his life, as being our foe,
> Yet bury him as a prince.

$$\text{(4.2.250–52)}$$

That most gorgeous of elegies, "Fear no more the heat o'th'sun," lingers in the air as Cloten's body is borne in.

The later stages of *Cymbeline* convert the issues of social class into a promise of future greatness for the island. Posthumus is granted by Jupiter a vision of his dead father, mother, and brothers. "Sleep, thou hast been a grandsire, and begot/A father to me" (5.4.123–24). He is left with a prophecy that links the "lion's whelp" (Posthumus Leonatus) to a "stately cedar" (Cymbeline), whose

lopp'd branches which, being dead many years, shall after revive, be jointed to the old stock, and freshly grow; then shall Posthumus end his miseries, Britain be fortunate and flourish in peace and plenty.

(5.4.138–43)

The Soothsayer interprets this in the dénouement, explaining that the "lopp'd branches" are Guiderius and Arvigarus, now reunited with their father Cymbeline "whose issue/promises Britain peace and plenty" (5.5.455–56). Thus "stock" and "issue" support the metaphor of tree and family. The play's musings on nobility and birth, sophistication and boorishness, corruption and virtue, all flow into the great reconcilements of patriotism. It is British nationalism that unites, as it expresses, all classes. The most surprising tribute comes from Iachimo. Vanquished in combat by an unknown Briton (Posthumus), Iachimo sees in it the country's revenge for his crime:

> I have belied a lady,
> The Princess of this country, and the air on't
> Revengingly enfeebles me; or could this carl,
> A very drudge of nature's, have subdu'd me
> In my profession? Knighthoods and honors borne
> As I wear mine are titles but of scorn.
> If that thy gentry, Britain, go before
> This lout as he exceeds our lords, the odds
> Is that we scarce are men, and you are gods.

(5.2.2–10)

So much for the *Almanach de Gotha*. Continental families may trace their descent back to Aeneas of Troy: "An English peer takes precedence." In home matches, at least, the English class arrangements may be allowed to overbear the Continental challenge.

THE WINTER'S TALE

Class is one way of approaching the individual through the general. In *The Winter's Tale*, it is clearly the general aspects of human life that engage Shakespeare. Perdita and Florizel are young, comely, royal: they exist to represent their species, the golden youth of the human race. The play turns on what seems to be a class reversal, shepherd's daughter into princess, but is as we know nothing of the kind. As the Chorus puts it, "A shepherd's daughter,/And what to her adheres, which follows after,/Is th' argument of Time" (4.1.27–29). This is a romance, and the great harmonies of identity and reunion are to overcome the apparent opposi- tions of birth—while leaving them intact. Shakespeare is by now playing with class, absorbing it into his final statements, rather than fascinated with its minutiae. In the later stages of *The Winter's Tale*, he has some genial topical fun with a "gentleman born." But the subject is beginning to recede into the middle distance.

The opening contains a few reminiscences of what Shakespeare has already done. Camillo gets both barrels of the class gun in rapid succes- sion. When he dares to question Leontes' suspicions of Hermione, he is "a gross lout, a mindless slave" (1.2.301). When he shares his fears with Polixenes,

> Camillo—
> As you are certainly a gentleman; thereto
> Clerk-like experienc'd, which no less adorns
> Our gentry than our parents' noble names,
> In whose success we are gentle—
>
> (1.2.390–94)

he is now a gentleman and a man of education. Class is absorbed into the rhetoric of praise and blame, of anger and ingratiation. We have seen it before.

Part One of *The Winter's Tale* is the record of a tragic breakdown, a state of dementia that overturns a royal family. There is no direct link with questions of class. In Part Two the comedy shoulders aside the tragic effects, and at once the class interest begins to rise. The subliminal message is that the strata of rank are material for the human comedy. The cross-currents of tragedy and comedy meet off the seacoast of Bohemia, where the unfortunate Antigonus makes his celebrated exit pursued by a bear. The Clown is much affected by this sight, as well he might be: "to see how the bear tore out his shoulder-bone; how he cried to me for help, and said his name was Antigonus, a nobleman!" (3.3.93–95). Not every-one would identify himself by name and rank at such a moment. The outcome is bad for Antigonus, but good for the comedy, and the same kind of signal has already come from the discovered baby. "Though I am not bookish, yet I can read waiting-gentlewoman in the scape" (3.3.72), says the shepherd, and once the coverings are examined, "look thee, a bearing-cloth for a squire's child!" (3.3.111). The child is of gentle birth.

Perdita is raised in surroundings closer to rustic realism than Arcadian romance. The country scenes of Bohemia are absolute England, set in a seasonal time scale that moves from the daffodils of early spring (Autolycus's song) to the sheep-shearing festival of summer. The Clown and Autolycus have a marvelous evocation of the fair they are heading for, and the feast itself is a rural genre painting.

> *Shepherd*: Fie, daughter! When my old wife liv'd, upon
> This day she was both pantler, butler, cook;
> Both dame and servant; welcom'd all; serv'd all;
> Would sing her song and dance her turn; now here
> At upper end o'th'table, now i'th'middle;
> On his shoulder, and his; her face o' fire
> With labor, and the thing she took to quench it
> She would to each one sip.
>
> (4.4.55–62)

The Shepherd speaks in blank verse. He is subtly raised by the context, which is a seasonal celebration, and by the other speakers, Florizel and Perdita. The realism is filtered through a sense of ritual drama, in which the Shepherd is a distinguished participant rather than a stock rustic. "Class" is now the local coloration of an actor in this cyclic drama.

Something of the same sense of ritual drama comes through in the exchange between Perdita and Polixenes. Polixenes praises the art of intergrafting flowers with a metaphor of deep consequence:

> You see, sweet maid, we marry
> A gentler scion to the wildest stock,
> And make conceive a bark of baser kind
> By bud of nobler race. This is an art
> Which does mend nature—change it rather; but
> The art itself is nature.
>
> (4.4.92–97)

Whatever happens in performance here, the impact on the reader must be marked. This is where the play declares its hand, indicating that flowers and humanity have equal status, twin halves of a grand metaphor. The immediate irony is obvious, that Polixenes' ideas on horticulture do not extend to his own son, the "gentler scion." Polixenes is progressive with flowers, conservative with Florizel. But of course Shakespeare has it both ways, since Florizel's instinct is to mate with one of his own rank.

Class formations are extended into the two dances that follow. The first, the stage directions tell us, is *a dance of Shepherds and Shepherdesses*, in which Florizel and Perdita take part. This is an image of social harmony, with royalty and commoners moving in concert. The second is *a dance of Twelve Satyrs*, all of whom are laborers: "Master, there is three carters, three shepherds, three neat-herds, three swine-herds, that have made themselves all men of hair; they call themselves Saltiers" (4.4.318–20). This is a genuine rustic dance, but also suggests an antimasque, a grotesque dance which is part of a court masque. They are a sinister element, says Brissenden, which foreshadows the outburst of Polixenes' rage.[8] In this reversed masque pattern, the coming of the King, Polixenes, is the signal for disaster not harmony.

The confrontation that follows has a masterly two-sidedness. Polixenes is a father, intolerably provoked by a wayward son who coolly proposes to marry a shepherd's daughter without informing his parent. He is at the same time a tyrant, brutally imposing his will on the desires of the young people. The class judgments that Polixenes makes, before and after the explosion, differ in the same way. To Camillo, he observes privately;

> nothing she does or seems
> But smacks of something greater than herself,
> Too noble for this place.
>
> (4.4.157–69)

But anger converts this sentiment to

> And thou, fresh piece
> Of excellent witchcraft, who of force must know
> The royal fool thou cop'st with—
>
> (4.4.414–16)

Yet again, class abuse is the first recourse of rage, and Florizel has to share it: "thou a sceptre's heir,/That thus affects a sheep-hook!" (4.4.411–12).

But Shakespeare wishes to redress the balance here. After Polixenes' exit in rage, Perdita is allowed an *esprit d'escalier* rejoinder:

> I was not much afeard; for once or twice
> I was about to speak and tell him plainly
> The self-same sun that shines upon his court
> Hides not his visage from our cottage, but
> Looks on alike.

(4.4.434–38)

That is as far as the play cares to go on the issues of class and birth. But some pleasant fun remains, at the expense of those who seek to clamber into rank via the court. There is raillery at practices not a thousand leagues away from King James's court, but there is no offense given, and *The Winter's Tale* was played before the King himself. Autolycus, having changed garments with Florizel, is able to stun the suppliant Shepherd and his son with his assumption of court grandeur:

> *Autolycus*: I am courtier cap-a-pe, and one that will either
> push on or pluck back thy business there; whereupon
> I command thee to open thy affair.
> *Shepherd*: My business, sir, is to the King.
> *Autolycus*: What advocate hast thou to him?
> *Shepherd*: I know not, an't like you.
> *Clown*: Advocate's the court-word for a pheasant; say
> you have none.
> *Shepherd*: None, sir; I have no pheasant, cock nor hen.
> *Autolycus*: How blessed are we that are not simple men!
> Yet nature might have made me as these are,
> Therefore I will not disdain.

(4.4.725–33)

Simplicity, indeed. A pheasant would be an acceptable present. With a lyric swoop into blank verse, surely Autolycus then addresses the audience directly. King James's court would also have enjoyed that one, especially the Clown's impressed comment: "A great man, I'll warrant; I know by the picking on's teeth." They close the deal, and Autolycus—for a consideration—agrees to "whisper him in your behalfs, and if it be in man besides the King to effect your suits, here is man shall do it" (4.4.786–88).

The apotheosis of the new born Gentlemen comes just before the great final scene (which they unaccountably miss). The Shepherd and Clown have been received into royal favor, for their part in the upbringing of Perdita. The Clown is in a mood both exultant and bellicose, looking for a fight to prove his newfound rank:

> *Clown*:   Give me the lie, do; and try whether I am not now a
>   gentleman born.
> *Autolycus*: I know you are now, sir, a gentleman born.
> *Clown*:   Ay, and have been so any time these four hours.
> *Shepherd*: And so have I, boy.
> *Clown*:   So you have; but I was a gentleman born before my
>   father.
>
>   (5.2.129–33)

A good joke, milked very thoroughly in the passage that follows. The Clown offers to swear to Autolycus's honesty, at which the Shepherd demurs:

> *Shepherd*: You may say it, but not swear it.
> *Clown*:   Not swear it, now I am a gentleman?
>   Let boors and franklins say it: I'll swear it.
> *Shepherd*: How if it be false, son?
> *Clown*:   If it be ne'er so false, a true gentleman may swear it
>   in the behalf of his friend. And I'll swear to the Prince
>   thou art a tall fellow of thy hands, and that thou wilt
>   not be drunk; but I know thou art no tall fellow of thy
>   hands and that thou wilt be drunk.
>
>   (5.2.152–60)

A gentleman of the new born variety hastens to emulate the peer group: brawling, drinking, and vouching for each other would seem the insignia of gentility. When in trouble, a gentleman can always look to another for character witness. If this is social criticism, it is tranquilized by the mellowness of tone. Shakespeare had been a "gentleman born" for over ten years by the time of *The Winter's Tale*. One wonders if it was a company in-joke among the King's Men.

The tone, in fact, is decisive in the later stages. Shakespeare does not appear to take too seriously the social unheavals hinted at in the advancement of Shepherd and Clown, not to mention Autolycus. The honors racket at King James's court, which is the background to the "gentleman born" pleasantries, does not call for Jonsonian indignation. Any entry system to the expanding classes will have to be flexible to work. Beyond that are Perdita and Florizel, the best of their generation. Together they take the lead in the slow-moving interchange of generations, a dance to the music of time.

THE TEMPEST

Master and man: that is the relationship to which *The Tempest* returns again and again. Ariel and Caliban are servants, yearning for their freedom. Prospero is their master, wanting control over their minds as well as their services. It cannot be done, and their departure leaves in Prospero certain unassuaged longings. The drama of power becomes a drama of abdication, resulting in the hard won independence of Prospero.

The storm contains, in its human dimension, a core of class feeling. The cause of bickering between the Boatswain and the first-class passengers is class resentment, which finds its outlet in the special circumstances of the crisis. Alonso at first tries to assert his status: "Good boatswain, have care." ("Good boatswain" is standard patronage. "Have care" may mean that the Boatswain has bumped into Alonso, or is bidden, superfluously, to manage things properly.) "Where's the master? Play the men" (1.1.8–9). "Play the men," with its unflattering implications, is addressed directly to the mariners. Alonso is interfering in the running of the ship. But the Boatswain will take no nonsense from the gentry. He tells Alonso, curtly but civilly, "I pray now, keep below," only to have Antonio insist "Where is the master, bosun?" (with the implication, "Who's in charge around here?," a query calculated to madden the subordinate). At this the Boatswain fairly breaks out: "Do you not hear him? You mar our labor; keep your cabins; you do assist the storm." This is no time for the passengers to get in the way. But Gonzalo, trying to smooth things over, brings out precisely the contradictions he ought to be suppressing: "Good, yet remember whom thou hast aboard." And the Boatswain responds, "None that I love more than myself!" (1.1.18–19). Social rank has no meaning here, and the Boatswain follows up his advantage: "You are a counsellor; if you can command these elements to silence, and work the peace of the present, we will not hand a rope more. Use your authority!" (1.1.20–23). These things happen at sea. Sir Francis Drake, who had his

share of social frictions on shipboard a generation earlier, had to tell his
crew "I must have the gentleman to haul and draw with the mariner, and
the mariners with the gentleman." Here the role of social peacemaker is
given to Gonzalo, which he accomplishes mainly from what he says after
the Boatswain's exit: "I have great confidence from this fellow. Methinks
he hath no drowning mark upon him; his complexion is perfect gallows."
With this rueful pleasantry, Gonzalo absorbs the Boatswain's rebuke.
The matter has been evened out.

But the storm returns, as it were, with greater intensity. Sebastian,
Antonio, and Gonzalo re-enter to a blast from the Boatswain, and this
time Sebastian and Antonio react with a barrage of abuse: "A pox o'your
throat, you bawling, blasphemous, incharitable dog!" "Hang, cur; hang,
you whoreson insolent noise-maker." It is useless to contend with this,
and the Boatswain leaves them, contenting himself with "Work you,
then." But note that loaded word, "work," which has been featured in
Coriolanus and *Pericles*. It suggests a fundamental class exchange: "Why
aren't you getting on with your work?" "Do it yourself." Just as the storm
on the heath is in Lear's mind, so the storm at sea is between the classes.

Its allaying comes later, again from Gonzalo. The vision of the New
Commonwealth has a complex, shimmering reality that demands a full
quotation.

Gonzalo:	Had I plantation of this isle, my lord—
Antonio:	He'd sow't with nettle-seed.
Sebastian:	Or docks, or mallows.
Gonzalo:	And were the king on't, what should I do?
Sebastian:	'Scape being drunk for want of wine.
Gonzalo:	I'th'commonwealth I would by contraries
	Execute all things; for no kind of traffic
	Would I admit; no name of magistrate;
	Letters should not be known; riches, poverty,
	And use of service, none; contract, succession,
	Bourn, bound of land, tilth, vineyard, none;
	No use of metal, corn, or wine, or oil;
	No occupation; all men idle, all;
	And women, too, but innocent and pure;
	No sovereignty—
Sebastian:	Yet he would be king on't.
Antonio:	The latter end of his commonwealth forgets the
	beginning.

> *Gonzalo*: All things in common nature should produce
> Without sweat, or endeavour. Treason, felony,
> Sword, pike, knife, gun, or need of any engine,
> Would I not have; but nature should bring forth,
> Of it own kind, all foison, all abundance,
> To feed my innocent people.
> *Sebastian*: No marrying 'mong his subjects?
> *Antonio*: None, man; all idle; whores and knaves.
> *Gonzalo*: I would with such perfection govern, sir,
> T'excel the golden age.
>
> (2.1.137–62)

It is a kind of protocommunist dream. The state has withered away, and
so have property, trade, laws, subordination ("use of service"). Arma-
ments have gone, and so have jobs. Nature itself supplies the plenty for
people to enjoy. It will never work, as Gonzalo knows perfectly well. This
is the daydream of an intelligent man whose immediate aim is to divert his
stricken master. It is not the manifesto of a student anarchist. The
self-awareness of Gonzalo, *an honest old counsellor*, is the key to this passage,
which is also inflected by its interruptors. The dream will never work
because of the presence, as much as the arguments, of Sebastian and
Antonio. And yet this vision, like others in *The Tempest*, has its own
authenticity. Gonzalo dreams of a new social order. He does not expect to
get there, but he thinks it worth placing on record.

Nearer home is Prospero's relationship with Caliban and Ariel. It is one
of master and servant, though with a difference. Ariel has always been a
servant, first to Sycorax and then to Prospero. Caliban was once independent. They regularly address Prospero as "master," and beneath the
surface of magical control there are homely necessities, as Prospero says of
Caliban: "We cannot miss him: he does make our fire,/ Fetch in our wood,
and serves in offices/That profit us" (1.1.311–13). He is indispensable, as
Prospero explains to Miranda. The fellow is impossible, but—we need
him. Even at the end, Caliban is sent to clean up Prospero's cell: someone
has to do it, and Prospero's high magic does not include automated
domestic labor. The prosaic realism of Caliban's services links the nameless island with England. In fact, Caliban's opening line (which is spoken
offstage) is that of a surly and uncooperative servant: "There's wood
enough within" (1.1.314). It is always worth looking closely at a character's opening line. Shakespeare likes an incisive, shaped start; he likes to
attack. Caliban's role is grounded in the term by which Prospero (and the

Folio) refers to him, "slave." His resentments broaden later into a cry for
freedom. But the initial suggestion is that of a servant who reckons he has
done enough already.

Ariel too is tired of service. One would not guess this from his opening
effusions:

> All hail, great master! grave sir, hail! I come
> To answer thy best pleasure; be't to fly,
> To swim, to dive into the fire, to ride
> On the curl'd clouds. To thy strong bidding task
> Ariel and all his quality.
>
> (1.2.189–93)

His face falls, however, when he discovers that Prospero is in the mood to
take him up on it.

> *Prospero*:   Ariel, thy charge
>   Exactly is perform'd; but there's more work . . .
> *Ariel*:   Is there more toil?
>
> (1.1.237–42)

After which, with a muscular display of biographical recall, Prospero
beats his recalcitrant servant into submissiveness. The final phases are
instructive: "I thank thee, master . . . Pardon, master; /I will be correspondent to command,/ And do my spriting gently . . . That's my noble
master!/What shall I do? Say what. What shall I do?" (1.1.293–300).
Gratitude and a delighted renewal of the pledge to work upon the promise
of freedom are the elements of the relationship. In *The Tempest*, no servant
has his heart in the job; the Adam of *As You Like It* belongs to folklore.
Without his books (his magic powers, that is) Prospero has not, says
Caliban, "One spirit to command; they all do hate him/As rootedly as I"
(3.2.90–91). Though Ariel aims to please and Caliban mutinies, they
have a common goal.

Both Caliban and Ariel speak blank verse, which one can read in two
ways. First, it may be a mark of their human worth and social potential,
which reflect Caliban's progress toward the light. And certainly his
speeches improve noticeably, from the club-footed stumping of "As wicked
dew as e'er my mother brush'd" to the free-moving energy of "What a
thrice-double ass/Was I to take this drunkard for a god,/And worship this
dull fool!" The other view of Caliban's verse is that it reflects the speech

he has been taught by Prospero. (Or Miranda: the speech heading at
1.2.351 is disputed.) This is what Caliban himself complains of, and "You
taught me language, and my profit on't/Is, I know how to curse"
(1.2.363–64) has often been quoted as anticipating Fanon's view of
language as a form of cultural domination.

But who are Caliban and Ariel? They are plastic figures, and the stage
has shaped them in ways that vary widely. Caliban, *a savage and deformed
slave*, used to be depicted as a near-anthropoid. Benson played him
hanging down from the branches of a tree, gibbering. The humanizing of
Caliban began with Beerbohm Tree and is now universal. In recent years
directors have seen in him a symbol of colonial domination. In Peter
Hall's production at the National Theater (1974), Caliban resembled a
Red Indian. However, the most advanced instance of this perspective
remains Jonathan Miller's production at the Mermaid (1970), set in a
colonial island shortly before independence in which both Caliban and
Ariel were played by black actors. On this showing, Caliban is the field
hand and Ariel the house boy (who will eventually take over the admin-
istration). Caliban and Ariel are seen as parallel figures, whatever their
apparent unlikeness.

Ariel, *an airy Spirit*, can also change greatly. The hermaphrodite so often
seen on stage is not mandatory. The Victorians were accustomed to seeing
Ariel played by an actress (which opens up a new vista on the relationship
with Prospero). The basic hint is obviously that Ariel is "air" to Caliban's
"earth." But the RSC Ariel of 1978 was distinctly earthbound, a shop
steward concerned with hours of work, overtime bonuses, and accelerated
retirement benefits—which, if one thinks of it, suits a good deal of the text.
The view of Ariel as an unworldly spirit, Shelley in tights, does not square
with the cool negotiator who in the end imposes himself upon his master.
Ariel's route to freedom is through ingratiation not unmixed with subtle
moral pressures.

> *Ariel*:   Do you love me, master? No?
> *Prospero*: Dearly, my delicate Ariel.
>
> (IV.1.48–49)

The "No?" is marvelous. It is the interested, yet detached query of a
coquette curious to learn of his or her power over the emotions of others,
but perfectly unconcerned as to its effects. The relationship is clarified, I
think, at this point. There is always one who loves and one who is loved.
Prospero, like Antonio with Bassanio, becomes aware of his ebbing

powers to create reciprocity. But no line at the end conveys Ariel's reaction to his release.

Caliban, for his part, goes through the learning experience of the uprising. He has realized by Act 5 that to be a foot soldier in someone else's insurrection is no great feat, and Stephano's habit of calling him "servant-monster" is ominously suggestive. Is he exchanging one oppression for another? Stephano's claim, "The poor monster's my subject, and he shall not suffer indignity" (3.2.34–35), is a parody of royalty protecting a follower. One might be better off with the genuine article than with the butler. Caliban's song, which is so effective as an interval-break, says it all: "'Ban, 'Ban, Ca-Caliban,/Has a new master—get a new man" (2.2.173–74). One of Cade's followers in *Henry VI* might have sung it.

The Tempest is easily read as a myth of decolonization. That remains, I think, the most urgent and compelling of the possibilities in the text. So much responds to what we now know about the process: the accelerating pace of the departure, for example, and Prospero's need to promise Ariel early release in order to get anything done. Again, the use of the loyalist Ariel to put down Caliban's mutiny has obvious parallels. But Shakespeare was writing far ahead of his day, envisaging a series of episodes that had to wait three and a half centuries for the large-scale demonstration of their historical truth. In terms of his own time, the dimension that matters is of service and freedom (and not the more pretentious "liberation"). If the climax is Prospero's breaking of his staff, the ultimate transaction is with Ariel:

> My Ariel, chick,
> That is thy charge. Then to the elements
> Be free, and fare thou well!—Please you, draw near.

The last paradox is "'My' Ariel," with its awareness of possession and loss. There follows a last word of endearment, the last command, the order of release, good wishes. And then a new word, "please," which has not till now been spoken by Prospero. *The Tempest*, which begins with an order, ends with a request.

HENRY VIII

Chorus is the soul of a play, and the Chorus in *Henry VIII* is a gentleman. The Prologue here has something new for Shakespeare, an overt appeal to social class that fixes the audience as reasonably well-heeled, "privileged" in the terms of its most recent historian, Ann Jennalie Cook. This audience has paid a shilling to get in (line 12), which is well beyond ordinary purses, and is also "known/The first and happiest hearers of the town" (Prologue 23–4). "First" is a compliment to the audience's sense of importance, and an indication that they are present at the opening run (when admission charges were higher). So *Henry VIII* is not addressed to the general audience, which Shakespearean drama takes for granted. It is targeted for the "gentle hearers" (Prologue. 17), a more select audience.

After the Prologue, the choric functions within the play are assigned to a string of gentlemen. All are nameless, though I think we could reasonably add Griffith, Queen Katherine's Gentleman Usher, to the list of commentators. Plebeians are absent until they burst in, symbolically, to join the action at the play's end. That is their first and only appearance. What the choric gentlemen contemplate is a series of great episodes of state: the Field of the Cloth of Gold, Wolsey's dinner party, the arraignment of Buckingham, the trial of Katherine, the Coronation procession, the Council scene, the presentation of the young Princess Elizabeth to the public. Two of these are reported, the rest are presented. Only the last is open to all; everything else is confined to those in high places with specific rights to be present. A sense of exclusiveness pervades the whole. *Henry VIII*, then, is a play about the great, performed before a privileged audience, and commented on by minor gentry.

The great set pieces mask as well as disclose the politics of the play. The inner story is Henry's struggle with his ministers and the nobility, with which is linked the struggle between Wolsey and the nobility. It is class antagonism, as much as the power struggle, that sets Buckingham against the Cardinal. "This butcher's cur is venom-mouth'd, and I/Have not the power to muzzle him" (1.1.120–21). What galls Buckingham is "This Ipswich fellow's insolence" (1.1.138), reflecting a persistent belief that Ipswich does not belong in the first division. For Henry, Wolsey's offense is to make policy on his own. The clash in the council chamber is detailed with masterly reticence. Wolsey wants to raise money for the state coffers and has authorized a capital levy of one-sixth of personal property. The King affects to know nothing about this: "Taxation!/Wherein? And what taxation? My Lord Cardinal . . . /Know you of this taxation?" (1.2.37–40); "Have you a precedent/Of this commission?" (1.2.91–92). In those days, higher taxes caused or were held to cause unemployment, and the King is disturbed to hear the Duke of Norfolk's report that the clothiers "have put off/The spinsters, carders, fullers, weavers" (1.2.32–33). The unemployed are making trouble in the streets, anyway. But it is a long way from the primitive class politics of the Cade rebellion. The covert alliance of workers and nobility is successful; the King backs off from buying income with trouble; Wolsey's policy is disavowed. During this phase of politics the King assumes the role of Scourge of Bureaucratic Abuse, with which is linked Guardian of Precedent, both astutely chosen roles for this monarch. Earlier he had become Defender of the Faith, to which title, since the faith in question is the Roman Catholic Church, he has the same order of claim.

Wolsey, like so many in Henry's reign, is headed for the role of scapegoat. The play understands Henry's pattern and has no intention of saying it out loud. Its hallmark is discretion, which brings us to the essential value promoted in *Henry VIII*: decorum.

Decorum is what the Prologue is about and from the first line: "I come no more to make you laugh." Correct behavior is insisted upon throughout. Katherine, for example, hates Wolsey, yet schools herself to listen patiently to Griffith's fine eulogy of the late Cardinal. Buckingham almost forgets himself during his trial but recovers to assert his self-control:

> *2 Gentleman*: After all this, how did he bear himself?
> *1 Gentleman*: When he was brought again to th'bar to hear
> His knell rung out, his judgment, he was stirr'd
> With such an agony he sweat extremely,
> And something spoke in choler, ill and hasty;
> But he fell to himself again, and sweetly
> In all the rest show'd a most noble patience.
> (2.1.30–36)

Noble is always an important word, but in *Henry VIII* it is, I think, the code word of the play. It occurs forty-seven times, more than in any other play of Shakespeare's save only *Coriolanus* (fifty-eight times). Noble conduct is the measure of right behavior, and "noble title"—the phrase is Katherine's (3.1.140)—is its source. Nobility as rank and as quality is the model held before the audience.

On the same count, indecorousness is a grievous sin. More than mere social peccadillo, indecorousness affronts the play's value system. There is not too much of it here, though the Lord Chamberlain feels keenly the unauthorized presence of people around the palace yard. Wolsey's rebuke to the Earl of Surrey is worth noting, "If I blush,/It is to see a nobleman want manners" (3.2.307–8). And Henry is incensed at the treatment of Cranmer, that he should "wait like a lousy footboy/At chamber door" (5.3.139–40). These are marginal adjustments, a necessary but not salient reminder of what the play is about. What we have in general is noble conduct, justly applauded by the observers.

Two scenes in particular bring out the values of *Henry VIII*. The first, Act 1, scene 4, is set in St. James's Palace (York Place). This is not a great state banquet, but an intimate dinner party where the King might just drop in, and does. The general tone is closer to Fort Belvedere than one of the royal palaces. The social badinage is knowingly presented, and so is the shading of protocol with sexual opportunity. The dance that follows is an image of courtly revelry. All in all, the audience is flattered with the sense of privileged participation in a special occasion; we join the great at their revels.

The second such scene is the account of the Coronation procession, in Act 4, scene 1. I cannot resist quoting the extraordinary stage direction, the longest in Shakespeare:

THE ORDER OF THE CORONATION

1. *A lively Flourish of Trumpets.*
2. *Then, two Judges.*
3. *Lord* Chancellor, *with Purse and Mace before him.*
4. Quirristers *singing.* Musicke.
5. Mayor of London, *bearing the Mace. Then* Garter *in his Coate of Armes, and on his head he wore a Gilt Copper Crowne.*
6. Marquesse Dorset, *bearing a Scepter of Gold, on his head, a Demy Coronall of Gold. With him, the Earle of* Surrey, *bearing the Rod of Silver with the Dove, Crowned with an Earles Coronet. Collars of Esses.*
7. Duke of Suffolke, *in his Robe of Estate, his Coronet on his head bearing a long white Wand, as High Steward. With him, the Duke of* Norfolke, *with the Rod of Marshalship, a Coronet on his head. Collars of Esses.*
8. *A Canopy, borne by foure of the* Cinque-Ports, *under it the Queene in her Robe, in her haire, richly adorned with Pearle Crowned. On each side her, the Bishops of* London, *and* Winchester.
9. *The* Olde Dutchesse of Norfolke, *in a Coronall of Gold, wrought with Flowers bearing the Queenes Traine.*
10. *Certaine* Ladies *or* Countesses, *with plaine Circlets of Gold, without Flowers.*

Exeunt, *first passing over the Stage in Order and State, and then, A great Flourish of Trumpets.*

Henry VIII becomes a drama-documentary, bordering on straight reportage. The play's original title, we now know, was *All Is True*, and nothing illustrates it better than this scene. The gentlemen who discuss the Coronation procession are the ancestors of the media commentators who, in a later age, transmit the interior of Westminster Abbey to the world. Some sample dialogue:

1 Gentleman:	They that bear
	The cloth of honor over her are four barons
	Of the Cinque Ports.
2 Gentleman:	Those men are happy; and so are all are near her.
	I take it she that carries up the train
	Is that old noble lady, Duchess of Norfolk.
1 Gentleman:	It is; and all the rest are countesses.
2 Gentleman:	Their coronets say so.

(4.1.47–54.)

Little is needed to adjust this commentary to the idiom of the twentieth century. Reinforced by a 3rd Gentleman (who has found the pressure of the crowd in the Abbey too much for him, and now joins his colleagues in the outside broadcasting unit), the choric team brings together a balanced picture of a great occasion. The choric elements realize their identity as admiring commentators.

Henry VIII aspires to the condition of a social column, and at the end achieves it. The final stages have a striking symbolism. The crowd, wanting a closer look at the show, presses in upon the stage, and therefore the consciousness of the playhouse audience. It calls for all the devoted efforts of the Porter and his man to keep them at bay, offstage. The people, whose token representative is "a haberdasher's wife," are a threat to decorum, however, rather than public order. That guardian of court standards, the Lord Chamberlain, is professionally appalled at the intrusion of the middling classes: "Are these/Your faithful friends o'th'suburbs?" (5.4.68–69). ("Suburbs," evidently, is well on the way to that later term of reproach, "suburban.") But the main need, as the Lord Chamberlain sees, is simply to create a passage for the troop returning from the christening. This is a media event, and "Go break among the press" (5.4.81) sounds prophetic to our ears.

Cranmer's prophecy ratifies the future, which is the reign of Elizabeth: "She shall be, to the happiness of England, /An aged princess" (5.5.56–57). In social terms, the future is a concordat between monarchy and people. The nobility, whose claims have been so assiduously checked by Henry, will not return to the pre-eminence of the early history plays. The present crystallizes into that most appealing of occasions, a public holiday linked with a royal birth. It brings together all classes on stage. And to them, as well as to the playhouse audience, the monarch reaches out with his sense of social order. King Henry has the last word in his play, and strikes a major chord of social harmony: "This little one shall make it holiday."

Notes

INTRODUCTION

1. Peter Laslett, *The World We Have Lost*, pp. 84–85.
2. Muriel St. Clare Byrne, "The Social Background," in *A Companion to Shakespeare Studies*, ed. Harley Granville-Barker and G. B. Harrison, p. 189.
3. Sir Thomas Smith, *De Republica Anglorum*. Quoted in Laslett, p. 31.
4. Lawrence Stone, *The Crisis of the Aristocracy 1558–1641*, p. 52.
5. Ibid., p. 49.
6. Quoted in Stone, p. 49.
7. A. L. Rowse, *The England of Elizabeth*, p. 244.
8. Quoted in Rowse, p. 245.
9. Stone, p. 50.
10. Friedrich Nietzsche, *Complete Works*, ed. Oscar Levy, 18 vols. 1909–11, reissued New York: Russell and Russell, 1964, vol. 13, pp. 22–23.
11. Thomas Fuller, *The Holy State*, 1642.
12. Brian Vickers, *The Artistry of Shakespeare's Prose*, p. 6.
13. Randolph Quirk, "Shakespeare and the English Language," in *A New Companion to Shakespeare Studies*, ed. Kenneth Muir and S. Schoenbaum, p. 70.
14. G. L. Brook, *The Language of Shakespeare*, p. 73.
15. Byrne, p. 214.
16. Stone, pp. 38–39.

CHAPTER 1
THE EARLY HISTORIES

1. Robert Speaight 1977, p. 36.
2. John Palmer, *Political and Comic Characters of Shakespeare*, p. 319.
3. Laslett, p. 159.
4. Gordon Crosse, *Shakespearean Playgoing 1890–1952*, p. 69.

CHAPTER 2
THE EARLY COMEDIES AND ROMEO AND JULIET

1. Sir Arthur Quiller-Couch, ed., *The Two Gentlemen of Verona*, New Cambridge Edition, 1921, p. xiv.
2. Ibid., p. xvi.
3. Ibid., p. xvii.
4. Holman Hunt, *Valentine Protecting Sylvia from Proteus*, 1851.
5. George Bernard Shaw, *Our Theatres in the Nineties*, vol 3, p. 240.

6. Ann Thompson, ed., *The Taming of the Shrew* (Cambridge 1984), Introduction.
7. H. J. Oliver, ed., *The Taming of the Shrew* (Oxford 1984), p. 57.
8. Brian Morris, ed., *The Taming of the Shrew* (London: Methuen, 1981), p. 149.
9. Shaw, vol. 3, pp. 239–40.
10. G. R. Hibbard, ed., *The Taming of the Shrew*, New Penguin edition, Harmondsworth 1968, pp. 30–32.
11. G. R. Hibbard, *The Making of Shakespeare's Dramatic Poetry*, p. 203.
12. Harley Granville-Barker, *Prefaces to Shakespeare*, vol. 2, p. 427.
13. Robert Speaight, *Shakespeare: The Man and His Achievement*, pp. 122–23.
14. Granville-Barker 1946–47, vol. 2, p. 305.
15. Byrne, p. 190.
16. Granville-Barker 1946–47, vol. 2, pp. 334–35.
17. Speaight 1977, pp. 69–70.
18. Hibbard 1981, p. 127.
19. Granville-Barker 1946–47, vol. 2, p. 335.
20. Brian Gibbons, ed., *Romeo and Juliet* (London: Methuen, 1980), pp. 142–43.

CHAPTER 3
THE MIDDLE COMEDIES

1. John Russell Brown, ed., *The Merchant of Venice* (London: Methuen, 1955), p. 22.
2. Byrne, p. 214.
3. Ibid.
4. Speaight 1977, p. 183.
5. E. K. Chambers, *William Shakespeare: A Study of Facts and Problems*, vol. 1, p. 231.
6. Shaw, vol. 3, p. 321.
7. Quoted in Rowse, p. 246.
8. John Manwood, *A Treatise and discourse of the lawes of the forrest*, London 1598.
9. Jan Kott, *Shakespeare Our Contemporary*, p. 279.
10. G. L. Brook, p. 182.
11. Speaight 1973, p. 281.
12. Harley Granville-Barker, *More Prefaces to Shakespeare*, p. 30.
13. Kenneth Tynan, *A View of the English Stage*, p. 70.
14. Ibid.
15. Crosse, p. 84.
16. Rowse, p. 245.
17. Gareth Lloyd Evans, *The Upstart Crow*, p. 187.

CHAPTER 4
THE MATURE HISTORIES

1. Frances Shirley, *Swearing and Perjury in Shakespeare's Plays*, p. 2.
2. Paul A. Jorgensen, *Shakespeare's Military World*, p. 70.
3. Kott, p. 43.
4. Quoted in Jorgensen, p. 80.

5. Jorgensen, p. 80.
6. Gary Taylor, ed., *Henry V* (Oxford 1984), p. 208.

CHAPTER 5
THE MAJOR TRAGEDIES

1. Kenneth Tynan, *He That Plays the King*, p. 44.
2. E. A. J. Honigmann, *Shakespeare: Seven Tragedies: The Dramatist's Manipulation of Response*, p. 70.
3. Michael Long, *The Unnatural Scene*, pp. 129 ff.
4. Peter Brook, *The Empty Space*, p. 14.
5. Kenneth Tynan, *The Sound of Two Hands Clapping*, p. 130.
6. Speaight 1973, p. 245.
7. Jorgensen, p. 110.
8. Honigmann, p. 83.
9. A. C. Bradley, *Shakespearean Tragedy*, pp. 213–14.
10. William Empson, *The Structure of Complex Words*, p. 218.
11. M. R. Ridley, ed., *Othello* (London: Methuen 1958), p. xlvii.
12. John Russell Brown, ed., *Focus on "Macbeth,"* p. 233.

CHAPTER 6
THE PROBLEM PLAYS

1. Stone, p. 41.
2. Kenneth Tynan, *Curtains*, p. 238.
3. Speaight 1977, p. 255.
4. Tynan 1961, p. 238.
5. Kott, p. 81.
6. E. M. W. Tillyard, *Shakespeare's Problem Plays*, p. 2.
7. Empson, p. 284.
8. Shaw, vol. 3, pp. 321–22.
9. Vickers, p. 317.

CHAPTER 7
THE ROMAN PLAYS AND TIMON OF ATHENS

1. Brook, p. 95.
2. M. W. MacCallum, *Shakespeare's Roman Plays and Their Background* (London: Macmillan, 1910), p. 264.
3. Mary McCarthy, *Mary McCarthy's Theater Chronicles 1937–1962*, p. 18.
4. Palmer, p. 268.
5. Granville-Barker 1946–47, vol. 2, p. 184.
6. J. E. Neale, *The Elizabethan House of Commons*, 1949.

7. See Harold Nicolson, *Diaries and Letters 1930–62*, ed. Nigel Nicolson, 3 vols. (New York: Atheneum, 1966–68), vol. 3.
8. Palmer, p. 269.
9. Ibid., p. 270.
10. Vickers, p. 396.
11. Granville-Barker 1946–47, vol. 2, p. 237.
12. G. R. Hibbard, ed., *Timon of Athens*, New Penguin edition, Harmondsworth, 1970, pp. 33–34.
13. Tynan 1961, p. 23.
14. Ibid., p. 24.
15. Quoted by Anne Paolucci in "Marx, Money, and Shakespeare: The Hegelian Core in Marxist Shakespeare-Criticism," *Mosaic*, Spring 1977, pp. 147–48.

CHAPTER 8
THE ROMANCES

1. Speaight 1977, p. 335.
2. F. D. Hoeniger, ed., *Pericles* (London: Methuen, 1963), pp. 129–30.
3. Evans, p. 340.
4. Shaw, vol. 2, p. 200.
5. Vickers, p. 409.
6. Granville-Barker 1946–47, vol. 1, p. 514.
7. G. L. Brook, p. 59.
8. Alan Brissenden, *Shakespeare and the Dance*, pp. 93–95.

Select Bibliography

All references to Shakespeare's plays are from *William Shakespeare: The Complete Works*. Edited by Peter Alexander. London and Glasgow: Collins, 1951.

Blake, N. F. *Shakespeare's Language: An Introduction*. New York: St. Martin's Press, 1983.

Bradley, A. C. *Shakespearean Tragedy*. London: Macmillan, 1904.

Brissenden, Alan. *Shakespeare and the Dance*. London: Macmillan, 1981.

Brook, G. L. *The Language of Shakespeare*. London: André Deutsch, 1976.

Brook, Peter. *The Empty Space*. London: MacGibbon and Kee, 1968.

Brown, John Russell, ed. *Focus on "Macbeth."* London: Routledge and Kegan Paul, 1982.

Byrne, Muriel St. Clare. "The Social Background." In Granville-Barker, Harley, and Harrison, G. B., eds. *A Companion to Shakespeare Studies*. Cambridge: Cambridge University Press. 1934.

Chambers, E. K. *William Shakespeare: A Study of Facts and Problems*. 2 vols. Oxford: Clarendon Press, 1930.

Cook, Ann Jennalie. *The Privileged Playgoers of Shakespeare's London 1576–1642*. Princeton: Princeton University Press, 1981.

Crosse, Gordon. *Shakespearean Playgoing 1890–1952*. London: A. R. Mowbray, 1953.

Empson, William. *The Structure of Complex Words*. London: Chatto and Windus, 1951.

Evans, Gareth Lloyd. *The Upstart Crow*. London: J. M. Dent, 1982.

Granville-Barker, Harley. *Prefaces to Shakespeare*, 2 vols. Princeton: Princeton University Press, 1946–47.

————. *More Prefaces to Shakespeare*. Edited by Edward M. Moore. Princeton: Princeton University Press, 1974.

Halliday, F. E. *A Shakespeare Companion*. Revised edition. London: Duckworth, 1964.

Hibbard, G. R. *The Making of Shakespeare's Dramatic Poetry*. Toronto: University of Toronto Press, 1981.

Honigmann, E. A. J. *Shakespeare: Seven Tragedies: The Dramatist's Manipulation of Response*. London: Macmillan, 1976.

Hurstfield, Joel. "The Social and Historical Background." In Muir, Kenneth, and Schoenbaum, S., eds. *A New Companion to Shakespeare Studies*. Cambridge: Cambridge University Press, 1971.

Hussey, S. S. *The Literary Language of Shakespeare*. London: Longman, 1982.

Jorgensen, Paul A. *Shakespeare's Military World*. Berkeley and Los Angeles: University of California Press, 1956.

Knights, L. C. *Drama and Society in the Age of Jonson*. London: Chatto and Windus, 1937.

Kott, Jan. *Shakespeare Our Contemporary*. 2d ed. London: Methuen, 1967.

Laslett, Peter. *The World We Have Lost.* 3rd ed. London: Methuen, 1983.

Long; Michael. *The Unnatural Scene.* London: Methuen, 1976.

McCarthy, Mary. *Mary McCarthy's Theater Chronicles 1937–1962.* New York: Noonday Press, 1963.

Palmer, John. *Political and Comic Characters of Shakespeare.* London: Macmillan, 1945.

Quirk, Randolph. "Shakespeare and the English Language." In Muir, Kenneth, and Schoenbaum, S., eds. *A New Companion to Shakespeare Studies.* Cambridge: Cambridge University Press, 1971.

Rowse, A. L. *The England of Elizabeth.* London: Macmillan, 1950.

Schoenbaum, S. *Shakespeare: A Documentary Life.* Oxford: Clarendon Press, 1975.

Shaw, George Bernard. *Our Theatres in the Nineties.* 3 vols. London: Constable, 1932.

Shirley, Frances. *Swearing and Perjury in Shakespeare's Plays.* London: George Allen and Unwin, 1979.

Speaight, Robert. *Shakespeare on the Stage.* London: Collins, 1973.

_____. *Shakespeare: The Man and His Achievement.* London: J. M. Dent, 1977.

Stone, Lawrence. *The Crisis of the Aristocracy 1558–1641.* Oxford: Clarendon Press, 1965.

Tillyard, E. M. W. *Shakespeare's Problem Plays.* London: Chatto and Windus, 1964.

Tynan, Kenneth. *He That Plays the King.* London: Longman, 1950.

_____. *Curtains.* London: Longman, 1961.

_____. *The Sound of Two Hands Clapping.* New York: Holt, Rinehart and Winston, 1975.

_____. *A View of the English Stage 1944–63.* London: Davis-Poynter, 1975.

Vickers, Brian. *The Artistry of Shakespeare's Prose.* London: Methuen, 1968.

Index